THE
VENLO INCIDENT

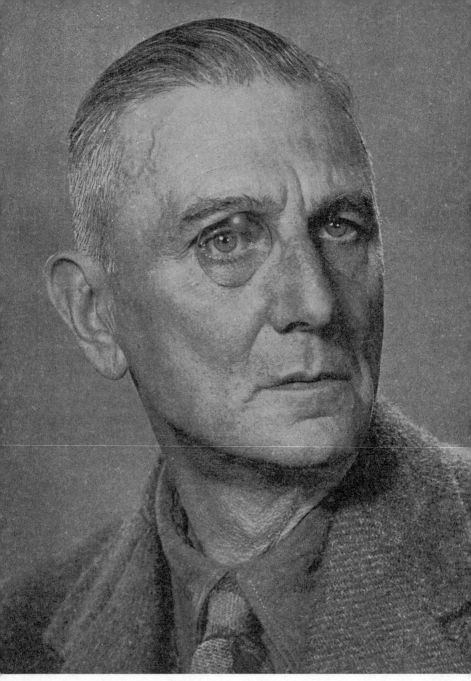

The Author.

THE
VENLO INCIDENT

A True Story of Double-Dealing, Captivity, and a Murderous Nazi Plot

CAPTAIN S. PAYNE BEST

Introduction by Nigel Jones

Frontline Books, London/Skyhorse Publishing, New York

The Venlo Incident: A True Story of Double-Dealing, Captivity, and a Murderous Nazi Plot

This edition published in 2009 by Frontline Books,
an imprint of Pen & Sword Books Limited,
47 Church Street, Barnsley, S. Yorkshire, S70 2AS
www.frontline-books.com
and
Published and distributed in the United States of America and Canada
by Skyhorse Publishing, 555 Eighth Avenue, Suite 903, New York, NY 10018
www.skyhorsepublishing.com

Skyhorse Publishing books may be purchased in bulk at special discounts for sales promotion,
corporate gifts, fund-raising, or educational purposes. Special editions can also be created
to specifications. For details, contact the Special Sales Department, Skyhorse Publishing,
555 Eighth Avenue, Suite 903, New York, NY 10018 or email info@skyhorsepublishing.com.

© 1950 Sigismund Payne Best
Introduction © Pen & Sword Books Ltd, 2009
United Kingdom edition © Pen & Sword Books Ltd, 2009
North America edition © Skyhorse Publishing, 2009

Frontline edition: ISBN 978-1-84832-558-6
Skyhorse edition: ISBN 978-1-60239-946-4

Publishing History
The Venlo Incident was first published by Hutchinson & Co (London) in 1950. This edition
includes a new introduction by Nigel Jones.

A CIP data record for this title is available from the British Library.
Library of Congress Cataloging-in-Publication data is available on file.

For more information on our books, please visit www.frontline-books.com,
email info@frontline-books.com or write to us at the above address.

Printed in the UK by the MPG Books Group

CONTENTS

LIST OF ILLUSTRATIONS

INTRODUCTION

In post-war accounts of the secret intelligence war between Britain and Nazi Germany, most of the spotlight – and the kudos – has focused on British intelligence agencies for such coups as the Double Cross system for 'turning' Nazi agents; and the breaking at Bletchley Park of Germany's military signals encoded on its reputedly impenetrable Enigma machines – the material code-named Ultra and called 'the golden eggs' by Churchill – knowledge of which helped the Allies to anticipate almost every German military move, and thus win the war.

Far less attention, for understandable reasons of national pride, has been paid to Germany's intelligence triumphs. Chief among these were the *'Funkspielen'* or 'Radio games' in which, by capturing and 'turning' Allied radio operators working in occupied France and Holland, the Germans managed to destroy entire networks of Allied agents, virtually crippling intelligence gathering in those two countries. But the most audacious and successful single stroke played by the German secret services was the story of the 'Venlo Incident' – recounted in this remarkable and revealing book by its chief victim, Captain Sigismund Payne Best.

The author was a British intelligence officer of the old school, familiar from W. Somerset Maugham's 'Ashenden' stories, which tell of the writer's work as a spymaster running agents from neutral Switzerland during the First World War. Payne Best was similarly employed by military intelligence in neutral Holland during the same conflict. Tall, tweedy, spats-wearing and monocled, Best was almost a caricature of the British officer and gentleman. Married to a Dutch woman, Maria van Bess, Best remained in the country after the war, becoming a well-known member of the upper-class British community in the Netherlands.

Best ran a legitimate import-export business, specialising in pharmaceuticals, which also provided a convenient cover for his second profession: espionage. Although apparently de-activated in the 1920s by the cash-strapped secret foreign intelligence service, MI6, spies never really retire, and with Nazism on the rise in the 1930s, Best was approached again by an old acquaintance from the Great War: Colonel Claude Dansey. The deputy chief of MI6/SIS, Dansey, a more ruthless player than the gentlemanly Best, was setting up his 'Z' organisation, an outfit that paralleled MI6's 'official' spy stations, which were based on the Passport Control Offices (PCOs) in British embassies around the world. Run from Bush House in the Aldwych, the home of the BBC World Service, Dansey's Z network was based on British businessmen working in foreign cities, and was supposed to be kept quite separate from the MI6 stations, so that if one was penetrated, the other could continue to function.

Best became Dansey's 'Z man' in the Netherlands, a position that, with his extensive contacts and experience, suited him well. But at the outbreak of war in 1939, Dansey took the decision to merge his Z organisation with the official MI6 PCO network. Probably this was a move designed to promote Dansey's claims to succeed Hugh 'Quex' Sinclair – who was dying of cancer – as 'C', the head of MI6. But, in the Netherlands at least, it proved a fatal error. Based in The Hague, the Dutch PCO network had recently been taken over by an inexperienced former Indian Army Officer, Major Richard Stevens. Neither he nor Best knew that Stevens' PCO network had already been penetrated by the German secret services. The Germans had even set up a camera in a barge permanently moored on a canal opposite Stevens' office from which every visitor to the PCO was photographed. As a result, several of MI6's spies and informers in Holland were double agents working for the Nazis.

The Germans were playing a classic espionage game. Rather than wrapping up Britain's spy network in Holland, they continued to monitor it, steadily accumulating more information, and identifying its agents for future arrest. Germany's most feared spymaster – Reinhard Heydrich, the ice-cold chief of the Nazi party's security service, the *Sicherheitsdienst* [SD] – personally kept his eye on the Dutch 'game' and made sure that his bosses, SS Chief Heinrich Himmler and Adolf Hitler, were informed of its progress. The Nazi leadership held the legendary British secret services in awe –rumour had it Heydrich even signed his letters 'C' and wrote them in green ink after the supposed style of all MI6 chiefs – which the bungling displayed by the service in the Venlo Incident shows was somewhat misplaced. In September 1939, with the outbreak of war, Heydrich decided to bring the game to a close and snapped his trap shut.

The Venlo Incident is an extraordinary story on several levels, reading as it does like a spy fiction by Eric Ambler or John le Carré. Indeed, the Incident finds its way – only slightly disguised – into William Boyd's acclaimed superior spy novel *Restless*. At its most basic level, therefore, *The Venlo Incident* is a real-life spy thriller. It was, however, much more than that. Best and Stevens were mere pawns in a greater game than local espionage. In the autumn of 1939 the newly co-operating but unwittingly compromised spy chiefs had been holding talks at a series of clandestine meetings with a group of shady Germans. Best and Stevens believed these men to be emissaries of the Wehrmacht High Command who were plotting a *putsch* against Hitler. They did not know, however, that the talks had been authorised at the very highest levels of Whitehall policy-making, in fact by Prime Minister Neville Chamberlain himself.

Most people in Britain assumed that when Chamberlain, speaking in the funereal tones that earned him the nickname of 'the undertaker', announced Britain's declaration of war on Germany on 3 September 1939, that was the death of the policy that he most embodied: appeasement. Chamberlain said as much himself in his broadcast when he spoke of 'the bitter blow to me that my long struggle to win peace has failed'. In fact, behind the scenes, and carefully hidden from a public who were preparing for a long and cruel war, Chamberlain's 'struggle to win peace' continued even after he had declared war on Germany. Unlike Winston Churchill, the man who he had reluctantly taken into his cabinet on the outbreak of war and who would eventually succeed him, Chamberlain was a man with no military experience, and no understanding of war. With his reedy voice, his ubiquitous umbrella and his old-fashioned wing collars, Chamberlain was hardly an inspiring war leader, even discounting his past record as the man of Munich, the arch appeaser who had bent over backwards to accommodate Hitler's appetite for chunks of European real estate: Austria, the Sudetenland, Czechoslovakia and finally Poland.

The first two months of the war underlined Chamberlain's bizarre policy of being at war without actually fighting. A proposal to bomb German forests with incendiaries was ruled out on the grounds that the trees were 'private property'. And beyond moving the tiny British Expeditionary Force over to France, Britain sat with folded arms while Hitler's Blitzkrieg destroyed Poland – the nation on whose behalf she had entered the war. It was dubbed the 'Phoney War' with justification. Unknown to all but a handful of close colleagues who shared his appeasing views – including his Foreign Secretary and favoured successor, Lord Halifax – Chamberlain was putting out desperate feelers seeking a compromise peace with Germany before too much blood had been shed.

The most promising such approach in Whitehall's eyes was the one being pursued by Best and Stevens in the Netherlands. As Best relates in this book, his direct contacts with the Germans had begun on the eve of war in August 1939 when London had asked him to meet a mysterious German exile named Franz Fischer. This man was a shady character who had been forced to flee Germany for Paris to escape charges of embezzlement. In the French capital he had made contact with anti-Nazi German exiles, but also become entangled with the SD, who offered to waive the fraud charges if he would work for them. Fischer agreed, betraying his new exile friends. The SD then sent Fischer to The Hague in 1938 to repeat the trick with anti-Nazi exiles there. He represented himself as the front man for a group of German Generals who were planning to overthrow Hitler and halt Germany's aggressive expansionism.

In the Netherlands Fischer succeeded in winning the confidence of an exiled Catholic leader, Dr Klaus Speicker, who was also one of Claude Dansey's Z informers. In this way, Fischer was put in touch with Best. With the instincts of an old spymaster, Best was instantly suspicious, regarding Fischer as an obvious plant, but his MI6 bosses, keen to win Chamberlain's approval, told him to pursue the relationship. 'I had the damn fellow up to my office' wrote Best, 'and spent a morning interrogating him'. The meeting only confirmed Best's suspicions that

Fischer was an *agent provocateur* seeking to sow mischief. Best wrote a damning report complaining that merely meeting such an obvious Nazi stooge had compromised him, and recommended that Fischer be lured to London and banged up for the duration.

Best's report was ignored. Dansey was away in Switzerland, MI6's main European listening post. Stewart Menzies, head of MI6's military section, who was acting as 'C' during Sinclair's sick leave, decided to tell Chamberlain what he wanted to hear: that there was a serious possibility that Hitler would be overthrown by a German 'peace party'. Menzies certainly 'sexed up' this possibility for Chamberlain's benefit as a way of strengthening his claim to succeed Sinclair as 'C', but his words fell on fertile ground anyway. Not only was Chamberlain eager to end the war peacefully, but there was a genuine German opposition in Germany's Wehrmacht and Foreign Office who had already made contact with Britain at the time of the Munich conference a year before the war. From this knowledge, it was but a short step for London to believe that Fischer was a real representative of these anti-Hitler elements.

It would spoil Best's story to rehearse the details of the Venlo Incident itself in advance. Suffice to say that a series of tense and tantalising meetings with a changing cast of German SD men masquerading as German officers, led by a certain bright young Major Schaemmel – actually the SD's head of counter-intelligence, Walther Schellenberg – eventually led to the dramatic denouement, the 'Incident' itself. On November 9th, in the car park outside the Cafe Backus – a sleepy pull-up in the unremarkable town of Venlo on the Dutch-German frontier – a snatch squad of SS goons roared across the border, abducted Best Stevens, and their driver in a few violent seconds, and fatally shot their Dutch intelligence 'minder' Dirk Klop.

Heydrich had chosen his most trusted thug to carry out the clinically ruthless kidnap. Alfred Naujocks was fresh from an equally ruthless and murderous operation on another frontier – that between Germany and Poland – that had started the Second World War. In late August 1939 Naujocks had commanded another hit squad, dressed in Polish uniforms, who had commandeered a local radio station at Gleiwitz, just inside the German border, gabbled a few phrases in Polish onto the airwaves, and made their escape. Naujocks left behind the bodies of a few murdered concentration camp inmates – also dressed as Polish soldiers – as 'evidence' of an intolerable Polish provocation. The Gleiwitz incident had provided the totally bogus *casus belli* for Hitler to invade Poland. Once again, at Venlo, Naujocks carried out his murderous mission to his superiors' complete satisfaction.

The previous night, in distant Munich, fate had provided the Germans with the perfect *post facto* justification for their illegal incursion into Dutch territory. On one of the most sacred dates in the Nazi calendar – November 9th was the anniversary of Hitler's bloody and unsuccessful first bid for power, the 1923 Beerhall Putsch – a devastating explosion had wrecked the Burgerbraukellar beer hall, killing seven people, just minutes after Hitler had concluded his annual anniversary address unexpectedly early and left the premises. A carefully constructed time bomb made and planted by a leftist watchmaker and artisan named Georg Elser had caused the blast. Working entirely alone for more than a year, Elser had laboriously assembled his bomb and concealed it in a pillar behind the podium from which Hitler spoke. Had the Fuhrer not left the beer hall when he had, the bomb would certainly have killed him and changed the course of history.

Elser himself was arrested that night attempting to cross into Switzerland. Tasked by Hitler with uncovering the 'conspiracy' behind the bomb, Heinrich Himmler refused to accept Elser's story that he had acted entirely alone out of moral revulsion for Hitler's policies. With their paranoid mix of respect and loathing for the mythical powers of MI6, Hitler and Himmler were convinced that the long arm of London had placed the bomb. Even after repeated torture sessions – included one administered personally by Himmler – had failed to shake Elser's story, the Nazis' belief in an MI6 plot remained undimmed. Elser even constructed a perfect replica of his bomb unaided to prove his capabilities, but the SS chiefs remained unconvinced. It was then that it occurred to Himmler that the two real MI6 men whom Heydrich, Fischer, Schellenberg and Naujocks had placed in his hands could be useful beyond their obvious utility as a source of information about British secret service methods and operations. (Unbelievably, the Nazis had found a list of his agents in Stevens' pocket after they had seized him).

Himmler decided to use Best and Stevens as co-defendants with Elser in a propaganda trial that would follow Germany's victory in the war and would prove to the world that the wicked MI6 had been behind the attempt on Hitler's life. For this purpose, after their initial interrogations, all three men were kept alive in relatively comfortable conditions in a special block for VIP prisoners in the Sachsenhausen concentration camp outside Berlin, though care was taken to ensure that they had no chance of meeting and comparing notes. Despite this, Best managed to make indirect contact with Elser. On entirely inadequate evidence Best became convinced that the courageous little craftsman was an SS scapegoat, and that his beer hall bomb had been an inside job planned and planted by the SS as a way of drumming up popular support for Hitler dented by the lukewarm public enthusiasm for his war. Most historians have concluded that Best's theory is wholly misplaced – would the SS really have risked Hitler's life by leaving a live bomb ticking away a few feet from where he was speaking? – and that Elser really did act heroically and alone.

The Venlo Incident had many long-term consequences, all of them malign. Firstly, it placed two of MI6's European spymasters, with all their inside knowledge of the service's agents and secrets, in Nazi hands. Best carefully skirts the issue, but it seems certain that they, especially the

weak and susceptible Stevens, must have given away valuable information under sustained pressure from their captors. The damage thus
inflicted to Britain's espionage network in Europe was immense. Not
for nothing did Churchill start his own rival spy and sabotage agency,
SOE, from scratch when he succeeded Chamberlain as Prime Minister
in 1940. The second malign consequence was that Venlo permanently
inoculated the British, especially Churchill, who had been suspicious of
the contacts with the Germans in Holland from the outset, against
having any truck with the German opposition to Hitler for the rest of
the war. When the military, Christian and conservative resistance
planning the July 1944 plot on Hitler's life sought support from
Whitehall, they were firmly rebuffed.

Another highly embarrassing result of Venlo was that it exposed the
fact that the Chamberlain government was still seeking to do a deal with
Germany, albeit an anti-Hitler Germany, at the same time as it was
exhorting the nation to bend every sinew for the war effort. Governments always keep the public in the dark as far as they can, and their
private policies often differ radically from their public rhetoric. *The Venlo
Incident brutally* exposed this contradiction at a time of supreme crisis for
Britain. No wonder that the official records of the incident are still
under lock and key at Kew – where Britain's National Archives are kept
– and we will have to wait another five years, until 2015, before they
become available.

Best and Stevens had to endure a five-year wait after Venlo, too. But
at the end of the war, the two men, a pair of embarrassing spectres at
the feast of victory, emerged from their long night of Nazi captivity,
bewildered, emaciated, traumatised – but alive. Doubtless their survival
was not entirely welcome to their former MI6 employers. They were
walking reminders of Britain's greatest single intelligence disaster of the
entire war. They were also, Best in particular, men with a justified
grievance. They had been sacrificed in the pursuit of an illusory peace
policy that Best had cautioned was highly dubious. But his warnings
had been discounted. The men chiefly responsible, Dansey and
Menzies, had also survived the war and now did what they could to
stifle discussion about their mistakes, silence the survivors, and generally
airbrush the whole painful episode from history.

Stevens, the more conventional, less intelligent and more deeply
compromised of the two Venlo victims, never breathed a word in public
about his experiences until the day he died of cancer in a Brighton
hospital in 1968. Best outlived him by a decade. Naujocks, after quarrel-
ling with Heydrich, fell into British hands, and no doubt his
co-operation and silence were ensured. He died forgotten: a Hamburg
nightclub bouncer. Schellenberg himself, the clever young lawyer who
had directed the whole operation in the field, prospered mightily in the
war, rising to become head of Germany's foreign intelligence service.
He gave evidence against his erstwhile comrades at Nuremberg, and
was jailed for six years – during which time he wrote his memoirs. He

was released in 1951 on health grounds. Schellenberg died in 1952 of liver cancer, though some suspect he was poisoned.

Best, the wily old fox, at least profited from his suffering. Dissatisfied with his MI6 pension, he apparently squeezed more cash from Stewart Menzies after a lunch at Whites, Menzies' London club, by threatening to spill embarrassing beans. He supplemented the pension by writing the book you are holding which, despite the discretion of a lifelong professional intelligence officer constrained by the Official Secrets Act, is still a remarkably revealing document: perhaps the most hair-raising memoir every penned by a spy. For obvious reasons it is unique: very few people survived abduction by the SS and prolonged imprisonment in the notorious Sachsenhausen and Dachau concentration camps. Best's final ordeal was a perilous odyssey through the Alps in the dying days of the war, in the company of other VIP Nazi prisoners. Their lives became gambling chips played for by the still murderous SS threatening to kill them at any moment; and army officers who saw their captives as passports to survival in a post-Hitler Germany.

Published now for the first time since its original appearance in 1950, Payne Best's account of his unenviable experiences deserved its bestseller status. It is at once a classic of true spy literature; a gruelling account of prolonged captivity in a Nazi concentration camp; and a nail-biting human story of survival against very long odds. Its author deserves our sympathy – and our respect.

NIGEL JONES, 2009

CHAPTER I

At the outbreak of war our Intelligence Service had reliable
information that Hitler was faced with the opposition of many
men holding the highest appointments in his armed forces and
civil service. The German General Staff had welcomed and gladly
accepted rearmament at his hands, but did not believe that
Germany was strong enough to wage a successful war. They rightly
feared that Hitler was steering the country towards disaster.
According to our information this opposition movement had
assumed such proportions that it might even have led to revolt and
the downfall of the Nazis. That this supposition was justified has
been amply shown by what we have learned since the end of
hostilities about the many plots forged against Hitler and how
narrow was the margin which saved him time and again.

Once we were at war it was obviously of paramount importance
to investigate these matters, and to find out whether there was
any hope that internal dissensions might create conditions favourable
to a quick end to the war. Although many vague rumours had
reached me in Holland, so far, I had failed to get hold of anything
definite and—something had to be done about it.

For reasons of secrecy and security I had hitherto kept very
much in the background, maintaining a number of links between
myself and my agents in Germany, and restricting my own direct
contacts to a few chief assistants. No one was supposed to know
the identities of any others than the person from whom he received
his instructions and those working directly under him. I now
decided to break with this practice and attempt myself to establish
direct relations with the opposition leaders in Germany.

Through a German refugee in Holland named Dr. Franz, we
had for some time past received reliable and often valuable information from a major in the Luftwaffe, named Solms. This man
had frequently indicated, that if he could be absolutely certain
that Dr. Franz had made contact with the British Intelligence
Service, he had some most important news to give. He was particularly insistent that a meeting between him and a responsible
British officer should be arranged, and he refused to give any further
details to Dr. Franz. When I came to know the latter, I could
very well understand this reluctance for, although Dr. Franz was
a likeable little man, he was most excitable and very far from a
model of discretion.

I met Dr. Franz one day at the beginning of September 1939,
and after a long talk I expressed to him my readiness to meet his
friend if it were possible for him to come to Holland for this

7

purpose. At first it was intended that our meeting should take place at The Hague or Amsterdam. This proved to be impossible as he could only make a flying visit of a few hours. He could, however, come to Venlo, as Germans living near the frontier were still allowed to cross the border to shop in neighbouring towns in Holland. We therefore arranged to meet at a small hotel there.

Major Solms was a big, bluff, self-confident fellow, a Bavarian, and inclined to talk as big as he looked. I very soon discovered that he was not nearly as knowledgeable as he pretended, and came to the conclusion that he was little more than an errand boy for more important people in the background. Indeed, he eventually admitted that he could not say much until he had reported to his chief about our meeting. It was then arranged that we should meet again in a week's time.

At our second meeting he impressed me much more favourably; he was calmer, less boastful, and seemed to be acting under definite instructions. Whereas at our first meeting he had ranted a good bit about his honour as a German officer, and had asked me whether I thought he would be a traitor to his country, on this occasion he was quite co-operative. He answered one or two questions on technical air force matters which I put to him and, in the end, told me that there was a big conspiracy to remove Hitler from power in which some of the highest ranking army officers were involved. He could give me no details, as the ring-leaders would only deal with me direct. We therefore made some arrangements to facilitate future communication and agreed upon a code message by which his friends could identify themselves. Sure enough, some days later, Dr. Franz received a telephone call from Berlin and a German officer, whom he knew well, gave him the code message.

A day or two later a letter from the same man reached us through the channel which I had fixed up with Major Solms. In this I was told that a certain German general would like to meet me, but to make absolutely sure that I was indeed a British agent I was asked to arrange that a certain news item, the text of which was enclosed, should be broadcast in the German News Bulletin of the B.B.C. This was easily arranged, and the paragraph was broadcast twice on the 11th October. About the same time too, I received a last message from Major Solms in which he told me that he was afraid that he was being watched by the Gestapo and would therefore have to lie low for a time.

These latest developments seemed to indicate that I might be on to quite a big thing and, as I feared that the job might prove to be more than I could manage alone, I asked Major R. H. Stevens, a British official at The Hague, whether he would be willing to lend me a hand. He agreed to this without demur and from that time on we worked together as partners.

Although it sounds quite simple to speak of arranging to meet some Germans in neutral Holland, actually many difficulties had first to be overcome. By this time the Dutch Army had been mobilized and the entire frontier zone organized to repel invasion. To reach the German border numerous road blocks and military posts had to be passed, and at each travellers had to establish their identity. Under such conditions any secret meeting with our friends seemed to be out of the question.

After some discussion, Stevens and I decided that our only hope lay in placing our difficulties before the Chief of the Dutch Military Intelligence, Major General van Oorschot, in the hope that he might be willing and able to help. General van Oorschot was one of a comparatively small number of men in Holland who from the very first recognized the probability that his country would be invaded and overrun by Germany. He was, too, a man who never feared to shoulder responsibility nor hesitated to take prompt action where such was necessary. We put our case before him in broad lines and he immediately consented to help us by sending one of his officers with us with authority to pass us through the Dutch military cordon and to assist the Germans to enter Holland. The only stipulations which he made were that this officer should be present at our interviews with the Germans, and that we would ourselves refrain from putting forward any proposals which might endanger Dutch neutrality. Considerable criticism has been levelled in Holland against General van Oorschot, especially since the Nazis attempted later to justify their invasion by citing his action as a breach of Dutch neutrality. His action may have been *ultra vires*, and indeed, it was immediately disowned by his Government, but had our enterprise proved successful, there is but little doubt that he would have deserved and received the gratitude of everyone engaged in the fight against Hitler. It was a time of crisis which called for action even at the danger of doing the right thing in the wrong way.

On the 19th October we heard that the Germans would be at a small village on the frontier called Dinxperlo at ten o'clock next morning. This was some 120 miles from The Hague and so we had to set off bright and early. Our party consisted of Major Stevens, Dr. Franz, and the Dutch officer who had been detailed by General van Oorschot to look after us. This officer, Lieutenant Klop, was an exceedingly nice, upstanding young fellow whom we soon came to look upon as a good friend. As he spoke English perfectly, we decided to pass him off as a British officer and Stevens gave him the name of Captain Coppens.

I drove, and we made quite good time. We reached Zutphen, a small town in Gelderland, at eight o'clock and Stevens and I decided to wait at a café there whilst Klop and Franz went by taxi to fetch our visitors from the frontier some twenty miles away.

We had breakfast and then Stevens and I hung about the café for hour after hour with no word nor sign from the rest of our party. We held the fort with numerous cups of coffee until, about noon, Klop rang up to say that he too had been waiting all the time at the frontier without a sign of the Germans. Two men had, however, now turned up and he was bringing them back right away.

When he reached us he had with him, instead of the general we had expected and of whom we had a good description, two men in the early thirties whom Dr. Franz introduced as Captain von Seidlitz and Lieutenant Grosch. He said that he knew them both well and that they would tell us themselves why the general had failed to come himself. The men seemed very nervous and at first were reluctant even to get out of the car. My intention had been to take them to Amsterdam where I had arranged for a quiet place for our talk, but they declared that this was impossible as they must be back again in Germany before eight that evening without fail. This put me in rather a quandary. Stevens and I had been hanging about that café for so long that we felt the waiters were beginning to eye us suspiciously. They had heard us talking English together and I felt sure that if we now came in with two Huns they would certainly report us to the police. Remember that this was near the German frontier and people were inclined to see spies everywhere.

I packed the whole party into my car and drove a little way into the country-side until we came to an isolated roadside café where I decided that we might stop for lunch. Dr. Franz, who had been quite normal on the drive down, had become terribly excited which we attributed to joy at meeting his friends. He was really quite a nuisance as he kept running round the table from one to another of us, making all sorts of absurd remarks and interrupting our attempts to interrogate our guests. A couple of Dutch soldiers came into the café and I noticed that they were eyeing us very attentively and apparently trying to listen in to our conversation. We were still in the frontier zone and I did not want any trouble with the military. As soon, therefore, as we had finished our lunch I telephoned to some friends in Arnhem, which was about ten miles farther on, and asked whether I might come to their house as I had some people with me with whom I wanted to talk undisturbed. 'Certainly,' was the answer and when we got there, the dining-room was placed at our disposal and we settled down for a round-table conference.

The Germans would not, or could not, tell us anything beyond admitting that they were connected with a revolutionary movement. They said that their chief had been afraid of being held up at the frontier, or that we might fail to keep the appointment. He had therefore sent them to see how the land lay. They made rather a joke of the fact that generals tend to leave sticky jobs to others, but said that when he heard from them how easily they had got through, he would certainly venture to pay us a visit next time himself.

We had scarcely started our talk when my friend came in, and in some agitation, told us that the house was surrounded by police and that there were two men at the door asking about some Germans. Klop and I went out and sure enough the street seemed full of side-car combinations and men of the Dutch gendarmerie. We learned that after we left the café the soldiers, who thought us very suspicious characters, had rung up headquarters and the police and then traced us through my trunk call to Arnhem. Klop had some difficulty in preventing the police from bursting into the house and arresting the lot of us, but after some argument they agreed to take him to their barracks where he quickly allayed the suspicions of the officer in command.

Whilst all this was going on the two Germans were in an absolute panic, and Stevens had the greatest difficulty in preventing them from jumping out of the window and trying to escape. Franz, too, became white as a sheet and seemed on the point of passing out. When Klop, by his return, brought some semblance of calm, we tried to get down to business again. The two Huns still seemed to be scared out of their wits and it was very difficult to get any-thing out of them except that they wanted to go home. They were certain that they would be late and this would ruin them. We did manage to get some further confirmation about the conspiracy and had a little general conversation on possible allied peace terms, but as it did not seem likely that we should get much further with these men, we asked Klop to take them back to the frontier. Dr. Franz was complaining that he felt very ill (he often suffered from gall-stones) so we packed him off to The Hague by train.

During the next few days we received several more communications from Germany. A fresh meeting was fixed for the 25th October and then postponed until the 30th. Again, a rendezvous was given at Dinxperlo, but this time only Klop went to fetch the men and Stevens and I awaited them at The Hague. We did not want another experience like the last, which might have compromised us seriously; so, if the Germans wished to see us, they would have to do what we thought best.

Again we had a long wait. When at last Klop got back, he told us that although he had been well on time, the Germans, instead of waiting quietly, had tried to make their own way into Holland through a wood. They had been spotted, arrested, and searched. Klop had taken advantage of their mishap to go through their belongings and inspect their papers. Everything seemed to be quite in order.

This time, instead of the officers we had expected, Klop had with him three men. One was the man Grosch who had come over on the first occasion, and he introduced the two others to us as Colonel Martini and Major Schaemmel. Of the three, Schaemmel was obviously the leader. It was difficult to assess his age, as although he had a babyish sort of face, most of it was obliterated by the numerous scars of those sabre cuts so dear to German students. But he was a well-informed man, had a quick decisive manner, and a ready answer to all our questions.

He started by giving us a clear and convincing résumé of conditions in Germany and the degree in which the army had suffered in the Polish campaign. Losses in men and material had been high and the present military and economic conditions made it imperative that the war should be brought to an end quickly. Hitler though, would not listen to the advice of his General Staff and allowed nothing to stand in the way of his ambitions. Therefore, he must be got rid of. It was, though, of no use to assassinate him, as this could only lead to chaos. The intention therefore was to take him prisoner and force him to give orders authorizing a junta of officers to reorganize the Government and start negotiations for peace.

Schaemmel said, "We are Germans and have to think of the interests of our own country first. Before we take any steps against Hitler we want to know whether England and France are ready to grant us a peace which is both just and honourable."

A long discussion followed during which we hammered out a protocol which could be submitted by us to a higher level. We made it clear to the Germans that we had no authority to give them any assurances and that our task was solely that of intermediaries.

The Germans had to be back at the frontier before noon next day as a friendly customs officer who would pass them through went off duty at that hour. It was clearly impossible for us to expect any answer from London before then and the Germans were therefore given a wireless transmitting and receiving set so that future communications would be facilitated. Although Klop was present at our talk, he did not, of course, take any part in the discussion. This was very useful, as he was free to observe the Germans and give undivided attention to their reactions. When we compared notes after the meeting, he agreed that the Germans seemed to be genuine and thought that the whole thing looked most hopeful.

A full report was made to London, and a day or two later we received a carefully worded and rather non-committal reply. We were authorized to impart the gist of this message to the Germans, but were instructed to give them nothing in writing. The matter seemed very interesting and we were to follow it up with energy, though at the same time we were urged to be cautious and to avoid risk to ourselves.

After a preliminary technical hitch, wireless communication with the Germans worked smoothly and messages were exchanged daily at a certain hour. Since we were not permitted to give the Germans anything in writing, it was obvious that another meeting would be necessary so that we could tell them about the reply which we had received. For this next encounter, Klop suggested that Venlo would be a better place, as it was close to the frontier and less than five miles away there was a very quiet customs post which was far easier to pass unobserved than that at Dinxperlo. We therefore made arrangements to meet the Germans there on the morning of 7th November.

Again it was the intention of Stevens and myself to put up at an hotel in Venlo whilst Klop went to the frontier and fetched the Germans. When he got there though, he rang up to say that they seemed very frightened and would not agree to come to Venlo with him. For his part, he strongly advised us to come along to the frontier as there was a café, from which he was telephoning, which was much quieter and better for our purpose than the hotel at Venlo. He absolutely pooh-poohed any idea of danger and said that the café was well inside Dutch territory and nothing could possibly happen to us there. Neither Stevens nor I liked to venture so close to Germany, but we had to admit that the Germans might be running a greater risk if they came to Venlo, so, on the whole, we had better take Klop's advice. After all he knew the ground better than we. So off we went.

It was a pretty drive from Venlo to the frontier, a winding road through pine woods. When we got to the café, certainly nothing could have looked more peaceful. A red brick building with a roofed veranda at the front and sides. At the back a large garden with swings, see-saws and other amusements for children. It lay on the left-hand side of the road and about 200 yards farther on, we could see the black and white painted barrier of the German frontier. Nearly opposite the café was the Dutch customs house.

Klop met us at the door, and inside, in a quiet room next to the café, we found Schaemmel and Grosch. We gave them a résumé of the answer we had received to their questions, which did not seem to come quite up to their expectations. They said though, that they would pass it on to their chief, and then asked whether it would be possible for us to come again next day to meet him. He had been unable to come this time, but he was anxious to see us as he wished to entrust some secret papers to us for safekeeping. The plot might fail. Plots often did, and he did not want all record of his work and that of his friends to be lost; besides, there were certain points which he could only discuss with us personally.

'So,' we thought, 'the general is getting windy and wants us to arrange a get-away for him.' But, as the request seemed reasonable, we agreed, and a meeting was fixed for the following afternoon.

Next day we drove straight through to the café, though this time Klop made a short stop at Venlo and went to police headquarters where he arranged that an armed guard should be sent to the frontier. It was not that we distrusted Schaemmel, but there was always the possibility that the Gestapo might have got on to him and make a raid so as to catch him with us red-handed. It would not be difficult to do this in such an isolated spot, so it was better to be on the safe side.

When we got to the café, to our disappointment we found only Schaemmel there. He was very sorry, but the general had been held up at the last minute. That morning an appeal for peace had been launched by the Queen of the Netherlands and the King of the Belgians. Hitler had called a big staff meeting at Munich to consider this, and the general had been obliged to attend. Could we come next day again? The attempt against Hitler was to take place on Saturday; today was Wednesday, so tomorrow would be the last chance of a meeting. With some hesitation we agreed to try yet once more to meet this most elusive general. Neither Stevens nor I liked the idea of coming here again. The weather had turned dull and in the waning evening light we seemed a long way from home and far, far too close to Germany. We tried to fix our appointment for the morning, but Schaemmel said, the general, who was now in Munich, could not possibly be with us before the afternoon. We therefore arranged to meet at 4 p.m.

CHAPTER II

(i)

THE 9th November, 1939. I got up shortly after five although I felt very tired and much disinclined to do so, but through these daily trips to the frontier I had been forced to neglect all my other work and there were some things which I could put off no longer. As I shaved I could not help wishing that I could somehow or other dodge having to go to that beastly frontier café again. There had been something about it the previous evening which had made me feel most uncomfortable; the unpleasant looking stout man who had looked us over so carefully as we went in, then the feeling of being completely cut off from the outside world in that little side room where we had our talks with the Germans, those big glass windows which looked out on to a wall of dense undergrowth. It would be so easy for some SS men to cross the border at the back of the café and creep up so that they could shoot us through the windows as we sat in the light. Rubbish! There was no real reason for my fears. During the First World War I had been to the frontier dozens of times like this; much closer too, for the café in Limburg where I used to meet people was half in Holland and half in Germany—but yet I was uneasy, and if I could have done so with decency, would have rung up Stevens and called the whole thing off.

My wife was not up, of course, but I spoke to her before I went out and said, that perhaps I might not be back to dinner; in any case, she was not to wait for me after 7.30. She said, "No, don't hurry back. You drive much too fast and it always makes me nervous. I have a bridge party here this afternoon and it will really be better if you have dinner out; I shall be much happier if I know you are driving carefully."

It was a dull morning and much colder than of late; the sky was overcast and threatened rain. When I got to the office I just had time to glance at the morning paper. It carried a stop-press notice about an attempt on Hitler's life which had been made at Munich the previous day. Hitler himself had escaped as he had already left the place before the explosion, but many others had been killed and injured. Very curious, and I wondered whether this attempt had anything to do with our people and, if not, what effect it would have on their plans.

Then I plunged into my work and it was after ten before I was free to join Stevens at his house. Klop had not yet arrived. Stevens felt just as I did, that the Huns were becoming an infernal nuisance with their shilly-shallying. If the general did not come up to the scratch this time, we would wash our hands of the whole business and leave them to run their show alone. We would keep this one last appointment, and then, finis.

Stevens produced some Browning automatics and we each loaded and pocketed one—just in case. Then Klop came in. He apologized for being late but there was a bit of a scare on and he had been kept at the office. Some news had come in to the effect that the Germans might march into Holland at any moment. The story was unconfirmed and Klop did not believe it himself; nor did it agree with any indications which Stevens and I had. We talked about this for a time and then discussed what could be done to satisfy the Germans about an escape route into Holland in case of emergency. Of course it was out of the question to give them anything in the nature of a pass, so it was decided simply to give the telephone number of Klop's office; then, if they wanted to come into Holland they could ask the customs officer to ring up this number and Klop would then see to the rest.

We were just on the point of setting off when a message from the Germans started to come in over the wireless. It might be to cancel our appointment, so we had to wait until it had been transcribed and decoded. It was though, of no importance whatever;

merely a request for a change in the hours of transmission. This had delayed us quite a bit and I would have to drive all out if we were to be on time for the meeting. As we were all feeling rather tired I asked my driver, Jan Lemmens, to come with us so that he could bring the car back in case we wished ourselves to return by train.

We made such good time that we were able to stop for a quick lunch at a little road-side café near s' Hertogenbosch. While we were eating, Stevens and I talked about the possible danger that we might be raided and captured, but Klop assured us that there was nothing to be feared, especially not during daylight, as he had arranged for a stronger guard than usual to be at the frontier.

Until we stopped for lunch Jan had sat next to me, and Stevens and Klop behind. When we started off again, Stevens came and sat by me and we had a chat about what might happen if the Germans made a sudden attack on Holland and we discussed what measures would be best for the safe evacuation of the legation and other Britishers still in Holland; Stevens also scribbled down a list of people whom he knew, who would have to be got out of the country before the Germans got in. I said, "Better destroy that list of yours before we get to the frontier. I still have a feeling that something may go wrong." Stevens said, "Of course," and I believe tore up the paper and threw it out of the car.

I never like to talk when I am driving and always find that it slows up my speed appreciably; in any case, when we reached Venlo it was already four o'clock, the time set for our meeting. Although we stopped so that Klop could call at the police station and arrange about our guard, we could not wait until the men had cycled the five miles to the frontier, but pushed on ahead of them.

All the way down from The Hague we had noticed that military precautions had been intensified and we had been held up at every road block and tank barrier. Even now, between Venlo and our café, we were stopped twice. The first time the sentry said something about having orders to allow no cars to pass and although Klop showed him his authority insisted that he must first go to the guard room and speak to the N.C.O. in charge. Both Stevens and I, I believe, felt alike and hoped that he would come back with the news that we could go no farther; but in a few minutes he was with us: "Everything is all right. The N.C.O. had a message for me which had been phoned through from the office. Carry on."

The second sentry did not actually stop us, but only made signs that we should drive slowly. He was stationed at a bend in the road just before we entered the straight along which one had a view of the frontier. Somehow or other, it seemed to me that things looked different from what they had on the previous days. Then I noticed that the German barrier across the road which had always been closed, was now lifted; there seemed to be nothing between us and the enemy. My feeling of impending danger was very strong. Yet the scene was peaceful enough. No one was in sight except a German customs officer in uniform lounging along the road towards us and a little girl who was playing at ball with a big black dog in the middle of the road before the café.

I must have rather checked my speed, for Klop called out, "Go ahead, everything is quite all right." I felt rather a fool to be so nervous. I let the car drift slowly along to the front of the café on my left and then reversed into the car park on the side of the building farthest from the frontier. Schaemmel was standing on the veranda at the corner and made a sign which I took to mean that our bird was inside. I stopped the engine and Stevens got out on the right. My car had left-hand drive. I had just wriggled clear of the wheel and was following him out when there was a sudden noise of shouting and shooting. I looked up, and through the windscreen saw a large open car drive up round the corner till our bumpers were touching. It seemed to be packed to over-flowing with rough-looking men. Two were perched on top of the hood and were firing over our heads from sub-machine guns, others were standing up in the car and on the running boards; all shouting and waving pistols. Four men jumped off almost before their car had stopped and rushed towards us shouting: "Hands up!"

I don't remember actually getting out of the car, but by the time the men reached us, I was certainly standing next to Stevens, on his left. I heard him say: "Our number is up, Best." The last words we were to exchange for over five years. Then we were seized. Two men pointed their guns at our heads, the other two quickly handcuffed us.

I heard shots behind me on my right. I looked round and saw Klop. He must have crept out behind us under cover of the car door which had been left open. He was running diagonally away from us towards the road; running sideways in big bounds, firing at our captors as he ran. He looked graceful, with both arms out-stretched—almost like a ballet dancer. I saw the windscreen of the German car splinter into a star, and then the four men standing in front of us started shooting and after a few more steps Klop just seemed to crumple and collapse into a dark heap of clothes on the grass.

"Now, march!" shouted our captors, and prodding us in the small of our backs with their guns, they hurried us, with cries of "Hup! Hup! Hup!" along the road towards the frontier. As we passed the front of the café I saw my poor Jan held by the arms by two men who were frog-marching him along. It seemed to me that his chin was reddened as from a blow. Then we were across the border. The black and white barrier closed behind us. We were in Nazi Germany.

B

(ii)

They hustled us up the slope of a ramp and into the customs office, where we were made to stand with upraised arms facing a dirty whitewashed wall. Behind each of us stood a man, pistol in hand.

It was funny, but I felt no fear—not even anxiety; indeed, I did not seem to realize that I was an actor in the events that were taking place but rather that I was a deeply interested spectator, viewing things from afar. I can remember when, as a small boy, I was for the first time taken to the pantomime, I had had this same disembodied feeling. I was at one and the same time leaning against a plush covered barrier, whose soft roughness I can still feel on my chin, and, taking active part in the exciting happenings on the brightly lit stage. Although Stevens and I had talked about the possibility of capture, I don't think that we had either of us really envisaged its practical physical implication nor foreseen the possibility of so sudden a translation into an unknown world.

We had been standing facing the wall for only a few minutes when there came a renewed order to "March!" We went out into the light of day and on to the ramp before which the German car was standing. Behind it I saw my own car. This seemed to jolt me into present reality for I felt extremely angry that the Huns, not satisfied with kidnapping us, apparently intended to steal my car. This offended my sense of the sanctity of property. "Into the car with you," was the next order. This meant a jump from the four foot high ramp which to me, handcuffed as I was, seemed quite a distance. A nudge in the back resolved my hesitation, though I nearly made a bad landing. I sat on the right of the back seat with Stevens next to me and, on his left, one of the gangsters whom I later discovered to be an army captain and leader of the raiding party. Two men threw some tommy guns in at our feet and then sat down on folding seats facing us. Another couple came along with Jan Lemmens, also handcuffed, and literally chucked him into the car so that he fell on his back, with his legs in the air, at our feet. These last two men went away and returned carrying Klop, holding him by his legs and one arm. The other arm hung down as though broken. There was a trickle of blood down the fingers and also one on the side of his face. He was unconscious, his face greyish yellow and it was difficult to hope that he still lived. It looked at first as though it was the intention to throw him into our car on top of Lemmens, but the captain said something and the men took him away again; I believe that he was put into my car.

I began to say something to Lemmens about how sorry I was that he should be involved in this mess, and Stevens said something about Klop; "Looks as though he were dead," or something like that. This raised a storm and the Germans shouted at us to be silent and said that severe measures would be taken if we did not hold our jaws.

Our driver and another man got in and we were just about to make a start when one of the men who had been carrying Klop came running up holding some papers in his hand. He gave these to the captain saying in an excited voice, "We have made a great find. The other one is a Dutch officer." All the men seemed to be excited and in a state of great nervous tension; just as though they had accomplished some very dangerous mission. There was a lot of talk between them about the hair-breadth escapes they had had from the shots fired by poor Klop; one man kept repeating that one bullet had passed so close to his head that he had felt the wind. Compared to them I felt myself to be quite calm and collected. I was in no way worried about what might happen to me; all my thoughts were about May and the shock the news of my capture would be to her. I thought, 'She will probably hear about it in the eight o'clock news'. Actually, she waited up for me all night, every hour in greater fear, and had no definite news till she was rung up from the legation next morning.

Our car started and off we went into the blue.

We had only gone a short distance when we turned down a lane on the left which seemed to lead only to some fields. I wondered whether this was 'journey's end' and this quiet spot considered suitable for the disposal of the bodies. The leader shouted "Halt!" and, after some discussion with the driver, we backed out on to the road again and continued our journey in the direction in which we had been going.

It was an open car and on the back seat one got the full force of the blast. I was lightly clad and the evening was chilly; perhaps too, I was affected by the shock of our capture; however it was, I felt abominably cold and besides, badly wanted to relieve myself. Mention of these two points to the captain resulted in a coat being thrown over Stevens and me which afforded us some protection, but for the rest, I was told to hold on and wait until we 'arrived'.

By this time, I was acutely conscious of the fact that I was a prisoner, sitting handcuffed in a German car, and being rapidly driven towards some unknown destination and fate. I began to think quite a lot about what might happen to us, but I can't say that I felt downhearted; rather, my state was one of enhanced mental alertness. I am essentially a practical man and seem to have insufficient imagination to be able to worry about the future. Stevens, from what I could see of him, was immersed in blackest gloom and poor Jan looked pathetically puzzled and startled. I felt so sorry for him. He ran a small garage at The Hague and for years past had looked after my cars and had played the part of a devoted and benevolent mechanical father to them and to me. Really, he was one of the best and staunchest friends I have ever had. He had a wife and four children, all still small, and worked single-handed, almost day and night to keep his little business going. He had nothing to do with my intelligence work and it was only by chance that he was with us today. I hoped that the Germans could be made to realize this and that they would let him go. It would be simply terrible for him if he were kept prisoner with us, perhaps for years.

I badly wanted to say something to comfort him and, as I was not allowed to speak to him, I began to tell the captain about him in German which I knew Jan could understand. As no objection was made to my breach of the silence I went on talking and said to the captain:

"I suppose you think that you have made a great capture in getting us like this. Really, your show was very well run."

"I don't care about you two," he said, "but I am glad to have got those German swine who were trying to betray their country. They will get short shrift. I wish I could hang them with my own hands, the pig-dogs."

Now this was most interesting and a very valuable pointer. So they intended to go on pretending that Schaemmel and Co. were genuine conspirators and like ourselves prisoners. Of course, by now I had no shadow of doubt but that Schaemmel was the nigger in the wood pile and that it was he who had given the signal for our capture. Still, if this were the line which the Germans had been instructed to take, it might possibly be better to play along with them and see how matters developed. It was always possible that they wished to keep a loop-hole open in case there was too much fuss made abroad about our capture; they might then plead that the raiders were sent to arrest some Germans and that Stevens and I owed our capture only to excess of zeal on their part.

After a drive of about two hours we came to the Rhine and I recognized the approaches to Düsseldorf. We drove a little way through the town and then turned under an arch into the court-yard of a large building. Here, we were bundled out of the car and with more prodding of pistols hurried at the double into a sort of basement where I was put into a small cell, furnished with a bunk, a table, and a chair. I was then made to strip to the buff and was subjected to an examination which most certainly was intended to leave no stone unturned. A dirty finger was thrust into my mouth and run around my cheeks and between tongue and teeth; ears, hair, nostrils, and indeed, all apertures of my body were probed and inspected—yet, they omitted to examine my feet although I might easily be hiding the poison phial for which they were searching between my toes. After this, I was given a blue serge training suit, which I was told with emphasis was quite new, and at last was permitted to visit the lavatory. Ah-h-h-h! what a relief!

(I'm sorry, but I cannot write about prison life without touching on such matters, for in prison you find that life is centred on and revolves about the elemental facts of food, sleep—and defecation. All three are of equal importance and, even to me, smoking came a bad fourth.)

As I came back from the lavatory I saw that my cell was one of a row. In the one next to me I saw Stevens, sitting on his bunk and looking just about as miserable as I really felt. Next door to him was Jan, but he was lying down on his bunk and I could only see him indistinctly.

My handcuffs had been removed whilst I undressed and dressed but now they were put on again, luckily, not so tightly as before, and I was told to lie down on the bunk.

Handcuffs are really most unpleasant things and the effect of having them on singularly demoralizing. You feel, not only helpless, but absurd. Then too, every part of your body out of scratching reach begins to itch and in time this becomes real torture. Having yet to make my début in crime my experience of handcuffs is limited to those in vogue with the Gestapo and I do not know whether they are subject to the vagaries of fashion. These, which I had on, with their highly chromed finish, combined elegance with lightness and, as I was assured, enormous strength. Shaped rather like a pair of spectacles they could be folded along a central hinge so as to fit the pocket. The two arms or hooks which fitted round the wrists had serrated ends which entered with a ratchet action into the central lock. They were so shaped that, when closed, they formed oval apertures which prevented the wrists from being turned. The degree of discomfort depended upon how far the ratchet was pressed in for the edges of the arms were razor sharp and they could, as I was later to discover, cut deeply into the wrists. Handcuffs can be worn either with the palms of the hand facing each other, or with the hands crossed, one above the other. Both methods are equally uncomfortable.

The next step in my initiation into prison life was a thorough examination of my clothes and the contents of my pockets. This was rather ostentatiously carried out in my presence. With grief and annoyance I saw my fountain pen roughly broken open and the back forced off my watch; worst of all, some 200 cigarettes which I had with me in the car were, one by one, broken into bits. How often did I think of these cigarettes and long for them in the months that followed. Then, all my money and other belongings were placed in a large envelope which was sealed. Everything perfectly honest and above-board. Yet, when the envelope was opened in my presence in Berlin a day or two later, f.500 (more than £50) which I had seen put in at Düsseldorf had faded away into nothing. Probably there was another envelope and more sealing wax at Düsseldorf.

I was next brought a couple of sandwiches which tasted like a mixture of sawdust and axle grease; there was also a mug containing that filthy dark fluid which in Germany passes for coffee. It was months before I could swallow it at all. This concoction made of an infusion of beach nuts and parched malted grain is a German heritage from the First World War, and is still generally what is called coffee. Real coffee is distinguished by the name of 'Bean Coffee' just as 'Black Tea' serves to distinguish real 'tea' from infusions of dried peppermint or other herbs.

I was very tired, for this was the third day in succession that I had been up at five, and my one wish now was to sleep. But this was not allowed. Every time that I was on the point of dropping off I would be given a shake by one of a number of men who seemed to spend the night tramping in and out of my cell. "Don't go to sleep. It is forbidden." At the time I thought this a most senseless regulation and I became so angry that I began to feel more and more myself again and ready to cope with anything that might befall me. Later, when I experienced the frequency with which prisoners attempted suicide, I realized, that in preventing me from sleeping, a normal routine precaution was observed. It was always just possible that, in spite of the search, I might still have poison secreted somewhere on me.

When I was first put into my cell I was for some time alone with one of the men who had taken part in the raid. He was a nice looking fellow of some twenty-five years of age. He told me that the men who had taken part in the raid were officers who had volunteered for dangerous duty and that they all came from different units; he himself was a naval officer from Kiel. He said that they had been told that they were to go into Holland to capture some Germans who were plotting against the Führer and who were responsible for the attempt against his life which had taken place the day before. Now though, he did not know what to think. Nothing had been said to him about Englishmen, and the German whom they had found at the frontier had returned with them as a free man and seemed to be a friend of 'the chief'. He didn't like the look of things at all and wished that he had had nothing to do with it. Now, we were to be handed over to the Gestapo and he hoped that I would not hold him responsible if they treated me improperly.

I think that this young man was perfectly genuine and felt that he had been duped into performing a dishonourable action. He was certainly very kind to me and helped me over some very difficult moments. They had taken all my cigarettes away, so he fed me with some of his own; he also asked for extra blankets for me, as he thought I looked cold. This was the first example of that kindness which I was to find, often in the most unlikely quarters, throughout my imprisonment.

It must have been in the small hours of the morning when I was told to get up. I was taken out through the courtyard and through another door, up several flights of stairs, and into a comfortable room where there were two men and a girl typist. I was told quite politely to sit down and was offered a cigarette. Then details were taken down as to my name, age, and place of birth. They expressed surprise when I said that I was British. "Your German is very good, but you speak like a Dutchman; not at all like an Englishman." This was not surprising after twenty years in Holland, for even Germans who lived there for any length of time seemed to pick up a Dutch accent. After a short talk which was quite amicable on both sides I was taken down again to my cell, passing Stevens in a sort of antechamber on my way down.

The dreary sleepless night dragged on and my thoughts of my poor wife waiting in vain for my return left me no peace; my thoughts and feeling of impotence were such that they almost caused me physical pain. Yet I knew that I must put away all thoughts of the past and of the might-have-been and concentrate only on the problems of the present if I were to have any hope of finding a way out.

At last the night came to an end and I was told to get up. "We are going farther," it was said. I was handed my clothes but was not able to wash or comb my hair. I dressed in one corner of a room and Stevens in another. Several of the men who had captured us were about; most of them now dressed in uniform. The leader of the party was a smart army captain instead of the dirty unshaven bandit with a shapeless felt hat pulled over his eyes who had sat with us in the car. He seemed to be the man in authority so I protested to him about not being allowed to wash; I also asked for food. He was quite civil and said that he was sorry, but there were no facilities for washing; as for food, I would get some later on—very much later on, as it turned out.

When I was dressed, I was again urged to move elsewhere by the now familiar prodding in the small of my back. This time we went out into the courtyard where I was told to get into the back of a touring car of which the hood and side curtains were closed. The captain got in next to me, the driver and another man sat in front.

I did not take much notice during the first part of our journey as by now I was pretty well all in and fell asleep immediately. I must have slept for quite a while, for when I awakened we were on the Reichsautobahn approaching Hanover. I felt pretty rotten, both tired and hungry—I was still soft from good living—the worst infliction though was the lack of my eye-glass which had been taken from me and which they had refused to let me have back. This strained my eyes and gave me a bad headache. I saw a notice board where the by-pass to Hanover left the Autobahn, but we went straight on and the signposts now said 'Berlin'. An hour or so later, about two o'clock I should think, we stopped at a filling station attached to which there appeared to be something in the nature of a café or restaurant. As we stopped I was able to catch a glance in the rear mirror and saw that another five or six cars, amongst them my own, were drawn up behind us.

The captain got out and with him the driver; the man who sat next to the latter was left to guard me, which he did with his pistol at the ready. After a while the captain came back alone and told the other man to go and get some food. As soon as he had gone the captain produced an apple which he cut into pieces and gave to me. He told me that I was not allowed to have any food and that we must be very careful as the other two men were from the police. He gave me a cigarette and later, when we were under way again, fed me with bits of sandwich which he cut up and popped into my mouth. Whilst we were alone together he also unlocked and slackened my handcuffs which had been so closely clamped together that my fingers were quite numb and swollen.

When we left the filling station, my car, a Lincoln Zephyr and very fast, passed us and soon vanished in the distance. I was much annoyed to notice that they had already succeeded in losing the cap of the petrol tank—I was in a mood when little things like this made me very cross.

We continued to jog along at a steady forty miles an hour which seemed terribly slow along the empty expanse of the Autobahn. Except for one or two heavy lorries stinking of paraffin and a group of military motor-cyclists looking like great frogs in their voluminous overalls, the Autobahn was quite deserted. When at last we reached Berlin it was already quite dark and the black-out was complete. Our driver, at one point, seemed to lose his way and got out to make inquiries. Whilst the captain and I were again alone for a few minutes, he said to me: "Up to now you have been in the care of the Wehrmacht. Soon I shall have to hand you over to the Gestapo. If you have disagreeable experiences with them, I hope you will not blame me too hardly, for I have only obeyed orders and done my duty. I am sorry to have had to capture you in this way for it is no work for a soldier." I said that I quite understood, and we gravely shook hands. I can't say that I felt exactly encouraged by this conversation for it seemed to me that both the army and the navy took a very dim view of what might happen when the Gestapo got me.

The car started off again and after about a quarter of an hour we stopped at a spot where it seemed to be darker than ever. The car door was opened and a rough voice asked: "Is this number one?" and, on receiving an answer in the affirmative: "Are his legs fettered? No? Then, out you come." My hat was torn off and a sort of hood pulled over my head. Then I was seized above the elbows by two men and dragged out of the car. We went through a doorway into a lighted passage (I could dimly see through the hood which covered my face) and then I was pulled, almost at the double, along passages, up stairs and down stairs, until I was exhausted and breathless. Although I had managed to clasp my fingers together and could so take some of the strain with the muscles of my arms, the two men holding me kept jerking at my elbows so that my handcuffs were forced deep into my flesh cutting my wrists badly. I must have been taken about three times from attic to basement, up one stairway, across the building, and down another one, for I found out later that the Gestapo Headquarters building in the Prinz Albrechtstrasse into which I was now making my entry was far from large. I suppose they thought that I needed exercise after the long drive. The hood over my face greatly impeded my breathing and when at last we stopped, and I was pushed into a lighted room and on to a soft seat, I had almost passed out. I was just conscious that my feet were being tightly strapped together and then a voice said: "Take off the hood."

When I had recovered sufficiently to take notice, I found that I was sitting on a couch in a comfortable looking room with, sitting facing me, a rather pleasant looking and seemingly quite harmless little man. There were a number of other men either sitting on chairs or standing in a semi-circle behind him, all looking at me as though I were some strange and possibly dangerous animal. It was some time before I had breath enough to speak, but when I had, I just let fly. I was in a furious passion and used up every ounce of German invective that I possessed. My performance must have been masterly and almost worthy of Hitler himself for the effect was magical. My handcuffs and the straps round my ankles were removed. I was offered a cigarette and the little man sitting opposite to me began to explain in a soothing voice that nothing offensive had been intended and that I had only been given a taste of the way in which German prisoners were treated at "Your Scotland Yard". This set me off again and I told him very plainly that his remark was slanderous and simply showed how ignorant Germans were about everything outside their own rotten country. So far I had never believed the stories told in England about the Gestapo because all the Germans I had ever met had been ordinary civilized human beings, but now I began to see how mistaken I had been.

In good German fashion we then conversed for quite a while, both shouting at the tops of our voices at the same time while the statists sat round us goggling, having apparently no speaking parts. As far as I could make out he was asking me to be calm, assuring me nothing offensive was intended and that on the contrary, every-thing had been done for my good. That is a great German slogan in criminal circles when anything disagreeable is done to you; it is the equivalent of the English: "It hurts Father far more than it does you, Jimmy."

"Do calm yourself, Mr. Best; nothing will happen to you if you will only be reasonable. But, remember, you are quite in our power and if you won't behave yourself we shall have to adopt very different measures with you. Surely you don't want me to have you fettered again. All that I want you to do now is to answer a few questions."

I told him flatly that it was useless for him to go on, he could do anything he damned well liked, but unless he treated me respectfully and until I had had a wash and a shave and had been given something to eat, I was not playing. This only set him off shouting still louder. In these German shouting matches, the man who starts first is always supposed to have scored the first point. No one listens to what is said and the important thing is to keep going without a break and so silence the other man. In German this is called 'Anschnauzen' which may be appropriately translated as snorting.

The general tenor of what he now said was that he was Dr. Max, the terror of all wrong-doers; surely I had heard of him and knew his reputation. When I confessed that, hitherto, his fame had not reached me, he was really quite taken aback.

"But you must have read the British White Book about the German concentration camps. There is a lot in it about me; all lies, of course, like everything else the English tell about us."[1]

I told him that I had not read the book, having so far been unable to get hold of a copy. If he had one to spare, I should very much like to read it, meanwhile though, could I please have a wash and shave and would he get me some food.

I don't to this day know what terrible things were reported about Dr. Max in the White Book, but personally, once we got to know each other, I always found him a very pleasant little man who paid me the compliment of always laughing at my jokes. On this first meeting he did his best to impress me with his frightfulness and threatened me with shooting; said, that under present German law, I had been guilty of high treason and a lot of rubbish of that sort. I was, however, so completely fed up with the whole business and had so little appetite for the long years of imprisonment which I saw before me, that his threats left me absolutely cold. If they were going to shoot me, why not go ahead. I had no objection and in many ways I should feel that they were doing me a favour. Why, for me, it was the simplest road to fame. I might even have a London street named after me.

Apparently I impressed Dr. Max with my sincerity for he went out of the room and, when he returned, had with him his chief, SS-Oberführer Müller. Müller was a dapper, exceptionally good-

---

[1] I have since been told that the book in question was not white but some other colour. The Germans however always spoke of 'Das Weiss Buch'.

looking little man, dressed in imitation of Adolf Hitler, in a grey uniform jacket, black riding breeches and top boots. He started his 'snort' immediately he entered and, as he walked towards me, increased the pitch and volume of his voice with great virtuosity. He managed to get right up close to me before his vocal chords tore into shreds. "You are in the hands of the Gestapo. Don't imagine that we shall show you the slightest consideration. The Führer has already shown the world that he is invincible and soon he will come and liberate the people of England from Jews and Plutocrats such as you. It is war and Germany is fighting for her existence. You are in the greatest danger and if you want to live another day must be very careful." Then he sat down on the chair in front of me and drew it up as close as possible, apparently with the intention of performing some mesmerizing trick. He had rather funny eyes which he could flicker from side to side with the greatest rapidity and I suppose that this was supposed to strike terror into the heart of the beholder.

"I have something the matter with my eyes, too," I said, "Could I perhaps have my glasses?" This set him going again. He jumped up. "Don't you worry about glasses or anything else. You will probably be dead before morning and won't need glasses or anything else. Then you won't be a nuisance to us any longer. You don't seem to realize your position. It is war. You are no longer an honoured guest in Germany but the helpless prisoner of the Gestapo. Don't you know where you are? At the headquarters of the *Gestapo*. Don't you know what *that* means? We can do anything we like with you, *anything*."

I was quite calm and answered as politely as I could, that of course I had read a good deal about Gestapo methods but, as in a lifetime experience of Germans I had never found them more inclined to cruelty than ourselves, I had paid no greater attention to such stories than I did to other reports published in the Press.

"Ah! I am glad to find an Englishman who is so sensible. You agree that our Führer was right to stop the papers from publishing lies about the people of other countries. We did not want war, nor did the English people whom we like and respect. It is all the fault of the Jews and the Plutocrats who batten on the unfortunate people in England as they did in Germany before the Führer rescued us from them."

Turning to Dr. Max he said in a normal voice: "Give Mr. Best what he wants."

The room in which I was sitting and in which I was to spend the next ten days was apparently the private office of some fairly important official; at all events, it contained the bookcase, leather-covered desk, the carpet, couch, and easy chairs which throughout the world mark success in the civil service. On my left was the door through which I had entered and just opposite me another one leading into an unlighted room. The cast always used this door and in the room beyond I could dimly see figures grouping themselves so as to be better able to peer at me. Dr. Max went to this door and seemed to shoo the crowd away and I was then led through it and across a large room, from its sweaty smell, obviously a general office, into a small lavatory. I had a good wash and someone lent me a comb and shaving gear. When I came back, feeling quite a new man again, a small table had been placed before my chair and there were some good cheese sandwiches and a bottle of beer. I pitched in, for I was really famished. When I had finished, Dr. Max handed me a packet of twenty cigarettes; German cigarettes it is true, tasting like a bonfire, but, how welcome they were and how they raised my spirits.

I sat back and for the first time since my capture began to feel myself a normal human being again. To be suddenly snatched from civilian life and find oneself a prisoner is probably much more upsetting than being captured as a soldier on active service. Then, one is more or less prepared for all kinds of unpleasant eventualities of which capture is far from being the worst; also, there is the knowledge that one is safeguarded by international laws and conventions. I, for my part, seemed to be playing a game for which the rules had still to be written and in which I might easily find myself cast for the part of mouse to the Gestapo cat. Yet I did not feel frightened nor particularly cast down. I know that this may seem like conceited boasting after the event, but in fact, I am only honestly trying to give a picture of my reactions to capture and imprisonment.

I was fifty-five years of age and so far nothing particularly unpleasant had ever happened to me. Moreover, I had known Germany and Germans all my life and had grown to look upon as my due that measure of respect which was always shown to an Englishman on the Continent. So far the men that I had met were just ordinary German officials and the fact that they shouted and ranted did not impress me in the least, for I had heard that sort of thing hundreds of times before; in fact, I was myself no indifferent performer when occasion arose. Above all though, my feelings towards my fellow men are friendly and my inclination is to like people. I think that this generally influences those with whom I come in contact and that they show themselves to me from their best side. I have never yet met anyone whom I would call really bad; stupid people, frightened people, and some who do bad things from greed or bravado, but downright vicious, no. We are gregarious animals and we each and all of us want to have someone who cares for us, someone who is interested in our fate. During the years of my imprisonment I met many men who behaved at first like savage dogs straining at their chains to get at me and rend me in pieces, but in the end I was able to establish friendly relations with most of them and some showed me the greatest kindness often at considerable risk to themselves.

After my meal, I found that the crowd had melted away and I was alone with Dr. Max and two other men. One of these went out of the room and returned with a stoutish, pleasant-looking woman and carrying a typewriter on a small table. This was planted next to Dr. Max who then started my first interrogation. If I did not feel any particular fears for my own safety I was extremely concerned about how I would be able to stand up under questioning, for any indiscretion on my part would certainly cost many other people their lives. My position was of course entirely different from that of a soldier prisoner of war. In his case, from the point of view of military discipline and morale, it is important that he should adopt an intransigent attitude towards his captors and, since he is one of a multitude where brave example counts, it is his duty to remember at all times that he is in the hands of the enemy. I could serve no one by making a heroic stand. Any sign of unwillingness on my part to answer questions would almost certainly encourage my captors to resort to methods of compulsion which I should find very unpleasant. With memories of past cowardice in a dentist's chair my estimate of my fortitude under torture was modest in the extreme. As I saw things, my best policy was to appear, if not a willing witness, at all events one too frightened to put up much resistance, and to attempt to satisfy my interrogators without giving them information which could jeopardize others.

I was therefore extremely relieved when Dr. Max confined his questions entirely to matters connected with my conversations with Schaemmel and his colleagues. He started off by telling me that I was in most serious danger as, by negotiating with traitors for the overthrow of the German Government, I had, even though I was a foreigner and my actions had taken place outside of Germany, been guilty under a new law of high treason. The penalty for this was death by beheading, but if I showed myself ready to help the administration in bringing the traitors to book, there was a possibility that the Führer might be merciful and treat me only as a prisoner of war. Of course this was right down my street for I had not a shadow of doubt but that Stevens and I had been the victims of an 'agent provocateur' plot and that Schaemmel and Co. were Gestapo agents. Dr. Max's intention was obviously to test my veracity by posing questions to which he knew all the answers. I therefore showed the utmost reluctance to answer any questions damaging to these people and pretended that my conversations with them were only about possible peace terms.

Only gradually as Max's questions became more pressing did I admit that I had also been told about plans to remove the Nazi Party from control in Germany but said, that as far as I knew, Adolf Hitler was to remain in power. Bit by bit I told the whole story of our talks and I could feel **Max** preening himself as he felt how splendidly he had managed the interrogation. I had to exercise a certain measure of caution regarding the instructions received from London as I did not want to queer anything that Stevens said. It was of course often very difficult to know what to say with Stevens, and as I then thought, Klop being interrogated separately. Any marked discrepancies in our stories might be fruitful of trouble for all of us. At this time I believed that Klop was still alive for I had been told at Düsseldorf that a shot had just grazed his head and knocked him out. It was not until three years later that I learned that he had died at Düsseldorf the same day without regaining consciousness. He was a very gallant officer who, to protect us, took the seven raiders on single handed although had he made his way unobserved to the woods at the back of the café, he could probably have escaped and saved both life and liberty.

This first interrogation lasted, as far as I could tell, until about 2 or 3 a.m. Then I went on strike, said that I was too tired to go on any longer and that, if they intended to shoot me at dawn, I should like to have a good sleep first. Dr. Max was quite nice about it and immediately sent out for a bed which was brought in by two men; then he wished me good night and left me alone with these men who were apparently my guards. What a relief it was to get into a comfortable bed and sleep. Sleep too, I did, and I knew nothing until I was awakened at seven next morning and told that it was time to get up. I asked whether this was the hour fixed for my execution and was told no, but as the clerks would be coming to the office next door at eight, if I wanted a wash, it would be better to get up as otherwise I should not be able to reach the lavatory. I washed, shaved and then felt fit for anything.

The fat jailer, who the previous evening had led me on my initial march through the building, came in with my breakfast; a slice of black bread thinly spread with a pink *ersatz* jam and a tin mug of the unspeakable 'coffee'. Shortly afterwards Dr. Max arrived and after a friendly good morning to me said something which I could not hear to my guards. They then took me upstairs to the attics where I was photographed in true criminal style with a large number beside me. Some twenty or thirty photographs were taken; full face and side face, with and without monocle and with each of the three pairs of spectacles which I had had with me. Then my finger-prints were taken and I was weighed and measured. When, after all this, I got back to my room, the doctor came in and put me through a thorough medical examination. Then Dr. Max with his typist appeared and my interrogation was resumed.

I must confess that at the outset I was distinctly scared. One had heard so much about the Gestapo and it's methods that it was only natural to expect that I should find myself in the hands of a real expert in interrogation. Nothing was further from the truth. Dr. Max had hardly got going before it became evident that he was entirely ignorant of military intelligence work and that, not only did he not know what questions to ask me, but he didn't even know what he was trying to find out; his ideas seemed to be based on his reading of stories by William le Queux, Edgar Wallace and their German counterparts. Anyhow, he wanted action and excitement and I tried to give it to him. Most of the time we found ourselves talking about our war (1914–18), in which we had both taken part and we had a great time swapping yarns. Although I make no pretence of being a wit and am used to my attempts at humour being received in cold silence I do like people to laugh at my jokes and with Dr. Max they rang the bell every time and this of course predisposed me in his favour. Every now and then he would break off our chat saying, "but now to business, we must be serious and you must remember that your life hangs by a thread." He would then ask me one or two stupid questions and dictate my answer to his typist.

She, by the way, had also become quite matey and produced some biscuits and made us tea. Frau Roland was a real good sort. Just a fat Berlin housewife who had taken on a war-time job after her husband had been called up. She was very kind to me and while I was at Gestapo Headquarters seldom a day passed without her coming in to see me, bringing me biscuits, apples and other delicacies.

At noon there was a break for lunch and I was brought a tin bowl of carrots boiled in starchy water which I ate with appetite if not with pleasure. The guards who had been with me up to then were relieved by another couple. One of them, a stout, cheery looking middle-aged man said, "Ach, look at him trying to swallow that hog's wash. Here, eat this, my wife always gives me more than I can eat and in any case I can always get more at the canteen," and he handed me two meat sandwiches and an apple. I had hardly spoken a word to the men who had been with me during the night but this little man and his companion were friendly from the first and most ready to give me pointers for my behaviour in my new position. Both were old pre-Hitler C.I.D. men, and both seemed to have a very poor opinion of the Gestapo and all its work, which they did not hesitate to express. I was told not to pay any attention to these people here who called themselves 'Commissars' and what not—they were just a pack of flat-foots from the provinces who " 'Heil Hitler' everyone and have been promoted over the heads of all of us real police officers." "Don't you worry about any threats they may make, they can't do anything to you for yours is an important State affair and only the Führer can decide your fate."

I was completely flabbergasted at the way these men talked

and of course read into their behaviour some subtle plot to induce
me to be indiscreet. Not a bit of it though. They were simply so
pleased at being able to talk to an Englishman, who they could
be certain was not a Nazi spy, that they just let fly and said some
of the things which they had had to keep bottled up for so long.
I was often to have this same experience in the future just as I had
often been the recipient of similar confidences when travelling in
Germany before the war.

Around two o'clock Dr. Max and Frau Roland appeared and
we got down to business again. My talk with the guards had done
me a world of good and I faced the coming interrogation without
a trace of anxiety. Dr. Max now dropped the previous subjects
and wanted to have from me details of all visits which I had paid
to Germany and other countries during the previous five or six
years. Now, when one lives in a small country like Holland, trips
to neighbouring countries by car are so easy that they form a normal
part of one's life. Although I could more or less remember the dates
when my wife and I had been away on longer holidays it was
hopeless for me to attempt to recall all the short trips, often confined
to a single day, which I had taken to Germany and Belgium. The
subject was therefore one admirably calculated to waste time—
just what I most wanted. As far as I could make out, Dr. Max
had never in his life been abroad except as a soldier during the
First World War, and he seemed quite thrilled to be talking to
someone who had been about as much as I. At the start we had
quite a tussle. He had my passport before him which bore a number
of frontier entry and exit stamps. His idea seemed to be that these
would enable him to check the truth of my statements.

I mentioned a visit to France and Switzerland the previous
winter. "Ah, now I have you," he said. "Where is your other passport?" I was quite at a loss to know what he meant and said that
of course I had only a single passport. "Don't try to tell me lies.
You must have another passport for you have just said that you
were in France and Switzerland last December and there is no
stamp of these countries here. We know all about you. You are
really a Dutch officer and this passport is a fake." I patiently explained to him that there were no French or Swiss stamps in my
passport for the simple reason that, when you entered or left these
countries by car only your motor papers were cleared and that as
a rule, you did not even have to produce your pass. "Look," I
said. "You see, this stamp shows that I left Germany on the
14th December by the frontier post at Basel and re-entered Germany
again on the 20th at Bregenz. I must therefore have been in
Switzerland between these dates. As a matter of fact I went from
Basel to Lausanne and from there round the Lake of Geneva
into France, but you can't check that from the stamps on my
passport."

Dr. Max continued his study and suddenly in great excitement said, "But there is no stamp to show that you ever left Germany again". "I'm sorry," I said, "but you can't blame me for that. I remember that I gave my passport to the SS men at the frontier and they certainly took their time before handing it back to me. You must admit that I was in Holland when your people kidnapped me and it is easy to prove that I was there for months before."

This is just an instance of the kind of futility which marked all the interrogations to which I was subjected by the Gestapo. I have never in my life come across people who could so easily be put off the scent and set chasing hares in all directions.

As the afternoon wore on the news seemed to get about that a strange animal was on view and there was a constant stream of visitors. Some just stood and gaped, others shot absurd questions at me. Amongst them was one who seemed to be of exceptional importance. He was brought in by the Oberführer and when he entered, everyone stood up and with a great uprising of arms there was a loud chorus of "Heil Hitler, Herr Direktor." I don't know for certain who he was, but I believe, to judge from photographs which I later saw in the Press, that he was Martin Bormann; the man, who even at that time probably exercised the greatest influence on Hitler. He asked me some questions, but I have forgotten what they were. Generally, I was asked whether I did not realize that Germany was certain to win the war.

It very soon became clear to me that belief in German victory was distinctly shaky. I had only to say that England would never give in before she had beaten Germany to be met with a flood of arguments showing that Germany must be victorious. Obviously, it was quite unimportant what I thought, so these arguments must have been attempts at self-encouragement. The simple fact was that in their hearts these people regarded me as their superior; as a representative of a nation which they could not hope to equal. How often was I not to hear the statement that the English were a 'Herrnvolk' a race of masters. An inferiority complex is, I think, the most marked German characteristic. All the military pomp and martial posturing, the shouting and stamping, are just a smoke-screen put up to conceal it. From earliest youth all Germans are brought up to believe that blind and unreasoning obedience to orders is the highest human virtue and that even thought must be directed along lines ordained by higher authority. From earliest youth the education of a German is accompanied by persistent bullying designed to make him feel that he is as dirt in the eyes of the man above him; and natural leaders, rare everywhere, are in Germany almost non-existent. Every German has burnt into his soul the memory of countless occasions when he has been shouted at and insulted by someone in authority and, however high the rank he may attain, a certain feeling of inferiority and insecurity never really deserts him. This fact is to my mind the real explanation of Hitler's rise to power and his complete dominance over everyone with whom he came in contact. His leadership was inborn, he had no doubts, and he acknowledged no superior. All other leaders in Germany were synthetic, he alone was real.

Most of my life has been spent on the Continent and I know many countries there better than my own. I believe that in outlook I am more European than insular. Yet, above all, I am an Englishman with that inherent conviction that . . . no, I can't find words for what I mean. I was going to write, that I was the superior of every foreigner, but that does not express my meaning at all; there is nothing of conceit in what I feel. I think that the nearest that I can get is, to say, that always, deeply rooted in me, is the consciousness that I am British and that I am proud of it. No matter what these people said to me nor how threatening their attitude, it was impossible for me to take them seriously or to believe that they would resort to unpleasant methods in order to obtain information. I felt no personal antagonism towards them; they were to me simply a lot of German officials carrying out their duties in the ordinary German manner, hemmed in by regulations and the fear of their superiors' displeasure. It was unthinkable that any of them exercised independent authority or, without direct orders from above, would resort to strong-arm methods of interrogation.

So, in many respects, I really felt quite at my ease and could concentrate all my attention to the question of satisfying their curiosity without giving anything away. This in itself was a large enough task, for all details of my story had to link together and, as my fiction grew, it was quite a feat of memory to recall everything that I had said when the next awkward question had to be countered.

Another thing which helped me was that none of the people with whom I came in contact at this time really believed that the war with England and France would have to be fought out to a finish. All seemed to have their hopes fixed upon a second Munich —they felt that something simply had to happen to end the war. They had therefore no inclination to get on the wrong side of a British prisoner, especially one, whom for some unknown reason they considered to be an important person. I believe that had we fallen into the hands of the Gestapo some months later, after the defeat of France, our treatment might have been far worse.

Since my return home, many people have said to me, often it seemed with a faint tinge of regret in their voices: "I can't understand why the Germans didn't kill you." Now from the moment that I was able to collect myself and use my intelligence, it never seemed to me probable that my life was in any real jeopardy. How could it be? I had committed no crime; indeed, the boot was on the other foot for by kidnapping me in a neutral country the Germans had put themselves hopelessly in the wrong. People in England do not seem to recognize sufficiently clearly that until Hitler went hay-wire after the attempt on his life on 20th July, 1944, the Nazi regime took great pains to invest itself with an outward show of legality. Although a man might be spirited away from his home and taken to a concentration camp and there suffer such indignities and hardships that he died, technically he was accused of no crime nor was he undergoing punishment; he was merely, for his own good, held in protective custody, and if he died this was just too bad but death comes to all and who could prove that imprisonment was the direct cause of his decease? In any case, only seldom was a man of influence or importance treated in this way, and such men could never be held for an indefinite time without inquiries being made about them through normal legal channels. It is a great mistake to imagine that the Gestapo was omnipotent in Nazi Germany; on the contrary, only Hitler held real power and the Gestapo could continue to function only so long as it enjoyed his favour.

When the Gestapo organized their raid into neutral Holland they created a precedent in International Law. Obviously their action must have diplomatic repercussions and in the event of serious difficulty Stevens and I might become pawns of some bargaining value. It was therefore to no one's interest to liquidate us, and indeed, as will appear from my own experiences, the greatest pains were taken to preserve us in good physical condition.

Dr. Max apparently had had his fill of night work, for round about six o'clock he downed tools, and heading the procession of typist, table and typewriter, he left the room leaving me to attack the bowl of watery soup that had been brought me for my supper. My sleep on this second night was not so good, for being less tired I was conscious of the brightly lit, overheated, and very stuffy room with its all pervading odour of stale feet, and of the movements of my two guards. When I got up in the morning I fel bleareyed and miserable; I longed for a bath and for clean clothes. For breakfast there was the same slice of black bread and jam with its accompanying mug of *ersatz* coffee. Dr. Max turned up bright and early and told me in a businesslike manner, that my real interrogation was now going to begin; I must be very careful and remember that my life was at stake. He had hardly asked me a question before Oberführer Müller came in, apparently in a great rage. He had in his hands what seemed to be the typescript of my interrogation of the previous days. He ripped this in half and scattering the pieces on the floor he let fly at Dr. Max, berating him for allowing himself to be made a fool of by a British gangster and crook. Then, turning to me, he delivered a long harangue to the effect that I mustn't think that he did not see through my tricks, that if I set any value on my life I had better stop fooling about and give them the information which they wanted. "Your life is in my hands and if you are not very careful I will order you to be shot without any more hesitation."

I said mildly that I was sorry that I had disappointed him for really I had done my best. After all, I could not do more than answer the questions which I had been asked and I was sure that Dr. Max had found me co-operative in every respect. Dr. Max confirmed this and Müller, calming down a bit said that he would give me one more chance and that at my next interrogation I must "confess everything I knew"; otherwise, it would be the END. Müller and Max, typist, table, and typewriter then filed out of the room leaving me undisturbed for the rest of the day. The intention was probably to give time for the threats to soak home. It is amazing what faith the Gestapo had in such theatricals which were so obvious and so badly staged that they never had the slightest effect on me; on the contrary, they confirmed my general impression that there was no intention of proceeding to any extreme measures to extract information.

My room was a pleasant one and, facing south, I could sit by the window in the sun. It looked out on to a sort of recreation or sports ground on the other side of which I could see the Anhalter Station. This enabled me to fix my position in Berlin. There were always two men with me as guards, but they were all very decent fellows and before we parted most of them had become my friends. They were members of the Gestapo clerical staff and had the rank of criminal secretaries, one step below that of commissar. Most of them had previously done duty as police constables or in the detective department at the Wilhelms Platz, the Berlin Scotland Yard. Although they were not supposed to talk to me, their curiosity was far too great to allow them to bother about this rule. They were none of them really Nazis but just men who had held on to their pre-Hitler jobs and who, by joining the party, had achieved promotion to posts far beyond their capabilities or experience.

One, a chubby little fellow in spectacles, whose kindness I have mentioned above, originally belonged to the homicide squad and had some first-rate stories to tell about murders he had investigated. Another, named Philip Steinmetz, had done similar guard duty with van der Lubbe after the Reichstag fire. He said that van der Lubbe was a very nice young fellow and very far from the fool which he seemed at his court appearances. Although van der Lubbe had certainly played some part in setting the building alight, Steinmetz made no secret of his belief that the whole business had been arranged by the party. He then discussed with his partner whether it was Goering or Goebbels who had staged the fire but it was obvious that both approved of what had been done, because, 'something had to be done to get rid of the Communists'.

There was a nice little man named Grothe who seemed to be a sort of general factotum in the building. If anything was needed, a chair, a table, or even a pencil, at once there was a cry for Grothe and invariably he could produce what was wanted. He seemed also to have taken over the charge of satisfying my material needs and whenever he came into the room had always some surprise for me. He treated me like a small child, making me guess which of the hands he held behind his back I would have. Always he brought with him sandwiches, apples or, most welcome of all, cigarettes. Although, no doubt, he was merely obeying orders in giving me these things, I shall always be grateful to him for the personal touch which he gave to his gifts and for his obvious wish to help me to raise my spirits. As time went on we became real friends and throughout my imprisonment it was a great comfort to me to feel that I had this friendly gnome in the fastness of Gestapo Headquarters. I do not know how he managed it, but in the end he seemed to run everything that concerned me, including my correspondence with my wife, and I cannot express how much I am indebted to him for his help and the comfort he gave me. I am glad to say that I was able to give him some little help after the end of the war and that we have remained good friends. He was an old police official and like all the other men of this class that I met, a thoroughly decent fellow quite uncontaminated by any Nazi ideas.

The only really objectionable men that I met at Gestapo Head-quarters were the so-called 'Commissars'. The place was thick with them and their principal occupation seemed to be to spy and report on the experienced officials who did the actual work. My guards told me that most of them were SA men who had been mem-bers of Hitler's bodyguard in the early days. Those with whom I came in contact were surly uncouth fellows, most of them Bavarians, who did their best to look tough by clenching their lower teeth over the upper ones. One or another of them would occasionally burst into my room, suddenly opening the door wide and then standing glowering and saying nothing. It was plain that my guards were afraid of them and after such incursions there was always for a while an uneasy silence.

On the following day a typical young German lawyer came in accompanied by another young man with the most Jewish cast of features that I have ever seen; more like a caricature of a Jew than the real thing. With them came the inevitable table and typewriter and a very pretty little typist. I later discovered that only the top men were allowed to interrogate prisoners alone, and that all minor officials had to have an observer with them. Ober-führer Müller then came in and said to the young lawyer, "I want to have everything from the very beginning; when you have finished, I want to know more about the prisoner than he does himself," then, turning to me, he repeated his customary warning that my expectation of life was getting very shaky. Then, we all settled down to a nice cosy interrogation, for that is what it turned out to be. The young lawyer, who can only just have passed his final law exams, with true Prussian conscientiousness followed the Oberführer's orders and started at the beginning; he was not even content to start at my beginning, but first probed deeply into my ancestry. After each name I mentioned he asked whether the person was of Arian descent and in dictating to the typist told her to enter in brackets after the name, 'nicht Jude'.

Well, this sort of interrogation was of course right up my street, and I discovered that I could recall a wealth of detail from the days of my early childhood, all of which was gravely noted down. We worked steadily through my autobiography for the next two days and had traversed some thirty years since my birth. I was in the midst of a description of Henley Regatta in July 1914 when the Oberführer came and took the young lawyer aside. I heard some whispering, the Oberführer went out, and the young lawyer came back and said to me, "You are finished for the present," then the whole *cortège* departed. I don't to this day know what was the reason for all this, but from that day, the 15th, to the 27th November, there was a complete lull in proceedings. No more high officials came near me, no questions were asked me, and I was just left to laze away the time as best I could. It is a curious thing, but I suffered more from nervousness during this period than at any other time during my imprisonment; there was a beastly nightmarish feeling of something horrible waiting for me just round the corner and it got so bad that I would almost jump out of my skin if anyone entered the room unexpectedly. I got into a state where I worried about everything.

Most of all my thoughts were with May. What had happened to her? Where was she now? For all I knew, the Germans might already have invaded Holland. It was feared that they might do so on the very day on which I was captured. Since then I had had no news of any kind from outside. I knew that my chief would certainly have looked after my wife and that no one would be kinder than he, but however much I reasoned about the matter, I was horribly afraid for her. Then too, I became ridden by a sort of bogey which made me relive all the circumstances of our capture at the frontier. Why had we not tried to put up some sort of fight, just as Klop had done. The raiders had called out 'Hands up!' and Stevens and I had just done as we were told although we had loaded pistols in our pockets. I am sure that we were neither of us frightened of losing our lives . . . no . . . I think the raid had followed a certain pattern of which we had often read and we, well, we just behaved as people generally seem to do when they are kidnapped. Then my mind would go haywire and I would form fantastic pictures of Stevens and me fighting the raiders and unfailingly shooting them down one after the other . . . and then I would again realize that after all, I was a prisoner. It is a most strange feeling to know that you have lost all freedom of action and all the rights of movement which before you just took for granted. Often I had an almost irresistible longing to get up, open the door, and walk away somewhere.

I really have no right to complain about my treatment during the days that I spent in room No. 315. The weather was really beautiful and as we faced due south, I could sit for hours in the sun. My nights were still very disturbed and I spent much of the day dozing on the couch. I got up at seven; washed and shaved, and at about eight the stout warder came up with my slice of bread. A little later the doctor would pay me a visit and ask a few perfunctory questions; then Grothe would turn up, bringing his usual gifts of sandwiches, apples and cigarettes. On one of the first days he had with him a parcel containing pyjamas, socks, handkerchiefs, a safety razor, and other toilet articles which he had been authorized to buy for me. This was a great improvement, for up to then I had had nothing but what I stood up in and had had to sleep naked, a procedure which my guards seemed to consider slightly shocking—they certainly went to bed in their underclothes like most Germans of their class. In the evening Frau Roland and the pretty little typist, Fräulein Blumental (called Blümchen), generally came to see me, bringing tea and biscuits; Blümchen also brought me flowers which she placed in a vase on the table.

There was a wireless receiver in the next room and once, through an open door, I heard enough to understand that Russia was at war with Finland; I wondered how long it would be before she and Germany would also be at daggers drawn; it never seemed to me possible that their *entente* could last long. Even Dr. Max made no secret of his hatred of all Communists and indeed my guards were constantly telling stories about atrocities committed by the 'Reds' before Hitler put them out of mischief in his concentration camps.

Once a week I was taken down to the basement for a bath. This was really delightful. The lavatory was a big place with numerous wash basins and a number of cubicles with shower baths. The water was beautifully hot and I stayed there enjoying myself until I felt that I could keep my guards waiting no longer. On one occasion as I was being taken down the lift came up and out stepped Stevens. He was holding a slice of bread and jam in one hand and a mug of coffee in the other. I smiled at him, but he looked grimly through me. This was the last glimpse that I caught of him until we met again in April 1945.

On the 20 November the door opened and a man carrying a suitcase appeared who seemed to be most surprised to find the room occupied. One of my guards gently pushed him out of the room and after some discussion outside came back to say that this was the rightful occupant and that he wanted us to get out. There was for a time a lot of coming and going and all sorts of people poked their heads in at the door, said something which I did not catch and went away again. At last a decision was arrived at and orders were given for us to move which we did with bed and baggage. We did not have to go far, only along a passage at right-angles to ours, to room No. 238. As I later learnt, this room had up to then been occupied by Stevens who had had to vacate it for me. As a matter of fact, this was a most inferior room, nothing more than a junior clerks office, appropriately furnished as such and facing north. When we first arrived at Gestapo Headquarters, I was No. 1 and Stevens No. 2, but our order of precedence had gradually been reversed and by this time I had very distinctly gone down grade; now, I was told, Stevens had been given an even better room than my first one and my guards did not seem to like this at all. All our guards, of course, knew each other and compared notes. There even seemed to be a certain degree of jealousy between them as to whose charge was the more weighty and it required quite a lot of persuasion on my part to convince my men, that in spite of appearances, I was really more important and that to guard me was the greater honour.

Grothe came in one day with the large envelope which I had seen sealed at Düsseldorf after my personal possessions had been placed in it. He broke the seals and made a list of the contents; my watch, fountain pen, keys, etc. When it was the turn of my pocket book, only f.200 in Dutch money and a couple of £1 notes were to be found; two Dutch notes, one of f.300 and the other of f.200 had mysteriously vanished. I asked Grothe at once what had become of them to which he said, and I think truthfully, that he knew nothing about them and that he had brought in the envelope just as he had received it. If I wished, he could make a report embodying my complaint, but, at the same time, he said that he didn't think that it would do any good and might only get me into trouble. I should have insisted at Düsseldorf on a list of my belongings being made before they were sealed up; now, it was only my word against that of the responsible official there. I deferred to his greater experience and held my peace.

I was later to learn that the Gestapo, like the Chinaman, must always have its squeeze and although I was deprived of many things to which I was entitled, in the long run, I gained many greater benefits from my policy of tolerance. Probably, even had I protested, my things would have been stolen just the same and it was therefore wiser to make no official protest but merely to indicate discreetly that I was not blind to what was going on. During the greater part of my imprisonment all my letters and parcels from home passed through the hands of Grothe and even if he was not entirely ignorant of the fate of the numerous packets of cigarettes and tobacco which May sent me but which never reached me, he fully compensated me for my forbearance by the way in which he acted as a buffer between me and the men higher up and undoubtedly I am directly indebted to him for many privileges which I came to enjoy.

On the evening of the 26 November Oberführer Müller came into the room and asked me how I felt, whether my health was good, and whether my nerves were standing up to the strain. Upon my answering in the affirmative, he asked me to be shaved and ready next morning at seven o'clock. I did as I was told and was then again taken up to the attics where a fresh series of photographs was taken though this time there was no finger printing. At about ten o'clock Müller came in and after again asking me whether I felt quite well, took me across the passage to his own suite of rooms which was directly opposite. The first room into which I went was full of SS officers in uniform, some sitting and others standing and talking to each other. I was then led into a room which opened out of it and was told to stand at a certain point. A door opposite me then opened and the three men who had visited me in Holland goose-stepped in single file through it until the front man was about three yards from me and then, with much slapping of feet, formed into a line facing me. All three were in full SS black uniform, on my left was Schaemmel, next to him the tall Colonel Martini flanked by weedy little Grosch.

In chorus they all said: "You did not think when you met us in Holland that you were entertaining führers of the SS?" The scene was indescribably funny and I was hard put to it not to burst out laughing. Each man then fired a question at me in turn, silly questions, such as: "Weren't you stupid to venture so close to the frontier?" "Do you still think we are only lads?" Then, with a smart right-about-turn, they reformed in single file and goose-stepped out of the room. This confrontation was obviously supposed to have a shattering effect on my nerves, for hitherto I had always professed to believe that these gentlemen were bona fide conspirators. Müller, who must have been standing behind me all the time, ready to catch me should I faint from the shock, again asked me if I felt all right and then led me back into the first room. Almost as soon as I entered a young and very resplendent officer whom I recognized as Heydrich (his enlarged photograph hung in every room) jumped up and started shouting at me in a most threatening manner.

"So far you have been treated as an officer and a gentleman, but don't think that this will go on if you don't behave better than you have done. You have two hours left in which to confess everything. If you don't, I shall hand you over to the Gestapo who are used to dealing with such gangsters and criminals—you won't enjoy their methods a bit."

I turned to Müller who was standing at my side and asked: "Who is this excitable young officer?" At this Heydrich really went off the deep end and literally foamed at the mouth; at all events he sprayed me most liberally with his saliva. Müller quickly pushed me out of the room and into my own. Later on he came in again and told me that I must not take the matter too seriously, "Soup is never eaten as hot as it is cooked." He was satisfied that I had behaved properly and that I had been honest in my answers to interrogation. He added though that he was sorry to say that in future my legs would have to be fettered and that I should no longer be allowed to take any exercise in the passage. Orders to this effect had been given by the highest authority and he could not vary them. In my experience I always found Müller a very decent little man. I have heard from other prisoners that he was one of the most feared men in the Gestapo and that he had been guilty of terrible cruelty. My own feeling about him was that he always tried to ease things for me, and that his displays of anger and the threats which he uttered were merely examples of his obedience to orders from a higher level.

When Müller went out of the room he left a strap lying on the table. Nothing happened for a while, so I said to the guards: "Well, aren't you going to put the fetters on my feet?" At this both men protested that this was no part of their duty and that if the Oberführer wanted my feet strapped together, he should have done so himself. To this I said that I was damned if I was going to strap my own feet together. In the end we found a satisfactory compromise by keeping the door locked from the inside. We had had quite a lot of trouble with people who did not know that the office previously housed there had been moved, bursting into the room and, as no unauthorized person was supposed to see me, my guards had a good excuse for their action. If anyone wanted to come in they had to knock, and before the door was opened I had time to lay the strap in a loose figure of eight round my ankles. This seemed to satisfy everyone and although Müller and several other of the Gestapo bosses often came in to see me, none of them even glanced at my feet to see whether they were indeed fettered.

Later that same day Schaemmel came in, bringing with him a stoutish middle-aged man, a Dr. Schäfer, who was to continue my interrogation. Schaemmel now adopted a most self-important and patronizing air which from so young a man, and one who had played me such a dirty trick, I found distinctly irritating. In a fatherly manner he admonished me not to bring down misfortune on myself by my stubbornness. "I don't want to be hard on you and I really sympathize with you in the unfortunate position in which you now find yourself. I know, too, you have always appeared quite ready to answer our questions, but you have not yet told us anything that is the slightest use. We can't believe that you are so ignorant as you pretend, so take great care and answer Dr. Schäfer frankly. This is your very last chance and your life depends on the result of this interrogation." So, that was that.

Frequently during the past weeks I had heard the name of 'Schellenberg' and although this in itself conveyed nothing much to me I had deduced that this must be the name of the man whom I knew as 'Schaemmel'. It was not until after my return to England at the end of hostilities that I learnt more about him and could appreciate how important a man had taken a personal part in our capture. At that time he was the head of a newly created Intelligence Service of the Gestapo, and as time passed he became one of the most important figures in the German Intelligence, and moreover the man who probably stood closest to Heinrich Himmler and enjoyed his confidence to a greater extent than anyone else. Towards the end of the war, having sufficient intelligence to realize that it must end in German defeat he tried to induce Himmler to break faith with Hitler and himself take over the reins of government with the object of arriving at a peace with the Western Powers and eventually he himself went to Sweden where he tried to secure the co-operation of Count Bernadotte in an effort to conclude a separate peace with the West. Perhaps I am prejudiced but the impression which he made on me at the time was that of a conceited, self-opiniated and distinctly stupid man. I admit that he had completely taken Stevens and me in when we met him in Holland but this was not really surprising since he was exceptionally well informed and had been well briefed for the occasion. Besides, the man was a natural conspirator who, as events showed, kept faith with no one. He could therefore play his part with great realism.

Next morning I was taken to Dr. Schäfer who was installed in a tiny room next to mine. One of my guards came with me and as soon as I sat down I started to place the strap round my ankles. Schäfer asked me: "What nonsense is this?" I explained that I was considered such a dangerous person that orders had been given that my legs must be fettered. "I've never heard of such a thing; I'm in charge here and I am certainly not going to work under such conditions. Wait a minute." He went out of the room for a few minutes and when he came back he threw my strap out of the door and said to the guard, "You also can clear out. I shall be responsible for Mr. Best's safety." When he had gone, after looking through some typescript papers for a time, Schäfer sent his typist to fetch him some cigars from the canteen.

As soon as we were alone he said to me in a low voice: "Don't you worry yourself about what that officer said to you yesterday. You won't be shot and you won't be badly treated, but you may be placed on trial on a charge of *landesverrat* (treason). The Führer has taken you under his personal protection and no one can do anything to you except on his orders; you seem to have some very good friends in Germany. I have been given the task of examining you and I must report the result to the 'Reichsrat' (State Counsellor) who will decide whether you can be placed on trial. I have studied your dossier carefully and from what I can see you have done nothing on which any charge could be based. Just do what I tell you and look upon me as a friend. I know your wife's cousin at Wiesbaden and want to help you."

Naturally, I feared a trap, but as things turned out, Dr. Schäfer proved himself honest in what he had said and I came to look forward to the hours which I spent with him. Only seldom did he ask me awkward questions and when he saw that I was unwilling to answer, he frequently suggested plausible replies. Occasionally he adopted a bullying tone, but at the same time he pointed at the telephone, and I knew that there was a live microphone in the room. I could never discover how he knew when it was on; though at times his tone would suddenly change and from being his usual friendly self he would start shouting at me. On such occasions he asked me questions which I could not possibly object to answering, such as, how many German refugees I knew, particularly in Switzerland. Since I knew none, the question was easy to answer. Then he wanted the names of all people whom I knew in Germany, and all business firms with whom I had had dealings. Amusing interludes were numerous identity parades in which I had to take part. It seemed that after my photograph appeared in the Press, numbers of people had written in to the Gestapo claiming to have seen me here, there, and everywhere; even as far afield as Toronto. Since they had seen only the very bad photograph released for publication by the Gestapo which had been retouched until I looked a mixture of criminal and idiot, their idea of my appearance must have been hazy; nevertheless, one and all picked me out at once. Not very difficult when the men paraded with me were so obviously German. Schäfer paid very little attention to what these people declared, merely asking me whether I had been at the place mentioned on the date in question.

One thing I found rather interesting as an example of German thoroughness. Until shortly before the war, when they were recalled to the Fatherland, most of the domestic servants at The Hague were German girls. All these must have been carefully questioned after their return for Dr. Schäfer had a large bundle of reports from the ex-servants of friends of ours which contained all manner of information about myself and other visitors at the houses where they had been in service.

My interrogation by Dr. Schäfer continued for about a week or ten days. At first I would be with him all day, but later he only called me in for an hour or two at a time. On the 7th December I was again moved, this time from the third to the first floor and into a tiny, passage-like room. My old guards suddenly vanished and were replaced by men of a much lower grade, ordinary police constables, in fact. They were very decent fellows but we were not together long enough for me to get to know them properly; all I really remember about them is that one man had all his teeth encased in gold—his life-time savings were in his mouth. I have often wondered whether eventually they reached the Reichsbank via some concentration camp.

My treatment now was that of a condemned criminal. All my scanty personal possessions had been taken from me and I was no longer allowed to shave. There was no more extra food, nor anything to smoke. My feet were tightly strapped together and at night I was handcuffed. Obviously the heat was being turned on. After having threatened me so often, pressure of another kind was being tried. On the 9th December, exactly a month after my capture, no breakfast was brought me and when time came for my midday meal, there was still a blank. Late in the afternoon, Grothe, whom I had not seen for some days, came in and told me to get ready for a journey. I was tired, unshaven and very hungry and I must admit that my spirits sank to a new low ebb on hearing this. When one is a prisoner one becomes most conservative in one's outlook, and nothing is more upsetting than any change from accustomed routine. One gets used to certain people, a certain mode of life; one forms a real attachment to one's temporary home and there is that curious feeling that so long as there is no change, one is safe. Every move is a step into the unknown and, when one is in the hands of the Gestapo, unpleasant surprises are always possible.

Getting ready for a journey consisted in having my handcuffs put on and a black hood placed over my head. I was taken along a passage and down some steps which led to the courtyard. There I was told to get into a car and then, to my great comfort, Grothe and Dr. Schäfer got in with me. We drove for some distance through Berlin streets and I could see darkly through my hood that our direction was northward, apparently towards Spandau. In front of us was another car, a large Horch, which seemed to be acting as our guide. After leaving the town we drove for about twenty miles along a country road, passing several villages and one larger town. The road was unfamiliar to me and I could not make out where I was being taken. Then, we turned off to the left and came to a road bounded on the right by a high and forbidding looking wall. We came to a large white building and both cars came to a standstill. The people in the front car spoke to a man who seemed, as far as I could see, to be a sentry in uniform. By this time I had the wind-up quite badly and longed to be back in my dear, familiar Gestapo home. Our cars drove on for another couple of hundred yards or so until we came to a gate in the wall through which we passed. As far as I could see there seemed to be rows upon rows of men in greyish looking clothes standing to attention and the air was filled with a strong smell of sweat and dirt.

We went through yet another gate and stopped before a low concrete building. Although I did not know then where I was, we had arrived at the Bunker, or cellular prison of the Sachsenhausen concentration camp which for the next five and a quarter years was to be my home. That I was 'in' for the duration I had recognized almost from the moment of capture and even then I had decided that duration probably meant five years. I had expected internment in a camp for military or civilian prisoners of war and association with other prisoners of my own nationality— I had never expected imprisonment which segregated me from all contact with my countrymen.

CHAPTER III

Two men, Oberführers Müller and (I shall in future refer to Schaemmel by his real name) Schellenberg, got out of the front car, and were welcomed with loud cries of 'Heil Hitler' by a group of officers standing outside the entrance. Then our car drew up and I was told to get out. As I did so, someone pulled the hood off my head and as I went in I saw a long passage before me and similar passages to the right and left; towels were hanging at intervals along them on doors; it was clear that I was in a prison. I was not given much time for observation for, after a few steps, I was ordered to turn and stand with my face to the wall. I heard the jingling of keys and much marching of heavy boots and, after some five minutes or so, I was told to 'come along' and was taken to the end of the passage which had faced me as I entered and into the last door on the right. I found myself in a bare whitewashed cell which contained as only furniture a low wooden bunk, raised a few inches from the floor, and a bucket. The latter offered a modest contribution to the intolerable stink which filled the whole building.

I was ordered to sit on the bunk and a soldier stood on guard at the door with his hand on his pistol holster; an evil-looking fellow whose lip had once been split right open and which had healed askew. Later, I was to get to know him well for he was one of the warders. His name was Drexl and he came from Oberammergau; in spite of his ferocious appearance he was really a very kind-hearted, good-natured fellow and, because I knew his part of the country well, often came for a chat to satisfy his nostalgic longing for his mountain home. At our first meeting though his appearance made me believe him to be one of the Nazi thugs about whom one had heard so much.

After about a quarter of an hour, the door was thrown open and Schellenberg and Müller appeared and told me to come with them. We went right the way back along the passage, and I was taken to one of the last cells on the left. As I entered I saw a bed covered with a clean red and white squared coverlet and next to it a small table and a stool. I was told to sit on this stool with my back to the window which was some six feet from the ground. A man in uniform placed the table in front of me and the Ober-führer said: "That is your place, you are to stay there." A crowd of officers then came in, with them Schäfer and Grothe, and stood looking at me apparently with some degree of satisfaction.

Someone said, "He should take off his overcoat," and my hand-cuffs were unlocked so that I could take it off, but were at once put on again. Then it was discovered that there was no place to hang my coat and a little double shelf with hooks under it was brought in and nailed to the wall close to the door. There was a further conference and some apparent indecision. I heard Müller say, "No, the door must never be locked," and something about courteous behaviour and, no conversation. Two soldiers then brought in another table and stool which was placed facing me by the door and one of the men sat down there. Müller seemed satisfied at last and turning to me again he pointed to one of the officers with him and said, "Oberführer Lohritz now has charge of you and if you are wise you will obey his orders without demur—if you don't, or if there are any complaints about your behaviour—well, so much the worse for you."

Schellenberg then came up too and spoke his piece. "I have had you brought here for it will be much better and pleasanter for you than in Berlin. There you could never go into the fresh air, but here you can have regular exercise every day. I am trying to do everything that I can for you, but I advise you to be less cheeky than you have so far been—you are now in the hands of the State Police and under the jurisdiction of the Camp Kommandantur—don't expect them to stand any nonsense. They will treat you as an officer or as a criminal according to your behaviour."

Everyone then went away and I was left alone with my guard. He was a dapper little man, swarthy, almost a gipsy in appearance; although I did not know it then, he was to become the first of a series of guards who proved themselves my loyal friends and to whose kindness I owe every pleasant memory of my imprisonment. On this first evening though my feelings towards him were the reverse of friendly. I was tired, unshaven and dishevelled, I felt dirty, and I was very hungry; the combination of hunger and the fearful stench of the place made me absolutely sick. It is therefore not surprising that my normal kindly feeling towards my fellow men had given way to loathing, to the vicious hatred one sees in the eyes of a cornered animal. There we sat, each on his uncomfortable stool behind his little table, with nothing to do except glower at one another.

A warder brought in an aluminium bowl filled with potatoes boiled in their jackets and a saucer containing a greenish-looking sauce. Did I want some coffee? No! (Damn your eyes and to hell with you and everything!) How many slices of bread would I like for breakfast? I said, two. Try, handcuffed, to skin and eat tepid boiled potatoes, half of them rotten and you may perhaps share my hatred for the world and all its works. Then I sat again glowering at my guard, my hunger unstilled and sticky, potato-covered hands adding to my discomfort. The cell door opened and a young soldier came in and took the place of my previous guard; my dislike of him was immediate, particularly because he was smoking an evil-smelling pipe. An hour or so later, a warder whom I had not yet seen, opened the door and said: "Wash." I followed him, accompanied by my guard, to the lavatory which was next to my cell. That this was so, I had already deduced from the sound of rushing waters which intermittently punctured the silence of my cell. This lavatory was to be the plague of my existence for the next three years.

Between four and five o'clock in the morning some seventy or more prisoners came at the double from their cells each carrying his open pail which, still at the double, he had to empty into one of the two w.c.s; then, to the other side of the room, hold his pail for a moment under a running tap and back at the double to his cell. Loud shouts and threats from the supervising warder; one, of whom I shall have more to say, had a long leather-covered whip which he cracked in the air and with which he caught any prisoner who was too slow a slash across buttocks or back. The same process was repeated in the evening at four or five o'clock. The stench which came from the open unwashed pails as they passed my door and through the windows of the lavatory into my cell, hung about for an hour or more afterwards and rendered life an abomination to a sensitive nose. Occasionally I was fated to go to the lavatory before it had been cleaned up when the floor was covered with excrement which had missed its intended receptacle.

The building contained eighty cells; light, airy cells and adequately warmed, but none were provided with water closets. Consequently, all prisoners, except the privileged few, of whom I was one, had to do their doings in a pail. No one had ever thought of providing proper sanitary pails; all that was available were lidless tins which had started life as containers of the jam which we received for breakfast. They were rusty, battered and never washed, and how they stank. At the time when I came to the prison such a

Café Backus on the Dutch-German Frontier near Venlo, where the author and two of his companions were captured, and where Lieutenant Klop was killed by the raiding party.

Jan Lemmens.

(*Left*) Lt. Dirk Klop.

Georg Elser, der als Täter des verruchten Anschlags auf den Führer ermittelt und festgenommen wurde   3 Aufn. Scherl-Bilderdienst

Nr. 48

Kapitän Stevens   Mr. Best

Beide Leiter des Britischen Intelligence Service für West-Europa, die durch das entschlossene Eingreifen der Gestapo in deutsche Hände fielen

The first pictures released by the Gestapo to the German press, showing Major R. H. Stevens, Captain S. Payne

pail was the only article of furniture in the cells of most of the prisoners; cells, of which the windows were boarded up so as to make them almost completely dark. They were punishment cells for prisoners in protective custody at the camp who had committed some offence and the usual term was three weeks sometimes spiced with weekly beatings of twenty-five lashes. Compared to these unfortunates mine was the life of a gentleman of leisure. Not having suffered such a lot, I cannot say what it was like nor what courage was needed to bear it. I feel that it is shameful for me to complain about the brief discomfort which the intrusion of their misery brought me, but I am writing about my own reactions and experiences, and until a merciful dispensation put my sense of smell out of action my nose seemed to be permanently coated with the effluvium of human excrement.

The water closets, of which there were three, separated only by a thin wall from my bed, were flushed by a press-button system which emitted a stream of water with hydrant force for some half-minute and then turned it off suddenly with a dull thud. All day long and frequently at night I was startled by this noise to which I could never become accustomed. Never, while I occupied this cell did I have more than an hour or two's undisturbed sleep and my nerves suffered more from this than from any other circumstance of my imprisonment. Forgive this long dissertation on an unsavoury subject, but, unfortunately, it was one of the most important features of my life for over three years.

On my first visit to the lavatory I was handed a towel and a piece of soap. The warder removed my handcuffs while I washed at a sort of fountain from which five or six taps spurted thin streams of water to a circular trough below. I did the other things necessary before bedtime and returned to my cell, undressed and got into bed. The warder then put on my handcuffs again, but he was a decent fellow and closed them only so far that although my hands could not slip through, I could still turn my wrists in them. Then he gave the key another turn in the lock which he said would prevent the ratchet slipping in further while I slept. Sleep, no, I did not have much that night. Over my bed was an unshaded sixty-watt lamp. On account of the black-out, a blanket covered the window, there was no ventilation and my guards were chain smokers. The central heating was hot as hell and my bed, a straw mattress, felt like the top of a furnace; it was too, full of lumps, brickbats they felt like. Every so often the door would be pulled open with a jerk, a door that fitted so closely that one could feel the suction when it was opened, and a warder would come to my bed and flash his torch in my face or there would be a change of guard. This first night was typical of all my nights for many months to come. I never slept deeply nor undisturbed for any length of time but dozed for short spells by day and by night whenever I could.

D

It was before five next morning when Drexl, the plug-ugly warder, opened the door and shouted: "Wash!" When I came back to my cell, the window was wide open, my bed had been made and the floor swept. I asked whether I could lie down again, but the answer was, "It is forbidden to lie on the bed in the daytime." My handcuffs had, of course, been put on again, and there was nothing for me to do but sit on my stool and look at my guard. The man this time was a stout, florid fellow with a truly magnificent Kaiser William moustache. His name was Hoffman, and although he was on duty in my cell for nearly two years, I never succeeded in making friends with him, and he remained surly to the last.

About eight o'clock the warder came in and brought me a plate with two slices of bread thickly spread with butter and honey; the best food that I had tasted since my capture. He told me that I could have more if I wished, so I had another couple. He also brought me a mug of coffee but, in the light of past experience I funked this and asked for cold water instead. This time my handcuffs were removed while I ate and when I had finished I really began to feel a little better and my outlook on life became less venomous, but again I was handcuffed and left to sit on my stool with nothing to do but stare at my guard.

Sometime during the morning the commandant paid me a visit. He was a squat square figure and reminded me always of the frog who would a-wooing go. He had pop eyes, an enormous mouth full of glittering gold crowns, and obviously loved to surround himself with the pomp and circumstance of his exalted station. Whenever I saw him he was accompanied by a chorus of smartly turned out officers and N.C.O.s and when he came into my cell these draped themselves picturesquely at the door. On this first visit on the morning after my arrival at his establishment, his attitude was as friendly as that of a hotel keeper welcoming a new guest and it was with every appearance of solicitude that he inquired as to my health and well-being. I was feeling rather sour and met his overtures with merely a silent glance at my handcuffed wrists. "Oh yes, those can be taken off now. I am sure that you are going to be reasonable and will not make trouble for yourself and for us. Remember though, if you make the slightest attempt to injure yourself or to escape, I shall have you put in irons night and day, and both your arms and legs will be fettered. We want you to be comfortable here and everything is done for your own good. All you have to do is to obey orders. You can have as much to eat as you like and if you want more, have only to say so. Never hesitate to ask for me if you want to see me."

This sounded all very nice so I ventured to suggest that I should like something to smoke and something to read. Now Germans are on the whole extremely good-natured people and hate having to refuse any request which is made to them. It upsets them in fact to such a point that they immediately put on a pretence of being very angry and are apt to snort at you like grampusses. My humble request completely ruined the good humour of my host and he at once began a tirade about Englishmen who never knew when they were well off and seemed to think that when they came to Germany they could have everything their own way. The Führer would soon teach them how mistaken they were. "I was a prisoner of the French in the last war and I had to sleep on a plank and eat food only fit for pigs. That is the way you would be treated if I had my own way."

I regretted this breach of our amicable relations but at all events deduced from what he said, that he was by no means a free agent and that instructions regarding my treatment and the privileges permitted me came to him from a higher level. It was, of course, very important for me to know this as it determined my attitude to the people with whom I came in contact and the degree in which I could hope to ameliorate the circumstances of my life. If the commandant and the warders had no real authority over me but had to refer everything to the Gestapo, then obviously it would be safe for me to chance my arm to a much greater extent than would otherwise be the case. I know something of army methods and the dislike of every subordinate officer to referring his troubles to a superior and asking for help when small matters of detail are at stake. I really believe that it was at this time that I first had the glimmering of a plan of behaviour which, carried out with varying success and many setbacks, eventually brought me to the point where I became, as it were, the undisputed ruler of my little domain; but this time was yet very far away in the future.

My handcuffs were taken off and with my hands free I had an almost irresistible impulse to punch the commandant and knock his words down his throat. This man, Lohritz was his name, was one of those people whom I disliked from the first moment that I set eyes on him. Probably I was unjust, for I really believe that in his way he tried to be kind to me and that also he was really rather proud of having so distinguished a person in his charge. Anyhow, we never became buddies and in the end he had every reason to wish that he had never set eyes on me.

After he had gone it was not long before the door was opened again and the warder said: "Follow me." He took me past the door to the lavatory, to a little room in the passage which lay to the left and at right angles to the one in which my cell lay. I saw then, that the prison was built in the form of a letter T and that my passage was the longest of the three. The three wings thus formed were called Blocks A, B and C, and my cell was No. 51 in Block C. The room to which I was taken was called the 'Interrogation Room' and was simply an ordinary sized cell of which the six-foot high window had been replaced by a normal low one. When I went in I found Dr. Schäfer sitting with his back to the window at a large table. He told me to sit down opposite him and as soon as the warder had gone, asked me what sort of a night I had had and whether I had been given enough to eat. I told him that I was disgusted at the treatment, especially at being handcuffed. He said that he knew it must be very unpleasant but that he hoped steps would be taken to render life more tolerable for me. He then handed me a packet of cigarettes and gave me a light. For the present I must not smoke in my cell nor when out at exercise, but he would try to come and see me as often as possible and when I was with him I could smoke as much as I liked. He hoped that in any case it would not be long before I was also allowed to smoke in my cell and to have books, but for the time being, orders had been given that such privileges were not to be allowed.

Schäfer was, as indeed I had always found him, kind and considerate and I cannot express how much it helped me at the time to sit with him and talk and smoke. It seemed to me that I had only been there a few minutes when the warder came in again and told him that my food had been taken to my cell and would get cold if I did not come soon. Schäfer shook me warmly by the hand and promised to come again next day. I really felt quite cheerful when I got back to my cell, especially when I found there a big plateful of excellent roast pork with potatoes and greens which was followed by a sort of blancmange with a fruit sauce. Very different to the slops at Berlin. I really had a good feed for the first time since my capture and the only thing needed to make life perfect was a cigarette. I had a packet in which were at least fifteen cigarettes left itching in my pocket, but Schäfer had warned me so earnestly not to smoke in my cell that I had to put temptation aside and satisfy myself by licking my chops.

I had, however, barely finished when the warder came again, bringing with him Grothe. The latter told me that he had brought my personal belongings with him from Berlin and that some of these must be deposited in charge of the warder. I was then taken to a room opposite the lavatory which seemed to be a sort of cloak room. Here Grothe produced a typed list which he checked with the things which he had brought. I was allowed to keep my few spare clothes, my soap, comb and hair lotion, but my razor was given to the warder and I was told that he would bring it to me each day so that I could shave but that I was not allowed to keep it in my cell. All the things which I had had in my pockets at the time of my capture, my watch, my pen and pencil, my pocket-book and passport were there and full details were entered by the warder on a card which I was asked to sign. Grothe then told me that my name was now 'Wolf' and that I must use only this name while I was here. This I flatly refused to do, saying that I had never gone under a false name and was not at my age going to begin now. I took the card and put my usual signature. Neither Grothe nor the warder seemed quite to know what to do or to say. I said: "You both know that my name is Best and I shall tell everyone with whom I come in contact who I am and why I am here. If you like to call me Wolf amongst yourselves, that is your own look out, but you can't force me to help you to keep my existence secret." I stuck to this throughout and this was my first small victory.

After Grothe left, the warder came in to say that if I wished I could now go out for my exercise. Seeing that I only had a very light pair of shoes he said that he would give me some boots as it was very muddy outside. He brought me a pair of nailed army boots, an odd pair for they were boots of two different sizes, but they fitted me reasonably well and lasted out the whole of my time at Sachsenhausen. A procession was then formed. First the warder, then myself, and behind me two guards. We had to go down the whole length of my passage to a door at the end.

As we went out I saw that my wing of the prison divided the space between the surrounding walls into two square plots of ground. That on the right was cultivated as a garden but that on the left, into which I was led, was a barren waste in which nothing grew except some coarse grass and the ubiquitous nettle. There was a broad path which ran diagonally across the 'L' formed by the two wings of the prison and a narrower path which followed the side of the building. I was told that I might only walk round and round the track formed by these paths. One of my guards stood near the door through which we had come out and the other posted himself at the other end of the broad walk. The plot of ground was roughly thirty-five yards square and was enclosed by high stone walls surmounted with two lines of wire which were attached to insulators and therefore probably electrified. All the cell windows overlooking my place of exercise were boarded up but, as I passed, I could hear from the movements inside that the cells were occupied.

Along the path near the point where the two wings of the prison met I noticed six holes formed by drain pipes inserted in a concrete bed. Quite a time passed before I discovered their purpose. This was to hold stout poles upright to which recalcitrant prisoners were hung during interrogation. The men's wrists were handcuffed behind their backs and they were then suspended from a hook at the top of the pole so that their toes just cleared the ground. I was told that this treatment was extremely painful and if continued for any considerable length of time resulted in partial or complete dislocation of the shoulder joint. Only the passage and the opposite cell separated my cell from this place, and I was to spend many uneasy hours in the future listening to the shrieks of the victims.

It was a delight to be out of doors again and once more to smell fresh air instead of the human exhalations which had been its substitute ever since my capture. I did not even want to smoke but just breathed in deeply and walked as briskly as I could. Only a very short time seemed to have elapsed when the warder re-appeared and beckoned for us to come in. Someone had opened wide the window of my cell while I was out and, with the light on, it seemed both fresh and bright. Really, I felt almost cheerful. Supper was brought in, half a dozen slices of bread and butter covered with sausage; quite good. The window was closed and darkened by a blanket. Then the warder appeared again and said: "Wash," leaving the door wide open as he went. I washed, etc., and when I got back to my cell the warder stood waiting until I undressed and got into bed. Then, to my horror and disgust, out came the handcuffs again and once more I was fettered and my brief hour of freedom a thing of the past.

A miserable night again. Bright light shining in my face, what little air there was poisoned by the guards who smoked incessantly, and the disturbance inevitable when someone sits and occasionally moves close to ones bed. I got to the point when I could stand it no longer. I sat up in bed and said to the guard in my sternest voice: "Give me a cigarette." He was a mild elderly man with a bad sniff, a tailor by trade. He looked quite frightened and seemed inclined to shout in alarm for the warder, then he got up, crept on his toes towards me and gave me a lighted cigarette. "For God's sake don't tell anyone or I shall be badly punished." That was good. Who said that smoking was bad for one? This guard was only on duty in my cell for a week or a fortnight, but I have not forgotten Master-Tailor Hartmann of Greifenberg in Pom-erania. After the ice had been melted by this first cigarette we chatted in whispers for some time and it was soon clear to me that my guard hated his life here just as much as I did. He was not a Nazi but had been bullied into volunteering for the Waffen-SS and been drafted for duty in a concentration camp: "A horrible place," as he said.

I must have slept a little after our talk, for it did not seem long before again the warder came in, unlocked my handcuffs, and called out, "Wash!" When I got back from the lavatory I was brought my safety razor, a mug of hot water and a mirror. I was quite startled to see how I had changed in the course of only one month; I saw in the mirror the face of a worn old man; an unshaven tramp.

Another day passed. No one came near me except the guards and the warders when they brought my food which, by the way, was very good; I did not even go out as the warder came to say that it was raining and too wet. I had nothing to read, nothing to smoke, and conversation was also forbidden. I just had to sit before my empty table on my stool. This stool was one that had had a long career of barrack room service during which many soldiers had carved their names upon its surface. One 'Schulz' had done so in particularly deep and bold letters which, even through my trousers, I could read as though they were in Braile. There was, too, in the centre of the seat an oblong hole, intended for use when the stool was carried, which was so large that I could never altogether avoid its imprint. The day was mainly passed in offering first one and then the other cheek.

I was not enjoying prison life, but I consoled myself by thinking how very much better my lot was than that of thousands of others; people with incurable diseases just lying waiting for death, or those condemned to pass their lives amidst conditions of squalor and want; no, if the Gestapo thought that they would get me down by this sort of treatment, I was damn well not going to give them that satisfaction. Sitting on my stool I practised a cheerful grin and although this may have made my appearance rather inane, I think I may say that no German ever saw me looking otherwise than bright and happy and by perseverance I came in time even to feel that way. This seemed to annoy two of the Gestapo men who visited me frequently during my first year in Sachsenhausen. When they asked me how I was and I answered "Very well indeed, thank you," one of them would get quite irritated and say, "You can't feel well and you can't be satisfied here. You know quite well that you are being very badly treated. It is just that misplaced sense of humour which all you English seem to have; one can't believe a word that you say."

Of course my main fear was that my present treatment was intended to soften me up for intensive interrogation. My interrogation at Berlin had been so farcical that I could hardly believe that I should be allowed to get off so lightly. It therefore seemed to be of the utmost importance that I should cultivate my powers of resistance and harden myself to take whatever might be coming to me. Actually, nothing did come, but I was to be really grateful for the experiences of these first months for they taught me to take difficulties in my stride and never afterwards did I feel even impatience, let alone boredom. My role was that of the happy prisoner, and I lived up to it well and truly. Life is after all nothing but a series of experiences and if one does not profit from all, one has robbed oneself; one has, as it were, committed partial suicide. I am by nature, and for this I can never be sufficiently grateful, contented. I enjoy what I have and envy no man for the things which I have not. I have had my ups and my downs, I have had money and I have been broke, I have had my share of joys and of sorrows, but in retrospect, all things seem equally sweet. As I sit now writing about a period of my imprisonment which was, to say the very least, uncomfortable, there is no trace of bitterness nor hatred in my memories; just an interesting experience which forms one of the links in the chain of my passage on earth which has left me richer, and I hope, a little wiser. *Cogito ergo sum*, and neither walls nor chains can imprison thought.

At the time my first month at Sachsenhausen was rather bloody, but there were a lot of things to be sorted out and hardly a day passed without my making some new discovery, adding some detail to my growing accumulation of knowledge of the little world around me. The warders and my guards became individuals whom I knew, I worked out the system of their duty rosters. I learnt to distinguish the rhythm of the cage, a periodic regularity in the sounds which for me had to replace sight. Soon I could distinguish many individual footsteps and by counting them, could estimate their position and direction in relation to my own cell. Like a man who has been blinded I found myself acquiring a new acuity of other senses, that of smell, unfortunately included. I am something of a musician and so my hearing was already to a measure trained in analysis. As time went on, I became so expert that practically nothing happened within earshot which I could not translate into an almost visual picture. There was never any lack of sound, for the building, a ferro-concrete construction, was an absolute sounding board which transmitted so many noises that at first they seemed to unite into a vague blur similar to the sound of traffic in a busy street. Very soon, though, the normal background noises faded from my consciousness to form a sort of silence against which every abnormal and interesting sound came to me sharply defined.

There was one regular noise which to the end I failed to suppress and which as time went on became such an annoyance as to test my patience to the utmost. It was that of the wireless in the warders' room which, when certain warders were on duty, was turned on from break of day until midnight; always at maximum strength. The acoustics of the building were such that I could understand nothing that was said and of music only the beat of the rhythm and sometimes a vague indication of tune reached me. While this noise was going on, my brain simply ceased to function and I could neither read nor engage in any other occupation. In the evening there was competition from two other loudspeakers somewhere in the camp. Here I occupied the unfortunate position that the sound of one reached me a fraction of time before that of the other, with the result that all I could hear was a most unpleasant and discordant gibberish. In the morning, somewhere not far away, there was daily singing rehearsal. I learnt later that this was for prisoners who were taught to sing in chorus so as to make a gay and satisfied impression on any who saw them marching to and from their work. They always practised the same songs, the England Song ('We Are Sailing Towards England') and another which started off to the tune of 'Pack Up Your Troubles in Your Old Kit Bag' and then diverged into an entirely different air. As at most rehearsals, nothing was sung from beginning to end and songs were constantly broken off short or certain passages repeated time and again. Soon I knew all the difficult spots and I often sighed with relief when one of these was surmounted without breakdown.

There were though other noises. A sort of shuddering whimper which starting from one cell seemed to travel in jerky waves and increasing volume until the whole building was filled with a moan of utter misery. Then suddenly it would be hushed and the only sound left would be that of someone tramping back and forth in his cell, that, and a feeling of expectancy as though everyone were listening for something to happen. Often, too, something did happen. There would be the sound of many people in heavy boots walking about near the entrance and of talking and laughter. A warder would march briskly along one of the passages, stop, open a cell door and say: "Come, you." As he walked back there was a prisoner clip-clopping along in his wooden pattens beside him. There would be some more talk and laughter. Then a dull sort of thud, the sound of a piece of lead pipe striking a roll of carpet. This would be repeated, about once every three or four seconds. At first this would be the only sound and then following it there would be a sort of grunt or a cry of "O-O-W-W!" Then pain would vanquish any determination to display fortitude and ever louder and louder shrieks would mount into that terrible falsetto which seems to typify the limit of human endurance.

Another time a warder would march briskly to one of the cells, open the door with a jerk, and call to the inmate: "Get ready to bathe. . . . No, take everything off. Turn round. Face to the wall." A crack of a pistol.

"Clear up that mess in number seventy-two and scrub out the cell." One of the trusties would come along. Then there was the sound of something heavy being dragged along the passage. In the deathly hush one could hear in the distant cell the trusty slopping water from his bucket and scrubbing. More marching near the entrance and cries of "Heil Hitler"; then the wireless would strike up some cheerful tune and prison life returned to normal. My left hand would tremble for some hours afterwards.

There were three warders in the building when I first went there. All had the rank of Hauptscharführer (Warrant Officer 1st Class) in the Waffen-SS, in which they had enlisted for a minimum period of twelve years. Their names were Kurt Eccarius, Franz Ettlinger and Josef Drexl. Eccarius was the senior man in rank and was supposed to be responsible for the running of the building, but actually he always played second fiddle to Ettlinger, who was not only a man of more dominant personality but also enjoyed the friendship of the commandant. Eccarius, a dour-looking man of thirty-five who seldom smiled was an excellent official who ran things quietly and efficiently during his turns of duty. Each warder did twenty-four hours on and forty-eight off and I think that everyone like myself longed for the days when Eccarius was on duty. Everything ran smoothly, everything was on time, and there was none of the shouting and noise which marked the work of the other two.

Ettlinger, in his smart uniform and with his cap on was quite a good-looking fellow of twenty-seven; good-looking until he removed his cap, for then one saw that his head ended about an inch above his eyes and then went flat back. He was, I think, the most despicable character that I have ever met. He was a sadist, a bully, a sycophant, a thief, and a drunkard. He contaminated everyone with whom he came in touch and during his turns of duty succeeded in making the prison a hell for every inmate. I shall have much more to say about him later on. As for the third, Drexl, he was just a Bavarian peasant, rough and uncouth, inclined to speak gruffly and shout, but really a kind, good-natured fellow; he was much older than the other two, nearly fifty and never had much to do with them outside his work. If one asked him for anything, his answer was invariably: "Can't be done," then, after a few minutes he came in and with a crooked grin did what he had been asked.

There were four men detailed for duty in my cell, each doing two hours on and two hours off in the daytime and two hours on and four hours off at night. Each day at 8 a.m. one man went off on leave until 4 p.m. the next day and, if he lived in the neighbourhood, was free to go home. Each man therefore, was on duty from 4 p.m. one day for the succeeding three nights and two days. Just as my night's rest was disturbed every two hours by the change of guards so these men too had equally disturbed nights, sleeping as they did, four to a cell. Most men broke down under the strain, suffering from acute boredom and lack of sleep.

During the first months of my sojourn, my four guards were Becker, Hofmann, Schnaars, and Schwartz. Becker, who was the smart little man who took the first turn of duty after my arrival, very soon became my firm friend and gave me most valuable help in finding my feet. Schnaars, too, an enormous fat man, a fishmonger in civilian life, also turned out to be a good sort. He was very drunk one day when he came on duty and simply could not keep awake. I told him to go ahead and have a nap and that I would warn him if there were signs of the approach of a warder. After this he was so deeply grateful that he would do anything for me.

Hofmann and Schwartz were both surly, unpleasant fellows; the latter soon left me, but Hofmann was on duty, either with Stevens or myself, for the whole of the first and longest year. He was a Bavarian smallholder and had been a cavalryman in the First World War; he was not really a bad fellow and certainly never gave me away. He was just unsociable and suffered from a sense of grievance that he had been drafted for duty at the camp at all; at his age, fifty, and as a farm worker he should have been exempt from military service. We got on without friction except when I wanted a light for a cigarette. At first I was not allowed to have matches and my guards had been told to give me a light when I required one. Hofmann argued that no one had the right to order him to waste his own matches and that, if I had none of my own, the guards should be provided with them by the camp authorities. Every time I asked him for a light he would sulk for the next day or two. Always when he saw that I had nearly finished a meal, after which I should certainly want a cigarette, he would quickly light one of his own and blow out the match before I had a chance to light one. Yet, if he saw that I was out of smokes, he would always give me a cigarette just before he left the cell; matches though were tied to a matter of principle.

Tearing mouthfuls from hard German bread and leathery rolls had a disastrous effect on my teeth which, truth to tell, although still attached to me by roots were more the products of art than of nature; gold inlays and crowns left their anchorage and fillings crumbled to nothing. Already at Berlin I had suffered the premonitory twinges of toothache so that it was with some satisfaction that I heard a few days after reaching Sachsenhausen that I was to be taken to the dentist. This was quite a performance. First I was taken up the passage until I was close to the entrance door; there I had to stand for some five minutes with my face to the wall. Then I was handcuffed and told to get into an ambulance which was standing before the door. All the blinds were down so that I could not see where I was going. When we stopped we were still in the camp and near a long, low timber building. I was taken in here and had to walk along a passage for almost its whole length. On my way I passed a number of rooms, some obviously hospital wards, others marked operation theatre, X-rays, oculist, etc., then dental department and I went into one of the best equipped dental surgeries which I have ever seen.

The dentist, Sturmbahnführer Gussow, was in SS uniform, but his attitude to me was that of doctor to patient. He made a most careful examination of my teeth, taking several X-ray photos. Then he stuck in some gold inlays which I had saved when they fell out and made one or two temporary fillings. I was given an appointment for the following week and then getting into my carriage was driven home. Before I entered the dentist's room my handcuffs were taken off and it was forgotten to put them on again on the way back.

Dental treatment became my hobby during the rest of my imprisonment as only in this way was I ever able to get outside the four walls surrounding the precincts of my bunker. True, I did not even then get outside the camp, but since after the first two visits I was allowed to walk I could at least look at things at eye level for a couple of hundred yards or more and I could see trees from the root upwards. When for months at a time one's vision has been limited to things close at hand and those which can be seen sticking out above a nine-foot wall, one gets a curious longing to be able to look straight ahead at the world as it has its origin in the ground. From my cell all that I could see were the tops of some pine trees and the rooks who made their home there, swarming morning and evening. From the garden all that was visible were two high buildings to the south, a smoky factory chimney to the west, and to the north, one of the watch towers which stood at intervals along the main prison wall. The window of my cell was six feet from the ground and it was some time before my guards had become sufficiently tame to allow me to stand on a stool and look out. Even when I did, the only view that I had was again bounded by a high wall.   .

Until a few days before Xmas I had almost daily visits from Gestapo officials. Ostensibly their purpose was interrogation but all that happened was that I would be shown a few photographs and asked whether I recognized any of the people, or a list of names would be handed to me to see whether they included anybody I knew. Actually, I think the real object of these visits was (a) to make me feel that I was not neglected, (b) to give deserving junior members of the Gestapo opportunities for free meals at the camp canteen. They always managed to arrive half an hour or so before the midday meal and, when the warder came to say that my food had been taken to my cell and to ask whether they would not also go to the canteen for a meal, they accepted the suggestion as an agreeable surprise. Schäfer, after his first visit, I never saw again, but Grothe came quite often, and so did the man who came with Grosch at the first visit of the Germans at Dinxperlo; then he called himself von Seydlitz, but I believe that his real name was Schulz. There was also a long and very beautiful young man with fair waved hair, tinted lips and cheeks, and pencilled eyebrows. He was the only one who put me through an interrogation; one which occasioned me great amusement.

A few weeks before our capture a friend of ours had come to us for dinner, bringing with her her son who had come to The Hague from Berlin where he had a remunerative practice as a consultant astrologer. The same evening I had been at Stevens's house and had been pressed to stay and dine. In refusing I had said, more as a joke than anything else: "I'm so sorry that I can't stay, but Hitler's pet astrologer is coming to dinner with us." Somehow or other the Gestapo had got on to this and had succeeded in ferreting out the man in question. He had at once been arrested and subjected to a thorough grilling for, as it appeared, he had indeed been employed to work out Hitler's horoscope or whatever else astrologers do.

The blond adonis started off in the stereotyped Gestapo manner. "Now, Herr Best, pay the very greatest attention. This is a very important matter and for you it is a matter of life or death. Don't think for a moment that you can fool me, for we know everything, e-v-e-r-y-t-h-i-n-g. What did you arrange with Herr K. von H.?"

Well, what was I to answer to this. I remembered that the man had been to dinner and that I had fetched him and his mother by car from their house. I was very busy at the time and had had to go out after dinner, only returning half an hour or so before our guests left. What we had talked about had completely vanished from my memory. I told my interrogator all this, but he was far from satisfied. Rising from his chair and leaning over me he said: "All lies, Herr Best, on the contrary, you had a most important discussion. Oh, yes, we know all about it, but now what I want to know from you is, what *you* knew and how did you get to know it." This was getting far too deep for me and I asked him how he could expect me to remember details of a conversation with a comparative stranger some two months ago. If he knew so much, why not give me a lead.

In a most impressive voice and scanning each word, he asked:
"*Why did you tell Herr K. von H. not to return to Germany until AFTER THE CHANGE OF THE MOON?*"

Now to give some sense to this question I must go back some time to the occasion of my second meeting at Venlo with Major Solms. One of the things which he told me then was that Hitler firmly believed that his enterprises depended on the phase of the moon at the time of their initiation. After the victorious end of the Polish campaign there had been some sort of celebration in Berlin at which Hitler had been present. When congratulations had been offered to him, to the surprise of everybody he had had one of his uncontrollable outbursts of hysterical rage and had shouted: "This is no time for congratulation, Poland is nothing and that she has been beaten means nothing. The war has not been won—it will never be won—we shall be beaten—the war started ten days too late—it should have started with a *rising moon*. Anything started at the time of a waning moon is foredoomed to fail." Solms said that this had created quite a sensation and that Hitler had had one of his attacks and had rolled about on the floor biting the carpet according to his usual habit.

Having myself not the slightest belief in astrology or in lucky and unlucky omens, I had taken this as an amusing and probably apocryphal story. It must though have stuck in my mind, for I remember that I had pulled K. von H.'s leg in a mild sort of way and had told him that it would be better if he postponed his return to Germany until after the full moon a few days later. I must have done so, for May remembered the story and throughout the war noted that all Hitler's main offensives were in fact started shortly after the moon was new.

Of course I did not tell my young friend anything of this, but simply said that it was quite possible that I said something of the kind, but I had had nothing at the back of my mind and had simply been talking nonsense. When I said, of course no reasonable being believes in astrology, I came in for a first quality snort. "How dare I suggest such a thing. Of course astrology was an absolutely accurate science. The Führer believed in it, and he *knew*," etc., etc.

Well, this young man came for three days running, morning and afternoon, worrying me about this balderdash. He pounded out pages and pages on his typewriter with not one word of sense on any of them except my denial of belief in astrology—I am not even sure that he dared to write this down for in his opinion heresy was an offence which should bring instant execution. Anyhow, I could smoke all day on these occasions and, on the whole, I rather enjoyed myself. The young man gradually calmed down and towards the end we were on quite amicable terms and he confided to me his hatred of his present work and his conviction that he was by nature destined to higher things.

Meanwhile, my cell life had gradually become less uncomfortable. The Oberführer had given instructions that I could sit or lie on my bed whenever I liked and had sent in a pair of windsor chairs for the guard and myself; for my chair, two cushions were even provided. I was also permitted to wash at the basin where there was hot and cold water instead of splashing round in the cold spray from the fountain. Every Friday, too, I could have a beautiful hot douche and was given a change of laundry. They managed to find me a second shirt of sorts and I already had some spare underclothes, as a parcel had been found in the boot of my car containing some which I had bought but forgotten to take home. Yes, I had some underclothes, expensive new woollen things, but they were mine only for the first week of wearing and what came back from the wash were war-worn veterans. Every week too, I was provided with a brand new pair of army socks. At first I sent them back to the wash when they were dirty but after a time I was wiser and washed them myself. In this way I gradually accumulated a good stock and could change my socks every day.

I had managed to annex one or two pencils when being interrogated and, as I was provided with a roll of toilet paper I had the requisite materials to enable me to keep some sort of record of events; indeed, from the end of 1939 to final liberation I religiously entered up my diary day by day. In what I write I am therefore able to check the accuracy of my memory by the notes made at the time. Of course I had to be very careful what I wrote as all my belongings were open to inspection; still, I succeeded in devising a sort of unobtrusive code by which to mark any events of importance.

Until the 23rd December the weather had been fine and mild, but on that day it started to snow and for the next days there was a raging blizzard.

For some days there was no question of going out and, until after the New Year, there were no visitors from Berlin with their chances of a smoke. I just had to sit or tramp up and down in my cell, and think. No, I did not think of home, of the life that had been, or that which might have been. To remain sane, I had to discipline my thoughts; I realized that I was in for the duration and that I must make a new life and like it. I did in fact seriously count my blessings and never before nor since have I been so appreciative of every small factor which tended to render life tolerable.

My guard Becker, who had shown signs of friendliness had gone home on leave and had been replaced by a most unpleasant fellow. The little tailor occasionally passed me a cigarette or an apple at night, but for the rest I was thrown entirely on my own resources; nothing to read and no one to talk to. To occupy my mind I tried to recall what I could remember from my youth of mathematics—very little it was. Still, just trying to raise numbers to higher powers by mental multiplication would help me to pass an hour or two. On the analogy of $(x+y)(x+y)=x^2+2xy+y^2$ I succeeded in extracting square roots, and I was even able to reconstruct the formula for arithmetic and algebraical sequences which I had entirely forgotten. Although I had paper and pencil, I did not at that early stage dare to let my guards see me writing, so all my calculations had to be done in my head. Although I did not accomplish much I found a new interest in mathematics, and when later I was able to get hold of books I settled down to as much serious study as I could manage without help.

When the snow stopped, I was once more allowed my daily hour in the fresh air. How lovely this was and how I loved everything of nature that I could see; the clouds, the snow crystals, and the occasional bird flying overhead. Yes, prison certainly teaches new appreciation of nature. There was a slight thaw for a few days and huge icicles formed from the eaves and my cell, being on the cold side, had some gigantic specimens before the window; then it turned cold, the 1939–40 record winter had started. The snow had been shovelled from the paths where it formed walls five feet high and it was cold. Until well into February we had, day after day, record low temperatures. I had no hat and only a light summer overcoat, but in spite of temperatures often as low as —3 degrees F., I stuck it for the full hour whenever I was allowed out, much to the disgust of my guards who, being forced to stand in one place, almost froze to death in spite of their warm clothes, mufflers and ear shields.

I forgot to say that after the 19th December I was no longer handcuffed at night. On that day the warder called me and my guard out of the cell and put us in the interrogation room for half an hour or so. When I got back to my cell I noticed at once that a stout ring had been cemented into the wall under the window near my bed. I wondered what on earth this was for. That evening, when I had undressed and gone to bed, the warder produced a leather-covered chain of about a yard and a half in length which he proceeded to fix with a padlock to the ring in the wall. Then he fastened a leather-covered hinged steel band round my wrist and padlocked it to the chain. There I was, just like old Fido, safely chained up for the night. I was simply furious at the time and indeed always felt this nightly chaining as an indignity, yet it was much more comfortable than being handcuffed and as time went on, I became so expert in the management of my chain that I really hardly noticed it at night.

Now I want to be fair and I have to admit that from the German point of view nothing more was intended than a precaution against any attempt at escape during the night which might result in my suffering injury. Instructions had been given at some very high level that neither Stevens nor I were to be locked in our cells. The idea seemed to be that as long as we were not locked in we could not say that we were being treated as criminals or that we were in solitary confinement. The commandant had, however, been made responsible for our safe custody and also for our being kept out of harm's way. Although a guard was always on duty in our cells, it was impossible to hope that he would always remain awake at night; in fact, my guards did doze off regularly. If therefore there had been no chain to limit our freedom of movement, one or the other of us might have been tempted to make a get-away and might easily have lost his life in the process. When I got to know the details of the camp security system I realized that escape was an absolute impossibility, since from our building one could only have got out into the concentration camp proper which surrounded us. During the more than five years which I spent here, although very many attempts were made, no prisoner ever succeeded in escaping from the camp for more than a few hours, and none got more than a few hundred yards away. When, in 1944, the greatest British experts at escaping, men such as Wing-Commander Day, Major John Dodge and Flight-Lieutenants Dowse, Churchill, and James were imprisoned in the Bunker, they had to give up any further attempts at escape as hopeless.

I have written thus fully on this subject for, since our return home, there have been frequent references in the Press to Stevens and myself as having been kept in fetters for a number of years. Neither of us was ever fettered during the daytime except on the few occasions which I have mentioned. I must admit, too, that

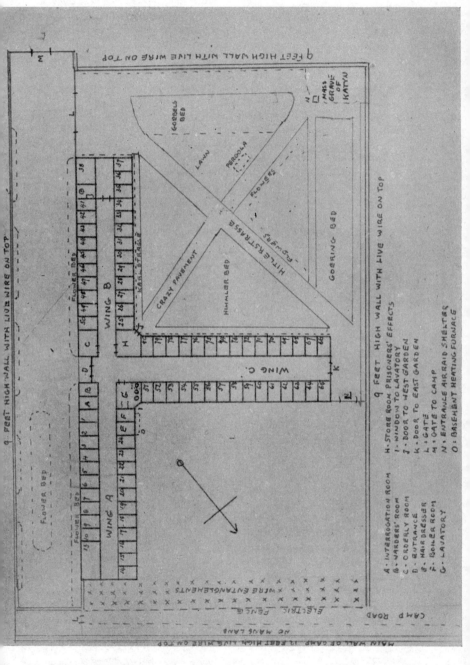

Plan of the 'Bunker' at Sachsenhausen where the author spent five and a quarter years, first in Cell No. 51 and afterwards in No. 43.

I was in a car with an extremely nice officer in uniform (Hauptmann) the same tho, in mufti, had lead the raiding party which captured us. He told me that Klop was not badly wounded, & that through the arm & a glancing shot on the head, and that he had recovered consciousness. Many months later Grothe told me that Klop's wounds had proved much more serious than was at first thought & that he was then still seriously ill. I was not allowed to wear my glasses. Smoking was also forbidden but the officer very kindly gave me two or three cigarettes, although a halt was made for lunch no food was provided for me but after we had got going again the officer gave me two apples.

We were quite a procession of cars going to Berlin. Stevens & Lemmens were presumably each in separate cars & then my own car also came

along with us. We arrived at Berlin after dark & when we reached the Gestapo H.Q. it was black night. We drove into a sort of courtyard & when we stopped a voice asked whether I was hot & whether my feet were free. Then some one tore off my hat and thrust a sort of sack of black stuff over my head. I was then seized by two men & roughly dragged out of the car which, as I was still handcuffed was rather a painful operation, wrenching my wrists badly. I was then marched by these two men each holding me by the wrist into a building & upstairs & downstairs and along long passages until, owing to the obstruction to breathing occasioned by the hood over my head I was quite breathless. At last I was taken into a brightly lighted room & was pushed on to a soft seat - that I later found was a sofa. Then my feet were tightly strapped together & a voice

Pages from one of the author's diaries, showing part of an account
of his capture written about a month later.

said "you can remove the hood". It took me some time to recover my wind as I was completely pumped. In the meantime I look round & took note of my surroundings. I sat on a sofa & next to me a very tall mean-looking one of my guards. There was also present another man (Hoffmann) who remained with me as guard. Sitting on a chair opposite me was an extremely intelligent looking man of sympathetic appearance & manner (or Max Schombacher) & next to him, sitting at a table with typewriter, a stoutish middle aged woman — Frau Rudolf. Also in the room was a fat man in jersey & trousers of prize fighter type who was apparently one of the two men who had dragged me from the car and up & down the stairs. He was, as I later discovered the head jailor of the H.Q. prison & really a mostly pleasant creature - we became quite

good friends during the course of my stay at H.Q.

The room in which I found myself (No 315) was apparently someones private office which had been prepared for my reception by the addition of a bedstead to its normal equipment.

Immediately I had recovered my breath I made violent protest to or Max as to the way in which I had been treated since I had left the car and the fact that I had been fettered. Or Max obviously felt the justice of my complaint & did not like the situation. He said in defence that they had only taken a leaf out of Scotland Yard's book and, as beginners, had copied English practice. I strongly protested against the suggestion that such behaviour was possible in England & the up that was, that my fetters were removed on the understanding that I would neither attempt suicide nor escape.

had not some measure been taken to restrict my liberty of movement I should very probably have attempted to get away. I had refused to give my parole and it seems to me that the Germans were justified in taking the precautions which they did, even if their nature seems most objectionable to our eyes. Everybody hated the business, both warders and guards (except, of course, Ettlinger, who obviously took pleasure in it). In December 1941, after Stevens had left the Bunker for a new home at Dachau, Eccarius came in one evening to chain me up as usual, bringing with him not my wristlet, but the one previously used by Stevens. I told him at once that he had brought the wrong one but he solemnly answered that it was the only one he had and that he was sure that I would find it quite comfortable. I certainly did, for being slighter in build than Stevens, I could quite easily slip my hand out of it when it was locked. After this we went through the same farce every night. At ten o'clock, or whenever I said I was ready, the warder came in and chained me up. I then slipped off my bracelet, hung it on the bed-post, and either sat down again for a read or went to bed. In the morning, I slipped the ring over my wrist again so that the warder could unlock me. Quite often though he would come in whilst I was still asleep and on such occasions had to wait for me to put on my fetters before he could carry on with the business of setting me at liberty. Neither of us said a word, nor even smiled. Orders are orders and the conventions must be observed.

During the first two months the warders were constantly finding excuses which resulted in my being docked of my exercise; it was too cold or it was snowing; on Saturdays and Sundays I was never allowed out and as a result my health suffered and I really began to feel very poorly. To spend day and night without a break in an overheated ill-ventilated cell was really quite a trial. When Grothe came to see me one day at the beginning of February he commented on my appearance, saying that I was not looking as well as I had. He asked me whether I was taking regular exercise and when I told him that during the previous month I had only been allowed out on five days he was very angry and going to the door called the warder into the room. In his presence he told me that orders had been given that I should have at least an hour's exercise if I wished daily and that the decision whether I went out or not depended entirely on me. Turning to the warder he said: "I advise you to be more careful in future as if anything like this comes to my ears again I shall report it to Oberführer Müller—you know what will happen then." This little incident had a most salutary effect on the behaviour of the warders towards me, for they realized that there was now always danger that I might report irregularities to one of my Gestapo visitors. This, indeed, I did, on one or two occasions and, as I was careful not to make unnecessary trouble, my applications were always successful.

E

On the 6th January, 1940, the commandant brought me in two books, Hitler's *Mein Kampf* and a rather trashy novel and told me that I was now permitted to read and could change books by asking the warder. This was a very great relief for I have always been an avid reader: I even found *Mein Kampf* interesting, for I was in Nazi Germany and everything which I could learn about the Nazi ideology might be of use to me. A month later and the commandant came again, this time to tell me that in future I might smoke; the warder would provide me with cigarettes. This was great news indeed. I had really suffered very much from the lack of tobacco, indeed, all my most unpleasant memories of imprisonment are of smokeless days. Generally I had managed to get hold of one or two cigarettes a day. When Grothe came to see me he invariably gave me a packet and my guards raised no objection to my smoking in the cell, indeed, when they saw that I had nothing left, I generally found that a cigarette would make its appearance, lying on my table or my bed. I am sure too, that the warders knew that I smoked, but they never made any comment—there is a brotherhood, a freemasonry amongst smokers.

After the Oberführer had gone I waited the rest of the day, with my tongue hanging out, for my cigarettes, but none came. Next morning though Ettlinger brought me twenty-one cigarettes which he told me was my allowance for a week, they lasted me two days. Then, like Oliver Twist, I asked for more. No, I did not get any, but luckily Grothe turned up and presented me with a packet of tobacco and cigarette papers. If the Germans had simply stopped my smoking altogether I should have had to break myself of the habit, and I am sure that I should have been saved a lot of unpleasantness, but what they did was to keep me short and, as it seemed to me, deliberately annoy me every now and again by leaving me with nothing to smoke for days on end. During the first two years my smokes were doled out to me by Ettlinger who made it his regular practice always to keep me waiting a day or two after the date when I should have received my next supply; not only this, but as I discovered later, although instructions had been given from Berlin that I was to receive an allowance of ten cigarettes a day, he had given me three and smoked the rest himself; but more of this later.

The 7th March was another red-letter day for Grothe brought me two packs of patience cards, for which I had asked some time previously. I was now a rich man. I could not read all day, for I always had to wait quite a time before my books were exchanged for new ones; patience though has always been a favourite pastime of mine and had often saved me from boredom in times of forced inactivity during the First World War.

I was gradually getting acclimatized and had got past the first hopeless feeling which attacks everyone when he is deprived of his liberty; but my health was not very good and although the food was really excellent of its kind, it did not seem to suit me and not only did I suffer from indigestion but I also lost weight rapidly. I was not alone in this for all the soldiers and officials at the camp were said to have lost from two to three stones during the first months of the war. The food always seemed very good and there was more than I could manage to eat, but something must have been lacking for my weight declined from about twelve to a little over nine stone and nothing that I ate seemed to make any difference. There was no lack of medical attention either, for during the first month or two I had several visits from senior medical officers who examined me pretty thoroughly, whilst the camp doctor came to see me at least once a week.

The weather became terribly cold and gradually my window, both inside and out, became coated with a thick layer of ice. It was so thick that practically no light shone through and the electric light had to be on all day. I found this most tiring to my eyes, for with the whitewashed cell walls there was a constant glare from which there was no relief. I had gradually left the place by the window where I had first been told to sit, and now had my table facing the wall close to the radiator so that my back was turned to the guard. I had given up pacing up and down my cell for it seemed to me that this had a demoralizing effect owing to its suggestion of impatience; it was far better to control oneself and sit quietly. I frequently noticed subsequently that when a prisoner got into the way of pacing up and down his cell all day long, as some did, this was often the prelude to a nervous breakdown or an attempt to commit suicide. I always tried to pretend that I was free and to behave as though I were just sitting in my own room at home; I refused to permit myself to desire anything which was impossible of achievement and, generally, I succeeded pretty well in maintaining my normal balance.

My greatest difficulty was to keep my thoughts away from May and to convince myself that all was well with her. Whilst in Berlin I had been allowed to dictate a short letter to one of the typists, and the Oberführer himself had promised that it should be sent off at once. After I got to Sachsenhausen I frequently asked the Gestapo people whether I might write but the answer was always that I must wait a bit as at present there were no facilities for sending letters to England. Grothe had already told me soon after I came to the Bunker that May had left Holland for England. This news was a great relief for it assured me that she was being looked after.

One day, at the beginning of March, Schellenberg came into my cell and addressed me in broken English. When I answered in German he said, "No, speak English." I then saw that a number of men were standing in the passage outside my door and peering at me. There were one or two Japs and the others looked like southerners, Italians or Spaniards, and it occurred to me that they were probably Axis press correspondents. I took the opportunity to ask Schellenberg why I was not allowed to write home, to which he answered that of course I could do so whenever I liked. I said that I had frequently asked for pen and paper but that this had so far been refused, and I then spoke of the chaining at night. At this Schellenberg hurriedly gathered his flock together and went away. Very soon afterwards I went out for my exercise and while I was tramping round my allotted path, Schellenberg and the commandant came out, followed by the men I had seen before, some dozen of them in all. When I showed an inclination to walk up to them, the commandant shouted to me to go on walking. I noticed one of the Japs taking some snaps with a camera which he held under his coat and I hoped that perhaps these might appear in some paper and so give an indication of my presence in the camp.

Next day the commandant told me that I could write to my wife once a week and ordered the warder to give me writing materials. From then onwards I wrote a letter every week which I handed to the commandant who assured me that they were sent on. I went on doing this until November 1940 when one of the Gestapo officials while looking for some paper or other let a file fall open, and in the quick glance at it that I was able to take, I saw that it contained letters which I had written and others in May's handwriting. A little later I mentioned this to Grothe who admitted that none of my letters had been sent off, but assured me that May was quite well and that she wrote cheerfully and regularly. This interception of correspondence between my wife and myself was far and away the dirtiest trick played on me by the Gestapo and, is indeed, the only one which I still find quite unforgivable. I was quite ready to accept the solitary confinement, the guard day and night, and even the chaining at night merely as signs that the Germans were anxious to retain me as their guest, but to deprive me of all contact with home and possibly, as indeed was the case, leave my wife in ignorance of my fate . . . well, I can't express my opinion in terms polite enough for print.

Apart from this the conditions of my existence gradually became easier as I accustomed myself to the routine of prison life. Routine, an indispensable factor, for it is the enemy of uncertainty. At first I never knew from one minute to the next what might happen. Suddenly the door would be flung open and the commandant or the doctor would come in, or the warder would say to me, "Come, you." It was only to take me to the interrogation room where I would find someone from the Gestapo, but equally well he might have been taking me to execution. I wasn't afraid of death, but the whole atmosphere of the place had made me jumpy. When Ettlinger was on duty things were always particularly unpleasant. He had a habit of suddenly pulling the door open with a jerk and, after standing looking in without saying a word, slamming it shut again.

He had another trick which occasioned me great discomfort. It was my privilege to be allowed to go to the lavatory whenever I wished, and unlike other prisoners I had no stinking pail in my cell. When Ettlinger was on duty and my guard rang the bell and said that I wanted to go to the lavatory, the answer was always that I must wait a bit; the lavatory was engaged, or it was just being cleaned. In this way he would often keep me waiting for two or three hours, with the result that I developed a nervous constriction of the bladder which caused me great suffering, and proved most difficult to cure. In the end it got so bad that I could not make water when I wanted to and was obliged to consult the doctor, who reported it to the commandant. There was a terrible row and from my cell I could hear the telling off that Ettlinger got. After that I had no more trouble of this kind, but Ettlinger had it in for me and did everything he could to render my life uncomfortable.

Eccarius, nominally the head man, had however, realized danger for himself if I should report things to the Gestapo, and his attitude towards me gradually became much more friendly, and whenever he was on duty went out of his way to satisfy my modest wishes. Previously I had had my hour's exercise at different times each day, often not until evening when it was getting dusk. This was changed and I went out at noon each day. Then, I had been chained and sent to bed at eight; this was altered to ten. He also brought me my meals as soon as they were received from the kitchen, whilst the food was still hot; previously everything had been tepid or cold by the time it was brought to me. As a matter of fact I always found Eccarius a very decent fellow. He was cowardly, he was incapable of exercising any authority over the other warders, and he was a drunkard, but during the five and a quarter years that I lived in the Bunker I never noticed any sign of cruelty, or even of roughness, in his treatment of prisoners. His main preoccupation always was to keep out of trouble. He had to carry out his instructions, but as long as prisoners did not do anything likely to get him into trouble, he interfered with them as little as possible. His policy was certainly that of 'Live and let live'.

All the menial work in the Bunker, and indeed in the whole camp, was performed by 'Trusties', called by the Germans 'Kalfaktors'. These were almost all 'Bible Students'; I believe that in England they are called 'Jehovah's Witnesses'. This sect was considered by the Nazis to be almost more dangerous to the regime than the Jews, for while no German could turn himself into a Jew, any German could become a Bible Student and, as such, refuse to take part in military service in any shape or form. The fortitude shown by these men was most remarkable and earned the grudging admiration even of their jailers. Most had been imprisoned since 1933 and their treatment had been the worst possible. They had been beaten, tortured, and starved; one man had been publicly hung, but I was told that there had not been a single instance of one of these men forsaking his principles and buying liberty by entry into the armed forces. I know nothing about the details of their belief except that they recognized only Jehovah as their deity, Saturday as their Sabbath, and placed their hope in a Judgment Day in the near future. All that I met were honest, kindly, and very brave men; fanatics, if you will, yet carrying with them something of that sacred flame which inspired the early Christians.

They had another quality, that of devotion to duty. They did not work slowly and ineffectively like other prisoners, but like free men to whom their jobs were important. Because of this they became indispensable in the camp economy and gradually many of the most important and responsible posts were filled by men bearing the little violet triangle which marked the Bible Student. The other classes of prisoners, the political, green triangle, the habitual criminals, red triangle, and the asocial elements, black triangle, often regarded them with distrust, accusing them of being tale bearers and of currying favour with the authorities, but from everything that I observed and heard I am convinced that these men unflinchingly offered themselves as shields for the protection of all other prisoners, and that their influence for good in the camps was incalculable. When I first met these men, who even then had already spent five or six years in concentration camps, and saw their selfless kindness and devotion, I felt that it would be shameful if I showed any weakness or complained of hardship. As I say, I know nothing of their belief and I could never rise to their height of faith, but I take off my hat to them as men who often made me feel very small and humble.

When I first came to the Bunker there were three of these men; Eckhard and Stokowski in the building, and the gardener, Clemens. There were besides, two other trusties, the furnace man and a carpenter, both political prisoners. The former was a great hulking 'Water Pole', that is to say a native of the Kattowitz district of Upper Silesia. He was also the executioner and carried out the floggings and other forms of physical torture practised in the Bunker at that time.

Very slowly, with almost imperceptible growth, there was improvement in the conditions of my life. In my cell, I could sit at my table and play patience, or, lying on my bed, read or doze. Becker and Schnaars became increasingly friendly and although we had to be cautious, we managed to talk quite a lot. All guards, too, did their best to be quiet at night and to cause the least possible disturbance when entering or leaving the cell; I had also got hold of a piece of brown paper, and made a sort of shade to the lamp, which kept the worst glare from my eyes when I lay in bed. In the garden I could interrupt my monotonous marching and either sit on a bench in the sun or amuse myself building a snow-man; there was even an attempt at snow-balling with my guards. In March a new guard came on duty who was to remain with me, on and off, for the rest of my stay in Sachsenhausen. This was Karl Böning, who became my faithful and loyal friend, and who remains so to this day.

In the First World War Böning was a sergeant in the field artillery and had seen service on both west and east fronts. After the war he had got a job as tap-man at a small café restaurant at Koepenick, near Berlin, and eventually married the proprietor's daughter who inherited the business. He had never had anything to do with politics and his presence in the uniform of the Waffen-SS was due only to the fact that he was a member of the Kyffhäuser Bund, the German organization equivalent to our British Legion. At the outbreak of war the branch secretaries had received instructions to report that all their members had unanimously volunteered for service in the SS, upon which they were promptly called up. Those who had never shown enthusiasm for the Nazi cause, or who, for any other reason were looked upon as politically uncertain, had been drafted for guard duties at concentration camps, so as to have a salutary warning before their eyes of what happened to opponents of the party. Although all these men were subjected to considerable pressure to induce them to join the party, Böning always refused to do so and managed up to the end to keep free from any political affiliations. As he himself said, as a young recruit he had sworn an oath of allegiance to the Kaiser, and although the latter had deserted, that did not relieve him from the obligation of loyalty to his sovereign; and beyond that he wished to have nothing to do with politics. In the past, when he had voted, it had been for the German National Party which represented those who had remained true to their emperor and to German tradition.

To most people in England the letters 'SS' symbolize everything that was most horrible in the Nazi regime; a gang of unmitigated ruffians whose main delight was the torture and murder of innocent people. Whilst it is true that most atrocities were committed under the banner of the SS, a large number of men who wore the SS uniform during the war had no sympathy for the Nazi party or its principles. They were *muss soldaten*, conscripts who had no illusions as to their status; in fact, they described themselves as 'Prisoners Second Class'—they had been drafted for service at concentration camps merely because they were considered politically insecure. Some forty of these men were on duty in my cell at different times, and with the exception of three or four real party members, all were decent fellows, who certainly showed not the slightest inclination towards cruelty; the worst that I have to say of any of them is that they were surly or untrustworthy. In the SS there were good men and bad just as in any other cross section of the population, and as always, the good predominated.

CHAPTER IV

WHAT was this concentration camp at Sachsenhausen where I now found myself?

Although I spent more than five years within the boundaries of its walls, my direct knowledge of the treatment of the inmates and the conditions of life there is very slight. Yet I lived so close to it and had so many contacts with men forming part of the camp community that, what I learned by personal observation, and what came to me by hearsay, perhaps allows me to give a picture more dispassionate and of greater continuity than many reports which have been published on the evidence of the conditions found at the end of hostilities and of the stories of prisoners found in the camps. Of course my experience relates only to this one camp and I have no means of judging what happened at extermination camps such as Frei Mann and Flossenberg in Germany, and those such as Auschwitz in occupied areas. It will be understood that I was throughout intensely interested in everything that went on around me, and that I seized every opportunity which came my way to learn something about the conditions in which the tens of thousands of men lived on the other side of the wall which was all that separated us. Great disbelief has met all protestations of Germans accused of war crimes when they expressed ignorance of the appalling atrocities committed in these camps, but having myself spent so many years virtually within one, and having experienced the close veil of secrecy which was drawn round everything that went on, I can believe that such ignorance was very well possible.

Take my guards, for instance. Except for one or two, I can definitely state that most of them had no idea of what was happening around us, and that they firmly believed that all prisoners in so-called protective custody, i.e. all the regular inmates of the camp, were well treated. These men, before they were detailed for duty in my cell, had performed guard duties around the camp in the course of which they were allowed no contact with prisoners; their duties did not take them into the camp itself, and many of them had never set foot inside its walls until they first came to the Bunker, to reach which they had to walk along one side of the main camp square. Whilst they were on duty in the Bunker they were never allowed to stray from this path, and their observation of camp events was confined to what they chanced to see during this walk. In the Bunker itself the names of prisoners were kept secret and reference to them was made by the number of their cells and, when particularly important or secret prisoners left their cells for any purpose, my guards and the trusties were shut into their sleeping quarters so that they should not see them. Going to and from the dentist, a visit which I managed to arrange some dozen times a year, I followed the same road taken by my guards on entering and leaving the Bunker and my observations agree with theirs. In the Bunker the maintenance of secrecy threw a great strain on the warders, and often they were careless, so that we in time generally heard all interesting news regarding other prisoners.

It will probably be argued that the fact that my guards did not tell me of the more horrible events which took place in the camp is no proof of their ignorance, but against this I can say that on a few occasions they did witness acts of cruelty, and I have no doubt whatever that their expressions of horror and disgust when telling me about such incidents were absolutely genuine. They were under no compulsion to tell me anything, and if they did it was only because they were so deeply shocked that they could not keep silence. Anyhow, this is what I learnt during my five and a quarter years at Sachsenhausen.

The camp at Sachsenhausen was opened towards the end of 1936, taking the place of a smaller one at Oranienburg, with which it has often been confused, as the village of Sachsenhausen lies only about three miles farther north. Neither money nor pains had been spared in its construction and it was intended to be everything that a concentration camp should be, if it is accepted that there should be such places at all; it was, indeed, a monument worthy of the genius of Heinrich Himmler. The original staff of Waffen-SS warders was mainly drawn from the much older camp at Dachau and both Eccarius and Ettlinger came to the opening of the camp bringing with them a selected nucleus of political prisoners. Until the outbreak of war, except for a short period in 1938 when a number of men belonging to the Algemeine-SS came to the camp to replace regulars who had been sent to the Czechoslovak border, when that country was subjected to peaceful penetration, the whole staff and all the guards at the camp were regular enlisted men of the Waffen-SS. When I reached the camp in December 1939 most of the regulars had been withdrawn for active war service, and their place taken by men between forty-five and fifty who had served in the First World War and younger men of low medical categories.

The commandant, from the time of the first establishment of the camp until the autumn of 1939 was a certain Oberführer Baranowski. According to all that I heard of him, he must have been a pathological sadist of the most beastly description, and it would be impossible to put into print some of the things which I was told about his cruelty to the prisoners under his charge. His son had been killed in some street fight between Nazis and Communists, and from this was said to arise his intense hatred of all such opponents of the party as had the mischance to come under the lash of his power in the camp. His hatred found its practical expression in devising means to render the lives of the prisoners entrusted to his care as intolerable as possible; acts of cruelty on the part of warders and guards were rewarded, any leniency shown by them severely punished. Towards the end of his term he became dangerously insane, and died shortly after his removal to an asylum from some kidney complaint. In November 1939, Oberführer Lohritz was appointed his successor as commandant.

Lohritz must have served in the First World War, for he frequently told me that he had been a prisoner of the French and had been very badly treated. According to one of my guards who had known him previously, he had served his apprenticeship as a butcher, but in 1920 had joined the police at Nüremberg. During the early stages of the Nazi movement, like many other members of the Bavarian police, he had been a sympathizer, and had given practical expression to his sentiments by turning a blind eye to Nazi acts of aggression, and by intervening on their behalf when their adversaries retaliated. His association with the Nazis was so blatant that he became the victim of a purge intended to encourage a certain degree of impartiality among the members of the Nüremberg police. He had already succeeded in getting in Himmler's good books, and having joined the SA and shown himself a doughty fighter in the war against the disturbers of Nazi tranquillity, he had been given such swift promotion that, by 1939, he had reached the rank of Oberführer (brigadier).

I never liked Lohritz, but to give the devil his due, I don't think that he was in any way a cruel man, or at all likely to initiate anything in the nature of a reign of terror in the camp. His sins were more those of omission than of commission; when he first reached the camp it was run on lines laid down by Baranowski, and Lohritz just took it that this was how it should be, and left it at that. As a matter of fact, he just hadn't time to bother about prisoners, for his appointment was a God-given opportunity for graft on the largest possible scale, and he devoted all his attention to getting while the going was good. He stole the coal and provisions provided for the prisoners and sold them on the black market; he sold the personal effects of the living and the gold crowns from the mouths of the dead. Within a few months of his appointment he had managed to acquire an estate in Upper Austria, and with materials stolen from the camp, and by prison labour, had built himself a country house and laid out a park. His furniture was made for him at the camp, and so was his yacht, in which he hoped to take his pleasures on the beautiful Mond See.

A human weakness of his was love of animals, and so he started a small menagerie at the camp where, for his bears alone, he was reluctantly compelled to dock the human prisoners of one and a half hundredweight of their sugar ration weekly. It was his ambition, too, to induce storks and herons to make their home in the camp, and a fatigue, popular with both prisoners and guards alike, was catching frogs to feed a mother stork who had shown the bad taste to start her nursery there. He did not do anything to promote cruelty, but he did nothing to prevent it, and left all power over the prisoners in the hands of the regular Waffen-SS officials and they, like him, were all eagerly engaged in making hay while the sun shone. The prisoners were underfed, overworked, and bullied by both warders and room bosses.

These room bosses were one of the worst features of existence in a concentration camp. Prisoners were of all classes, the vast majority being ordinary decent people who normally would never have seen the inside of a prison. A small minority was made up of the worst dregs of German prisons, habitual criminals, murderers and sexual perverts, whose death sentences had been reprieved under the lax criminal legislation of pre-Hitler days; these were the old lags, men experienced in all the tricks by which prison can be made a home from home. It is of course not surprising that these men managed to ingratiate themselves with the warders, and also, by strong-arm methods, succeeded in getting themselves appointed as freely elected room bosses in their respective hutments. According to official regulations, the warders, or block leaders, as they were called, were not themselves permitted to take any violent action for the maintenance of discipline but must leave such matters to the room boss who was to be held responsible for the men under him; if the methods adopted were rough, the attitude of the SS men was: "What else can you expect from prisoners, after all, the creatures are scarcely human."

It should never be forgotten that the worst cruelties were inflicted by Germans on Germans; later, when most of the prisoners were foreigners they were far better treated, at all events in the camps in Germany. It is true that thousands were murdered, but even death in a gas chamber was kindness compared to the slow extinction through brutality and starvation, which was the fate of tens of thousands of Germans whose only offence was that they were not Nazis. During this first, it might be called German phase, the death rate in the camp from these causes must have been simply appalling; all my informants agreed that the prisoners died like flies and that the crematorium never ceased smoking. At the beginning of 1940 though, there was a marked change, for the question of manpower having come under closer review, it was decided that the policy hitherto adopted at concentration camps was wasteful of a valuable asset; in June of that year new directives were issued, and orders given, that prisoners were to be so treated and fed that their capacity to work remained unimpaired. All the prisoners with whom I had opportunity to talk agreed in saying that from this time life in the camp became tolerable, and that the food showed great improvement both in quantity and quality.

Even so, the camp must still have remained a most horrible place, and even on my brief passages to and from the dentist (after the first couple of visits I was allowed to walk instead of being taken by ambulance) I saw heart-rending sights. Miserable fragments of humanity, mere skin, rags and bone, rendered ludicrous by their shaven pates and blue grey-striped pyjama-like garb. Many were covered with the sores, or had the steeply bulging stomachs of the starving. They wore clumsy wooden-soled mules and always had to move at the double.

As I walked along the main camp square I saw the punishment squad marching or running in the closest possible formation; generally, some fifty or sixty men. In the winter they were surrounded by a cloud of steam from their heated bodies, and if one passed close by them the stench made one sick. I was told that they had to march twenty-five miles a day, carrying packs weighing from twenty to forty pounds on their backs. This was a recognized and clement punishment. Far worse was the lot of the group of men standing to attention or squatting on their heels with outstretched arms, who had to remain in these positions for twelve hours at a stretch, or the men whose punishment consisted in lying full length on the ground and rolling, ten yards one way and ten yards back; if a man stopped, he was kicked and trampled on by the prisoner supervising the operation; the men vomited, they fainted, but throughout the day the order was, roll. Men who had experienced this punishment told me that it was the worst torture imaginable and far worse than any flogging.

Several times I saw, lying near the main entrance of the camp, the blood-stained body of some unfortunate prisoner who had attempted escape, left to lie there for two days as a warning to the others. In the spring there were always many such, for then some strange madness attacked the camp and not a night passed without the sound of shots, often followed by shrieks of agony; men would often just stand in the middle of the so-called neutral zone and wait quietly as a target for the machine-guns on the watch towers. Yes, life in the camp must have been very horrible.

In comparison my cell was a sheltered haven of peace, and the small inconveniences and annoyances which I suffered became mere futile absurdities at which I could laugh. It is, I think, a salutary lesson to live cheek by jowl with the hard verities of utter misery, and no man can have such an experience without realizing how little divides him from such a fate, and how hollow are the pretences on which all ideas of superior social station are based. It is perhaps a salutary lesson to live for a time under the terror of a police state, and many people who believe that such things as made life dreadful in Nazi Germany, could never happen here, would learn to know better. There are vicious and ruthless criminals in every land, and enrolled in the police force they are willing tools by means of which a dictator can strike terror in the hearts of all who seek to oppose him. We talk about war criminals, but forget that these criminals committed some of their worst crimes at the behest of Hitler and his gang, long before we in England would believe that war with Germany was inevitable, or indeed, even probable. I have met these men of the so-called Security Service, known them in the days when they were at the height of their power, so perhaps my impressions of them are clearer than those of the courts which tried them and saw them only as humble, broken, prisoners.

The vast majority of Germans under Hitler were, as they have always been, as harmless as a flock of sheep; good-natured, sentimental, hard-working. Unfortunately, unlike sheep they can be trained to kill and destroy, and with their sheep-like instinct blindly to follow their leader, they can become very dangerous. For six years before the war the mass of Germans had been deprived of all news from abroad, and even about their own country heard only what suited the Nazi policy. When war started they were told of an unprovoked attack by France and England, and the cry that the Fatherland was in danger brought all men to the colours. Yet there was never any general outburst of war-like spirit, and I can imagine that hardly ever has a country entered into a long and disastrous war with so little enthusiasm. A dictator armed with the modern weapon of his secret police can descend on any country, almost out of the blue, and in these days only continual watchfulness on the part, not only of the government, but of every single man and woman in the country, can ensure safety from this evil. The German propagandists called allied air attacks 'terror raids', but they terrified only for as long as they were in progress. The Gestapo terror was always there, it encompassed every minute of people's lives, whether waking or sleeping, and never let up for a moment. At the root of it was the informer.

Two friends got talking, both anti-Nazis and one would make some remark criticizing the regime. After they separated the other would start thinking: 'Of course I know Müller quite well and I feel quite sure that he is safe. Still, I wish he had not said that about Goering. After all, what do I really know about the man. Just look at the case of the Schulzes, denounced by their own daughter. Müller did not seem quite the same as usual today, seemed a bit strange in his manner. Supposing that the Gestapo have got something against him and have set him to spy on his friends. This is happening all the time. If he tells them what he said to me, and I do nothing, they may come and fetch me tonight— I like Müller, we have always been good friends—but—no, I daren't risk it'. Off he goes to the nearest police station and faithfully reports what Müller said to him. Müller goes to Dachau, Sachsenhausen, or Buchenwald, and the next thing that happens is that the screw is put on our friend and almost before he knows where he is, he has been roped in to spy on and denounce his friends.

Deprive people of news, destroy the liberty of thought and discussion, and the population of any country is indeed as helpless as a flock of sheep attacked by wolves.

CHAPTER V

ALTHOUGH it had seemed that winter would never end, by the beginning of April the walls of snow which had confined my walks had dwindled away to a few dingy mounds under the shade of the north wall, and there were days when the sun was really warm and it was a pleasure to sit on the bench in the sheltered angle of the two wings of the prison. The 2nd April was such a day, and as I halted my march near the bench I saw what looked like writing scratched in the sand before it. Yes, it was:

P.B.
Have you heard anything from home
I nothing
R.S.

Of course I already knew that Stevens was in the Bunker, for Paul Becker had told me very soon after I arrived that both he and Jan Lemmens were there. Then, on New Year's Day, when the warder called me in the morning to go to the lavatory, I walked in to find Jan standing by the fountain wiping his head and face. Of course he was at once shooed out by my guard, but we were able to grin at each other and I was glad to see that he looked fit, fat and cheerful. Poor chap, until he was released in the autumn of 1940 he never once left his cell except to visit the lavatory, he had nothing to read, was not allowed to write letters, and like me, had no news from home. When we met after the war and I asked him how he had managed to kill time and what he did with himself all day, his answer was "Holding up my trousers"—he had been deprived of his braces.

Later I was so foolish as to indicate to one of my Gestapo visitors that I knew of their presence and had been given a forcible and categoric denial. Unfortunately, suspicion was aroused that one of my guards had been talking, and all four of them were had on the mat and told that any indiscretion on their part would be most severely punished; the result was that all my information from this source dried up for a long time. I was therefore greatly excited to have this direct communication from Stevens and hoped that it might be possible to continue in correspondence with him. For the time being I contented myself with scuffling out what he had written and scratching my own reply:

No. P.B.

That evening while lying on my bed and keeping an eye on my guard to see that he was not looking, I wrote a few words to him on a scrap of paper which I rolled and charred to look like a cigarette stub. Next day I threw this on the ground near the bench, arranging two matches on the ground so that they pointed towards it; I hoped that Stevens would follow this clue. The following day my letter had gone and a series of matches directed my eyes to a scrap of paper stuck into a crack in the bench. Poor Stevens seemed to be making heavy weather in his anxiety about his wife, mainly because she had a very low opinion of the Germans and would certainly imagine that he was being put to all manner of torture. Myself, I had never worried about such things, as I felt confident that May would in her heart trust me to get out of any trouble into which I had got myself; in any case, she knew Germany well and would therefore be less inclined to place credence in all the stories of atrocities which were current. I hoped, too, that she would follow my principle of not worrying about things which she could not influence.

Stevens told me that he was in cell No. 44 in Wing B, and that he had caught a glimpse of me once as I was going into the interrogation room; the conditions of his imprisonment were the same as mine; a guard in his cell day and night and the chaining to the wall at night. In the days that followed we exchanged several notes in this way, and I was really deeply concerned as it became clear to me how intensely Stevens suffered, mainly because he had a sense of grievance and considered that, according to the rules of war, he was entitled to different treatment. This was, of course, as may be. When we were captured we had both, I think, rather anticipated being shot at dawn on one of the next days and would have been surprised if by argument about the Geneva Convention we had succeeded in averting this danger. Well, we hadn't been shot nor, on the whole, had we been very badly treated, so I felt that we should be thankful for small mercies and make the best of the situation.

Of course, I didn't enjoy imprisonment, but I did not feel that it would become any more enjoyable if, as Stevens wished, we were transferred to a prisoner-of-war camp, or even brought together and allowed to share a cell. I have never liked crowds and therefore felt reluctant to exchange that measure of privacy which I now enjoyed for life in a camp, even if, strictly speaking, the Germans had no right to place me in solitary confinement. It was most unlikely that the Gestapo would make any alteration in their plans, however much we might protest, and I therefore preferred to devote my energies to making the best of the position in which I found myself, and to finding practicable methods of rendering it more tolerable.

At the beginning of May our contact was roughly broken for a time, as a chill from which I was suffering took a wrong turning and I went down with an attack of pneumonia which, according to the doctor, almost relieved me of all my troubles. I didn't know much about it as I was off my head and only semi-conscious for about eight days. When the crisis passed and my interest in mundane affairs was reawakened I found that two of my old guards, Schnaars and Schwartz, had left, and had been replaced by two new men, Ebert and Prochnow. With them my life took a distinct turn for the better; they did not seem to have been so carefully briefed as the first men and from the start they were friendly and quite ready for conversation. Of course I could not ask them questions about the outside world and the progress of the war, but anyhow it was a great relief to be with people who did not seem scared out of their wits if we exchanged a few harmless remarks.

Very possibly, my illness had rather frightened my captors for, as I learnt later, there would have been very serious trouble for them had I died, as this would have been in disobedience to the orders of the All Highest, that I was to be kept safe and in good health. Anyhow, there was a marked improvement in the attitude of the warders towards me, and whenever I asked for a book or anything else that I needed, I got it at once. Only cigarettes were again in short supply, for the wretched doctor had cut me down to two a day. It was at this time that I started collecting fag-ends. I had previously kept my own and with them rolled cigarettes; now I started my guards collecting theirs for me; later on the time was to come when I picked up any old cigarette end that I could find without worrying about who might have cast it aside. Towards the end of the war, when the ration was six cigarettes for ten days, fag-ends, 'Kippen' as the Germans called them, became marketable articles, three good ones fetching a mark.

Ebert, one of the new men, was a nice, clean little Pomeranian bootmaker. He was a Nazi, and had been one of the first men in his village to join the party, but he was by no means a fanatic, and as time went on he lost faith in everything and believed nothing except that it was the fate of the common people to be lied to by all those whom they had trusted. We never became friends in the sense that I could take him into my confidence, but he always behaved correctly and in his way, was kind and considerate.

Prochnow, the other new man, was a very different proposition, and we got on well with each other from the moment that he started duty. He was a tall, very thin, saturnine looking fellow, who had neither principles nor beliefs but lived only for drink; when drunk, his normal state, one could not want a pleasanter or more amusing companion; sober, he was the picture of sullen misery. His thirst was enormous and his weekly pay did not cover his needs for even one day; the ingenuity which he displayed in obtaining the means to satisfy it for the rest of the time, afforded me amusement and delight throughout the time that he was with me.

A few days after he came to me he struck a very bad patch, and was without drink as I was without tobacco; then I had a happy thought. I still had my signet ring which the Germans, believing it to be a wedding ring, had not taken from me with my other belongings. I suggested a deal to Prochnow. If I gave him this ring he could sell it and satisfy his thirst, but I would only do this if he agreed to supply me with smokes equivalent to its value. No sooner said than done, and next day he came in very drunk and very happy, and told me that the ring had made eighty marks and "das geld ist alle", the money has gone; he had spent the evening at a café in Oranienburg, and when he got home his pockets were empty, but, he said, "I did not forget you," and with that he threw two packets of tobacco on to my bed. You would think that I had made a bad bargain but Prochnow, if poor, was honest, and whilst he was with me never let me want for something to smoke, and this is saying a lot, for everything he brought me was paid for in his life's blood—alcohol. What a time I had with him and what narrow squeaks we had. No matter how drunk he was, as long as he could sit and keep awake, he seemed sober as a judge; he was one of those men who get drunk from the waist downward.

The greatest difficulties occurred in the evenings when he had to go with me to the lavatory. Luckily, the warders had given up going with me and now contented themselves with telling us when the lavatory was free, and leaving me to go there under the sole charge of my guard. I would hoist Prochnow out of his chair and once we got moving, he could carry along pretty well for the short distance we had to go, but when we got to the lavatory it was the devil's own job to know what to do with him. He couldn't stand unaided and there was nowhere for him to sit except on one of the w.c.s. But these were of the upended drain-pipe pattern and Prochnow was so thin and so limp that I feared he might double up like a jack-knife and disappear. I tried propping him up against the wall, but twice his feet slipped away and when I looked round he was on the floor dreaming blissfully. Getting him on his feet again without making a noise was no joke especially as, when wakened, he was inclined to be fractious. Luckily he sobered up quickly and if he could have about an hour's nap when he came on duty he would be all right for the rest of the time. While he slept I had to keep watch, and if I heard anyone coming I would give a yank at a string tied to one of his fingers. He was very valuable to me, both as a source of tobacco and also because he kept me informed about what was going on in the world, so I was always in a panic lest he should be caught out and taken from me.

After I recovered from my illness Stevens and I soon picked up the threads of our correspondence again. We had, though, only exchanged one or two letters when Prochnow told me that one of Stevens's guards, a man named Lenkeit, had given him away and that our letters were being intercepted and, after being photographed, replaced. As a matter of fact I should have spotted this in any case, for on one of Steven's letters someone had written fifty-one, the number of my cell, and then crossed it out and put forty-four, Stevens's number. I tried to give Stevens the tip that this was happening, but I could never get it to register with him. From that time my letters were written more for the eyes of the Gestapo than for Stevens, though occasionally, when I wanted to tell him something important, I would give my letter to Prochnow to plant in the garden, which he could easily do unobserved. It was of course absurd to hope that two prison amateurs such as we could succeed in carrying on an illicit correspondence without being spotted. All prisoners try to do this and the warders know all possible ways in which it can be done.

It was nearly the end of May before I heard anything about the German offensive in the west; on the 23rd Becker, who had been away on leave, smuggled in a paper, and I read of the occupation of Denmark, Norway and Holland, and of a break through Belgium and France to the Channel. A few days before I had heard the Wilhelmus, the Dutch National Anthem, played on the radio, and this had filled me with forebodings, but what I now heard from Becker gave me a terrible shock. A few days later, Grothe turned up, bringing with him a Red Cross Inquiry from May, just twenty-five words, which told me that she was well and staying with a cousin of mine in England. It was the best tonic that I have ever had, and even when Grothe gave me more news of the war and told me that the French were in full retreat and the British Army encircled, I could not feel depressed; I just felt that everything must come right in the end.

On the 22nd June I was called to the interrogation room where I found Schellenberg and Oberführer Lohritz, the former in the uniform of a Sturmbanführer in the Leibstandarte Adolf Hitler, and wearing the First Class Iron Cross, which he had been awarded for his bravery in capturing Stevens and me. Schellenberg put on his most impressive air and pushing a newspaper before me asked me to read what I saw; France had asked for an armistice; millions of prisoners; the British Army routed.

"You would not believe that we should win the war. Now you see, *the war has been won!* What do you think that England can do alone? We are going to destroy England, very soon there will not be a house standing in London—I hope that your wife has the sense to leave before it is too late."

"What do you mean?" I said. "Are you going to bomb London? I thought that the Führer was against bombing civilian targets."

"Oh, but England started it and has killed hundreds of innocent people in Germany—now, we are going to teach your country a lesson and when we are finished with her, 'England wird total vernichtet sein'." (England will be completely destroyed.) He then went on to ask me, obviously with certain concern, whether I still thought that England would refuse to give in and might try to carry on the fight from Canada and other parts of the Commonwealth, and I assured him that he could make up his mind to this, that the British would never accept defeat but would fight on to the last man.

Schellenberg had a large bundle of newspapers with him and at first it seemed as though he intended giving them to me, but he changed his mind and said that he would let me have them in a few days' time; I heard later that Stevens had them first. He then said that arrangements had been made for me to have a paper, the *Völkische Beobachter*, daily in future, "So that you can see how Germany marches from one victory to another".

In the days that followed, after the exhilaration caused by the news from May had lulled, I passed through some very bad hours, and in my heart I really feared that Germany had proved too strong for us. On the 2nd July Grothe came again and gave me copies of the *Völkische Beobachter* from the 10th May to 30th June, and also three more Red Cross Inquiries from May. How often good news and bad news come together!

The next two days I spent in reading through all the papers which Grothe had given me and, at the end, I felt far less hopeless and depressed. The reports of the German victories were too exaggerated; they seemed to me to display the old familiar inferiority complex and doubt of ultimate success; there was something naïve, almost childish in their tone; joy at an unexpected and undeserved gift from heaven. No, to me, the argument that because the German Wehrmacht had overrun Norway, Denmark, Holland, Belgium, and France, they would also have a walkover in England simply failed to convince, and I can truthfully say, that from that time I never doubted that Germany would ultimately be defeated. The news was to be very black for a long time yet, but the gross exaggeration in all the German reports which never admitted losses or setbacks of any kind, always gave me comfort.

The weather became fine and warm, and often I would take my clothes off in the garden and have a sun-bath. Restrictions on my freedom had gradually become much less noticeable; of course I was a prisoner and the chain at my wrist at night was a daily reminder, but as long as I did not allow myself to want to do anything forbidden, I could feel that I was free. I read, played patience and talked to my guards; in the garden I no longer marched round and round, but amused myself watching ants and other insects, or just lying in the sun dreaming. What a curious thing was this loss of liberty which had befallen me; what did it really imply? In some respects I felt freer than ever before, for I had neither responsibilities nor duties; nor had I any real interest in life. The material and physical discomforts I discovered, mattered nothing; they might arouse temporary irritation but they made so little impression on my mind that most of the time I simply did not notice that they were there. What did matter was the intense sense of frustration, the feeling of uselessness, and something akin to shame that I should have allowed myself to be captured. It would have been so much better to have died fighting at the frontier.

Then, there was anxiety, generally subconscious, but nevertheless gnawing at my nerves and showing itself physically by an uncontrollable tremor of my hands. Where was May? Was she well and did she know that I was all right? Then, the war. I had the feeling that I had learnt many interesting facts which might be useful if I could only make them known. I wanted an outlet for my energy, I wanted to play my little part in the war, but here there was nothing to do but to kill time, surely the most wasteful, most futile occupation there is. I really believe that ill-treatment, giving me something to fight against, would have been easier to bear than this life of a prize pup; well housed, well fed, taken out on the lead for exercise, and finally, chained up to sleep. At this early stage of my imprisonment I was allowed to do nothing for myself; the warder saw me one evening making my bed according to my own ideas: "You mustn't do that. If you will tell me what you want done I will get the trusty to do it while you are in the lavatory. We don't want you to say when you get home that we made you do work of that sort." My job was just to keep alive in case the Gestapo or anyone else wanted me for anything; I was in cold storage.

For a time I threw myself into the game of the exchange of letters with Stevens and into devising new methods for their concealment. While I was ill a series of sheds, extending the whole length of the centre path on the prison side, had been erected. These housed large quantities of timber of all sorts ranging from deal to mahogany, as I later learnt, a private store which the commandant had abstracted from the camp supplies. At each of the German concentration camps there was an organization called the 'Deutsche Ausrüstungs Werke' (German Equipment Works) where all manner of trades were carried on by prison labour; one of these was carpentry and the manufacture of furniture for government offices. Actually, there was practically nothing that you could not get made or mended, whether it was a suit of clothes or a watch, a yacht or a roll-top desk, and at Sachsenhausen most of the work was for the commandant.

Well, these sheds were covered with freshly tarred roofing which, in the heat of the sun melted and formed a sort of black icicle. These, Stevens and I collected. Our letters we made into small rolls, and after wrapping them in silver paper from our cigarette packets, we gave them a thick coating of this tar. When they had been rolled in the dust they looked just like any other of the bits of slag which lay on the cinder-covered paths of our exercise ground. We just threw them down in a prearranged spot when, knowing what to look for, we could spot them quite easily. Unfortunately, this dodge was given away by the same guard, Lenkeit, who noticed Stevens preparing one. To arrange the spot where our letters should be left, Stevens occasionally sang in the lavatory, putting in a few words, such as: "On the left, near the bench," which I could hear quite clearly from my cell next door. It is interesting to read these old letters now, for I was able to keep those which I had from Stevens and bring them back with me to England—how far away it all seems now.

On the 11th July we had our first air raid warning and from my bed I heard the flak bursting, as it seemed, directly overhead. Next day there were very long faces in the Bunker and it was clear to me that Berlin had received its first quota of bombs. It had been a funny but exhilarating experience to feel that my own countrymen had come so close. There was nothing more until the 25th August, but from then on till the middle of November Berlin was raided on almost every fine night, culminating with two big raids on the 14th when the alert lasted from 8.45 p.m. till 6 a.m. next day. Meanwhile, the Battle of Britain had started and had been won, though all that I knew about it came from the daily 'Sondermeldungen' (special announcements) on the radio, heralded by blaring fanfares of trumpets and ending with the playing of the England Song which told of hundreds of British planes shot down without German losses; the paper, too, was full of sensational reports about the complete destruction of the R.A.F., and the ruin and desolation caused by German bombs. There was such obvious exaggeration, that I was, as I now know, inclined to discount the reality of this threat to British air supremacy. You see, my experiences of air warfare dated back to the First World War when the superiority of British pilots was never really called in question— the Germans said that they were having a walkover, and knowing that this could not be true, I disbelieved everything they said.

On the 19th September two men from the Gestapo handed me a large file of typewritten papers which they told me to read, saying at the same time that they would soon be able to take me home to my wife in England, unless, of course, I would prefer to have her join me in Germany—"when you see what we have done to London, you won't want to go there—it has been almost completely destroyed—let's hope that your wife got away in time". They told me to read the papers in the file and to give them back to the warder in the morning. They were the proclamations which the Germans were going to issue in occupied England. There were about fifty of them, I should say, and they dealt with every phase of the military administration of a conquered and occupied country, where every breach of the regulations was an offence punished with death. All fire-arms and wireless equipment must be surrendered within twenty-four hours. All railways, canals, and ports to be taken over, and all stocks of timber, coal, and oil to be requisitioned. There was a regulation for the registration of all men below the age of fifty, and another fixing the value of the pound at 9.60 marks. It is hopeless for me to try and remember them all, but one thing struck me about their wording; they obviously did not envisage a complete occupation of the whole of Great Britain, but only of the southern half. This was obvious, for there were frequent references to 'occupied' and 'unoccupied' territories, with regulations for civilian travel from one to the other, and also to a British Government, apparently that in the unoccupied zone. The German plan seemed to be based on the armistice arrangements which had been effected in France.

Now, why on earth was this shown to me? My own conclusion was that the whole thing was a washout, the idea of an invasion of England had been given up, and the Gestapo was just having its bit of fun with me. As a matter of fact, my guards had talked to me quite a lot about the possibility of an invasion of England, and they had certainly not seemed optimistic—no one could understand why the invasion had not been carried out immediately after the fall of France. The British Army had been annihilated, British warships were sunk by Stukas as soon as they left harbour, and the R.A.F. had ceased to exist—what was the Wehrmacht waiting for?

A new guard had come to me early in August, Paul König, who, throughout the rest of my stay at Sachsenhausen was to be my most loyal and self-sacrificing friend. That I am here today, that I learnt how to make my life in prison tolerable, that I was able to avoid all the pitfalls which bestrewed my path, everything I owe to the loyalty and wise counsel of my dear friend Paul. He was a short man and so fat as to be almost square; his gait was that of a duck, but of a very brisk determined duck. Although he was almost exactly the same age as I he had thick, fair, curly hair, which would have done credit to a boy of twenty; this was brushed to a cockatoo like crest which made him look rather like the caricatures of Mr. Herbert Morrison. He was the typical Berliner, just as Sam Weller was the typical Cockney of his day— he knew his way through life—as he always said himself, if you fall, fall on your feet, not on your head. He belonged to the lower middle-class, he was what he himself called, 'der kleine Mann' (the little man) and his philosophy could be summed up in the belief that the little man was between the upper and the nether millstone, and his life a constant struggle against being crushed out of existence. He had no use for Nazis, Communists, or indeed, for any political party. All promise the little man everything he desires and, as soon as they have power, try to take away from him what little he has.

He was not a man who could fight for his own selfish interests, nor had he the self-assurance to stand alone. Like a dog, he must attach himself to someone, and to that person he showed all a dog's fidelity and in him placed all his trust. Almost from the first day that he entered my cell, before that he had been for a week or two with Stevens, he adopted me as his master, and from then on my interests were his and to further them, this naturally rather timorous little man, was ready to face the greatest dangers. He was so convinced his duty in life was to serve me and that this was an honour, that in the end he managed to convince nearly everyone that I was an exceptional and extremely important person. Speaking to me he always called me Monsieur, this being in his opinion the respectful way of addressing a distinguished foreigner; when speaking to others, I was 'der Chef', the Chief, and the time came when even Eccarius, the head warder, always spoke of me by this term.

After his first turn of night duty he said to me: "But this is no good at all, no one can sleep with all that light shining on him; you should have a good shade over the lamp."

"That's all very well," I said, "but where is the shade coming from?"

"Very simple, just make one. I will bring you some cardboard and blackout paper and you can make a shade."

Well, so I did, and it was such a good shade that I was kept busy making more for others. It was a tube of cardboard covered with black paper which fitted over the globe of the lamp, and at the bottom it was so cut as to throw a beam of light by which the guard could see to read whilst leaving my bed in darkness. I used porridge as paste and made a reflector of tin foil.

The next thing with which Paul found fault was my bed; it appeared that the straw mattress, which I in my ignorance had accepted as a normal trial of prison life, was very far from being what it should be. The straw in it was so old that it had turned to chaff, and certainly, it was one of the hardest and most lumpy things I had ever lain on; it felt in fact very much like a cobbled road. Paul had a private talk with the head trusty and, when I came back from exercise, there was a brand new mattress absolutely bursting with fresh-smelling long-stalked rye straw. Then, as I complained of my pillow, this, too, was taken in hand. My ears tend towards the bats-wing model and offer great resistance to attempts to flatten them against my head; I had really suffered agonies at night from my debris-filled pillow and I would have even preferred one of Japanese pattern which would have left my ears free to flap without restriction. Paul produced a pair of scissors and said: "Let's see what's in the animal." I protested that this might cause trouble if the warder saw that I was operating on the pillow, but Paul gave his usual answer: "The soup is never eaten as hot as it is cooked. If you wait until they allow you to do anything you want to in this hole of a place you will have to wait until a beard grows on your backside. You just do what you want, and if the warder makes a row, well you weren't born dumb either, were you?"

The pillow was unstitched and out of it came two bundled up and very dirty sacks, and a small quantity of evil-smelling powder which Paul said had once been straw. He called for the trusty and got him to bring a bundle of straw and two new blankets. The straw was bunched up criss-cross so that it was nice and springy, and around it we wrapped the two blankets and sewed them into place; with a piece of new ticking which the trusty produced I had a soft and most comfortable pillow which served me throughout the next five years.

So it was with other things. My clothes were showing signs of wear and so far I had been unable to get needle and thread to mend them, but Paul said: "The wife can help there," and after his next day at home in Berlin he brought me needles and various kinds of sewing cotton and thread, and soon I was happily engaged on 'Make and mend'. I am by nature fairly ingenious and there are few things to which I cannot turn my hands; so far though I had rather accepted my impotence as a prisoner as an unavoidable circumstance of my condition, but with the encouragement given me by Paul and later by other guards, I became a revolutionary, or perhaps, better said, an old lag. Prison life is a constant clash of wits between warders and prisoners. The warders have power and they know all the answers, but they are few and the prisoners are many; besides, the prisoners know what they want and are prepared to try, try, and try again; their desires are positive and therefore far more potent than the mere negative attempts of the warders to keep them doing nothing. Warders are human and want to make their work as easy as possible, so that as long as prisoners don't flout regulations in any blatant fashion, they are but little inclined to interfere.

Our warders knew perfectly well that almost all the prisoners were doing things which were not allowed; smoking in their cells, tapping out messages on the radiator pipes, talking to each other through the windows, and exchanging notes. They must also have known that the trusties were on the side of the prisoners and helped them where they could. But, what could they do? Their duty was to make a report to the commandant if they discovered any of these delicts, but they also knew that to make many reports would certainly lay them open to the charge that they were inefficient and incapable of maintaining discipline. They themselves had no authority to punish and even if Ettlinger would beat up some unfortunate when he was in the mood, he did so, not in the interest of public order, but to satisfy his own inclination towards cruelty.

Under Paul's guidance and instruction I took every advantage of my position, until gradually the warders recognized that to interfere with me generally brought them only grief and sorrow, and that, too, where they least expected it. For Ettlinger I was no match, for he could get back at me by docking my smokes, and he also enjoyed the especial favour of the commandant, but he was only on duty one day out of three and Eccarius and Drexl I found easy to manage. In the end I got Ettlinger too, but that comes later in this story. My system was to appear most obedient and law abiding; if a warder told me that something I was doing was forbidden, I pleaded ignorance but said that I could not take orders from him and that he must report the matter to the commandant. If he did so and the commandant came to see me, my attitude was sweetly reasonable; I apologized for the trouble to which I had put him, but said that of course he would understand that I could not accept orders from an N.C.O. I was only too anxious to keep to regulations and he could be sure that if I had sinned, I had done so in ignorance.

When talking to the commandant I always tried to create the atmosphere of two brother officers talking together, which seemed to flatter him and put him off his stroke. He would be quite pleasant and say that he quite understood how difficult it was for me to understand German conditions, but that he was sure that I did not want to cause unnecessary trouble. Then I would gently insert my sting. "Excuse my asking commandant, but you see I have only had to do with the Wehrmacht and never before with the SS. In the army a soldier on duty is not properly dressed if he is not wearing his belt and cap, but I notice here that the warders often go about their duty in shirt sleeves; of course I agree that it is much more comfortable for them, but it does strike me as a bit unmilitary." Now, if there was one thing about which the SS was sensitive, it was any suggestion that their behaviour was less martial than that of the Wehrmacht. When I said something of this nature, and I could generally find some artless question of the kind, the commandant could not get out of my cell quickly enough, and as soon as the door was closed after him his wrath exploded and the warder on duty was cursed up hill and down dale.

After that the warders would be careful that I never saw them improperly dressed, and so in the evening I was free from the danger of sudden incursions into my privacy. One or two similar ripostes and the warders lost all inclination to report my doings to the commandant, and all that they did was to tell me that some action of mine was forbidden adding, if the commandant finds out, don't forget to tell him that I told you that it was not allowed. Of course all this was not achieved in one day, but by the end of 1940 a pretty well established non-aggression pact was tacitly observed by both sides. Much later there came a day when I turned to the attack and the warders learnt that it was they, not I, who must obey.

Yet, when all was said and done, my life during the first year of imprisonment was very drab and yet full of nervous strain. Just take a glance at my cell: it is five yards long by two and a half wide; at the end, six feet above the ground, is a large window outside which are five thick vertical iron bars; as you stand near the door you can see the tops of some pine trees about a hundred yards away. On your right with his back towards you sits my guard at a small table, about two feet by one; then comes my bed; hanging on the wall just above the guard's table are two small shelves on which are my few possessions such as soap, shaving brush, comb, etc. On your left, close to the door is the radiator, then against the side wall a similar table to that of the guard at which I am sitting on a kitchen chair either reading or playing patience. The walls and ceiling are whitewashed, but are rather dingy with a good few cobwebs in the corners. Scratched in the wall over the radiator and then whitewashed over are some obscene drawings apparently representing women of some Hottentot tribe; there is also what appears to have been a calendar with numbers scratched out. The wooden floor is a dirty grey. Only the bed looks bright and clean with its blue and white squared overlay, clean white sheet, and pillow-slip, but the cold north light makes everything look hard and inhospitable. I am wearing a well-worn grey herringbone suit, my trousers are pressed and my shirt, collar and tie are quite presentable; whatever the difficulties, I always take pains to keep myself looking as neat and well dressed as possible.

The status of a prisoner depends more than one would think on his dress; one could almost divide them into classes on this basis alone. At the top, the so-called 'Prominenten' which can best be translated as V.I.P.s (Very Important Prisoners), who wore their own clothes; next, the middle-classes, wearing their own clothes but deprived of braces, bootlaces, collars, and ties; unfortunates, whose girth prison fare had diminished, making them the slaves of slipping trousers; then came the trusties who wore clean and well-fitting prison uniform and often their own shirts and even collars; last of all the grey mass of the camp prisoners in their dirty shapeless grey-blue striped garb, their heavy clogs from which bits of sacking or straw stuck out, their shaven pates and jaunty little round caps. When I first became a prisoner I had no idea that such distinctions existed and I felt myself one with all the others, yet, as time passed, I must confess to my shame, that I came to regard the people in the camp outside as belonging to some lower order of humanity—not consciously, for I was intensely sorry for every one with whom I had any personal contact, but the prisoners in the mass became for me simply part of my normal environment.

At the time when Stevens and I were first brought to the Bunker, it housed only two V.I.P.s; Pastor Niemöller in cell No. 1, and Thaelmann in cell No. 76. Shortly after the occupation of Belgium and Holland, two new guests, said to be Belgian or Dutch bishops, joined us, and were given cells Nos. 62 and 63. The story was told that they had been sent to Sachsenhausen by Goering, to whom they had refused to give the Nazi salute, to be taught manners. They had comfortable cells which, from a glimpse I was able to take through an open door, were luxuriously furnished compared to mine; I saw a bookcase full of books and an easy chair. Their education in Nazi social etiquette was confined to their exercise time in the garden. Then, a stick was stuck in the ground half-way along the centre path, and on this was placed an SS uniform cap. The two men then took up positions on the path ten paces on either side of this saluting base, and at the word of command, started marching briskly towards each other; as they passed the cap they had to raise their right arms and cry "Heil Hitler", they continued their march for another ten paces, did a smart right-about-turn, and repeated the operation. This they did for two hours daily for more than a year and a half, and by the end of this time they had trampled two ruts, which were at least six inches deep, into the side of the path. From my cell I could hear their 'Heil Hitler's' and the warder's 'Louder!' always 'louder!' and once, when the warder had by mistake said that the garden was empty whilst they were still out there, I caught a glimpse of them when I went to the door to go out myself. A friendly prison doctor told me later that he had never seen two men whose physical condition had been so greatly improved by regular exercise.

Gradually the correspondence with Stevens ceased to amuse me, particularly since I knew that all our letters were going to the Gestapo, and I had continued it merely because it seemed to cheer him up a bit. Prochnow or König gave me almost daily news of him and their general description of his state was 'Verbissen' (looking grim). According to all accounts he would be quite well and cheerful for some days, and then suddenly he seemed to lose interest in life and would just lie on his bed all day refusing to eat or to speak to anyone; these moody attacks became quite a joke with the guards and were called his 'monthlies'. I did all that I could to cheer him up in my letters, but I had my own difficulties to counter, and in the long run began to find that his letters tended to depress me. It was really very sad for him that he could not achieve a more equable frame of mind, because his guards disliked his moodiness, and the nicest men among them all got themselves transferred to duty in my cell as soon as they could. During most of the time he had three of the most obnoxious men in the building as guards; men named Deckert, Schulz and Lenkeit, who were all real Nazis and reported everything he did or said to the warders. Of my own guards, Böning, Ebert and König had all started duty with him before coming to me, and if he had only managed to win their liking and allegiance, his life could have been so much pleasanter than it was.

Anyhow, towards the end of October 1940 I decided to stop our correspondence and in doing so, to have a little fun. When Ettlinger came into my cell one day I handed him one of my letters in its tarred cover and said: "Would you perhaps be so kind as to give this to my comrade?" He looked very blank and did not seem to know what to do or say. "You see," I went on, "you people make such mistakes that our correspondence is becoming completely disorganized. This is a letter which I wrote to Stevens three days ago and left in my usual hiding place, and this morning I found it in the place which Stevens uses for his letters. Now, I suppose, each of us has got his own letter back. I think it would make everything much simpler for the future if we just handed you our letters so that you could censor them and pass them on." This was too much for Ettlinger who found nothing to say but just went away taking my letter. I wrote and told Stevens what I had done, getting Prochnow to post the letter for me so that I could be sure that it would reach him. A few days later I heard that Stevens had been very poorly and that to cheer him up the Gestapo people had told him that I had had a letter from May, and that in it she had said that she had seen his wife and that she was very well. This was, of course, a lie, but since it might be a consolation for Stevens I did not contradict it.

Just before Xmas, when I went out for exercise, Head Warder Eccarius told me that I must keep to the middle path and not walk or sit anywhere else. Whilst I was out two of the Gestapo men came and began telling me off for corresponding with Stevens. In reply, I pointed out that from the first it had been obvious to me that my letters were being intercepted, but since nothing was said to me about it I supposed that they enjoyed reading them; in any case, as they must have heard from the head warder, I had myself put an end to the exchange of letters so that their reprimand came a little too late in the day. Then I turned to the attack and began complaining about the conditions of my imprisonment and the fact that I was treated like a condemned criminal, to which they counter-attacked by saying that I was being treated far too well, and that their people who had been caught in England were being beaten and tortured or kept in dark underground dungeons. Soon we were all three shouting at the tops of our voices and having a splendid time, but it all ended well and we finished by wishing each other a Merry Xmas and they handed me a hundred cigarettes with the compliments of the Brigadeführer; I did not at first grasp whom they meant, but it turned out to be Oberführer Müller who had been promoted to major general in the SS.

So 1940 came to an end and I was no longer a new boy. I had no illusions about the probable length of my imprisonment but had resigned myself to the idea that I was in for at least another four years. Could I make the grade and last out? Everything depended on my health and I determined to do everything that I could to recover some of the strength which I had lost during my illness. Things really weren't too bad and I felt pretty confident that, if they would only leave me where I was, I should soon find ways of improving the conditions of my life. Even at that time I realized that, if I ever regained my liberty, I might be tempted to dramatize my experiences and make out that my sufferings were greater than they were in truth, so at the end of each year I entered a little summary in my diary. That at the end of 1940 reads:

On the whole, time has passed quickly. My health on the whole has been fair, and except for constant worry about May, I have been free from depression. My nerves are in a pretty bad state. Treatment has in the main been considerate, though I consider the fact that I am chained to the wall at night a quite unnecessary indignity.

During December there had been a lot of noise of hammering in the building, and I had heard that alterations were being made to cells in the two other wings. On the 21st I heard that Stevens had been moved from cell No. 44 to the end of his passage where two cells, Nos. 38 and 39, had been knocked into one large cell. My guards were quite excited about this and told me that similar alterations had been made at the far end of the other wing, opposite that in which Stevens lived; this must surely be intended for me, and we were all overjoyed at the idea of a possible move to the front and sunny side of the building, and away from the damnable lavatory. But January came and I was still in my old cell No. 51, listening to the w.c.s next door flushing merrily away and inhaling my morning and evening dose of excremental effluvia. Then we heard that a new and very secret prisoner had been brought to the Bunker and occupied a very large cell, which had been made by knocking Nos. 11, 12 and 13 into one. Like me, he had guards with him day and night, but they slept in his cell and were forbidden to associate with Steven's guards and mine. It was all very well to make regulations such as these, but even if the guards were not allowed to fraternize while in the Bunker, there was nothing to prevent them doing so in the canteen and elsewhere outside, so not many days passed before we knew quite a lot about No. 13 as he was called.

The first news was that, as the guards put it, he was a 'Todes Kandidat', meaning a man condemned to death; next his identity was established; he was Georg Elser, the man who, according to press and radio, was guilty of the attempt to assassinate the Führer on the 8th November, 1939, by a bomb built into one of the pillars in the Bürgerbraukeller at Munich. What did this mean? Why had he not been executed? We were all greatly intrigued, particularly because, in the papers, my name had been coupled with his and the suggestion made that I had been his employer. If it were true that he had been condemned to death, what about me—was I in the same boat? Bit by bit information leaked out and my guards came to me with the story that I was to be tried for complicity in the attempt on Hitler's life, and that Elser would give evidence that he had acted on my instructions. Of course I had had nothing to do with the business at all, and all I knew about the story was limited to the short report which I had read in the Dutch paper on the morning of my capture. As for Elser, all that I knew about him was that I had seen in one of the German illustrated papers which a guard was reading, his photograph next to mine; this was at the time when I was not allowed to read, and I had only caught a glimpse of it as I passed the guard on my promenade up and down the cell.

In the course of time I was able to establish relations with Elser and although we never met or spoke to each other, a sort of friendship developed between us. From what he communicated to me himself, and from information which I picked up from a number of other sources, I was eventually able to piece together his very strange story which I will tell at the appropriate time.

From the beginning of 1941 there was a marked improvement in the general atmosphere (except for its smells) in the Bunker. I heard no further sounds of flogging or execution, and it was noticeable that the number of camp prisoners confined in dark cells was greatly reduced. From one after another of the windows facing my garden the boards were removed, and it was plain that the cells now housed an entirely different class of prisoner. My guards were never allowed to learn the names of prisoners who were always referred to by their cell numbers, but they told me that a lot of foreigners had been brought in, most of them as they thought, French. A lot of these new people were in cells on the opposite side of my wing; on my side of the passage, except for the two bishops, all the cells were occupied by SS men serving short sentences for military crimes.

It was, however, not only in the Bunker that conditions were improved but I was told that there had been a complete revolution in the treatment of the prisoners in the camp. Manpower had become a vital element in German war economy and someone had come to the conclusion that the abnormally high death-rate in the concentration camps constituted a waste of this valuable asset. Instructions were therefore given that measures should be taken to preserve, not only the lives of the prisoners, but also their physical capacity for work. New ration scales had been introduced and prisoners were allowed to receive food parcels from their relatives; this had previously been forbidden. Although much of the food was still purloined by the commandant and other camp officials, enough remained to enable the prisoners to keep body and soul together. The men too were employed on more important and consequently lighter work than the hard and often useless drudgery with pick and shovel which had been their main occupation. A large number, some 3,000 or so, were employed at a large brick field belonging to the camp, and others worked at the Heinckel aeroplane works and at other factories in the neighbourhood engaged on war work. More and more, as the war progressed, the concentration camps were regarded as important labour reservoirs, and prisoners as particularly suitable for employment on secret development work since their discretion could be assured. On my walks to and from the dentist it was very noticeable how much brisker and better fed the prisoners looked.

My days followed a fairly regular routine. I rose at 5 a.m. and went to the lavatory to wash, and when I got back to my cell it had been cleaned and aired. Then the warder brought me my razor, a mug of hot water and a mirror. After shaving, I dressed and lay down on my bed for a nap. Breakfast was brought in at about eight o'clock, six slices of bread with honey, jam, or butter— on Sundays, two doughnuts and a bowl of chocolate as well. I then either dozed on my bed, read, or played patience. At ten I went again to the lavatory—after quite a fight I had got this time established. From noon to one o'clock I went out for exercise and when I got back my dinner was waiting for me on the table; the food was always excellent, but I hated having everything brought to me ready cut up so that I could eat with a spoon, the only utensil which I was allowed. After dinner another snooze, and then read or played patience till my supper was brought at about five; this again consisted of five or six slices of bread with sausage, boiled bacon, or cheese. It was always most tastefully prepared for me by the chief trusty who, knowing that I had trouble with my teeth, cut up my bread for me in small squares. From then until ten o'clock I would generally chat with my guard or read. Then to the lavatory, undress, get into bed, and the warder came with my wristlet and I was chained up for the night. A lazy futile sort of life for most of which I was only half awake, but it must be remembered that I had to snatch my sleep when I could, and that at least once every two hours I was awakened by the change of guards.

On the 4th March there was a sudden burst of excitement. Two of my guards vanished and König and Böning had to do duty turn and turn about. In the evening I asked Paul what was up, and after some difficulty got it out of him: "Your comrade tried to commit suicide with a bootlace and now two guards must be with him day and night." I was, of course, very much upset at this news. When I later asked Stevens about this incident, he said that there was not a word of truth in it; he had been sitting reading and idly playing with a bootlace which he had put over the back of his neck; he had said something to the guard, the man named Schulz, that one could easily strangle oneself with a bootlace, who had reported to the head warder making out that there had been an attempt at suicide which had only been frustrated through his watchfulness. The result was unpleasant for poor Stevens, but it was equally so for me as they took my glasses away in case I broke them and cut my throat, and it was two days before I was allowed to have them back. Then, first Hofmann and Ebert left me, and subsequently Prochnow and Paul König. In their place I was sent two lads of eighteen and nineteen years of age and another young fellow named Pohle, who turned out to be quite a good sort. I strongly objected to the presence of these two lads in front of whom I had to bathe and do everything else.

There had been another change in the organization of the Bunker which I forgot to mention; since the beginning of February, an officer, Lieutenant Heydrich, had been appointed as chief; and the warders no longer had things all their own way. This man had been in to see me once or twice and had struck me as quite a decent little fellow. He was that most unusual figure in the German Army, a ranker officer, having been given a commission in the First World War for gallantry in the field; he was, of course, a dug-out, and, I believe, an SS man by compulsion. I asked whether I could see him and complained to him about the young men being sent to me as guards. He was very nice about it and quite understood my attitude; he agreed to let me have Paul back and another older man if he could find one. The man he sent was a fellow named Teppich, who had been for a time with Stevens; a most unpleasant fellow who, whenever he came on duty, whether by day or by night, brought with him some food or other which he noisily devoured, washing down each mouthful with some coffee which he sucked in bubbles through his lips. Very often he was tipsy in the evening and, unlike Prochnow, inclined to be quarrelsome.

I put up with him for about a fortnight and then had little Heydrich in again and reported that he had adopted a threatening attitude towards me, and had said that Stevens and I were only common spies and ought to be shot. This was, I am sorry to say, a slight perversion of the truth, but I could not afford to be too scrupulous if I wanted to get my own way. Actually, all that Teppich had done was to say that he could not understand that two spies like Stevens and me had not been shot and, one evening when he was pretty tight, he started showing off his strength by holding a chair out at arm's length over my bed. Anyhow, Teppich was known as a drunken, quarrelsome fellow, and my story was accepted without demur, with the result that Teppich was given three weeks in a cell on a diet of bread and water and then drafted to the front. I tell this at length, because this incident materially eased my own position as, seeing how easily I had dealt with Teppich, all the officials came to the conclusion that perhaps I was better left alone, and even Ettlinger became much more civil.

Unfortunately this business did not end merely with the disappearance of Teppich, for the question of guards drinking on duty became the subject of an investigation by the commandant, and they, as well as the warders, were had up before him and warned that should there be any more complaints of this nature the punishment would be far more serious, and the man involved might find himself deprived of his SS uniform and sent to the camp as an ordinary prisoner. As Drexl had been on duty the evening when Teppich had been drunk on his arrival in my cell he was dismissed from his post as one of the warders in the Bunker. I was very sorry about this, for he had always treated me very kindly; actually, it turned out very well for him because he was detailed to a sort of batman job with the widow of SS-General Eycke, where, as I later heard, he was extremely happy in the role of devoted attendant to two small children.

Teppich was replaced by another man who had previously been with Stevens. This was Johann Odörfer, one of the strangest and most amusing characters I have ever met. In appearance he was rather like a gorilla with his stooping gait and long swinging arms; his head was covered with a thatch of reddish hair which had never known brush or comb, and his face, for most of the week, was also a field of thick stubble. His uniform was dirty and covered with stains, and almost always there was a bottle sticking out of one of his bulging pockets; not something to drink, but varnish or oil, for he was by way of being an artist. Odörfer was a man who had been born 300 years too late, for he was the soldier of fortune who would have found his true place and felt himself at home in the times of the Thirty Years War. He was just a

G

fighting man. He had no interest in nor use for drill and the spit and polish of peace, all he wanted was the chance to go out and kill a few people, no matter at what risk to himself. He had been a sapper in the First World War but, as soon as these were formed, got into one of the 'Stoss Truppen' which were, in a way, the proto-type of the Commandos of the Second World War. Wounded five times he had acquired every decoration for gallantry within his reach; he spent the war either fighting, in hospital, or in the cells, for his general method of inducing a medical board to pass him fit for general service was to knock out the chief examining doctor.

After 1918 he joined one of the free corps, and saw a lot of fighting in the Baltic and in Upper Silesia, then, when his unit was disbanded, he took up with the Nazis as they seemed to offer a bigger prospect of a little honest manslaughter than any of the other political parties. He joined the party quite soon after its formation, and so had the party emblem in gold, which made him quite an important person, as this gave him the right of personal access to Hitler if he were in any difficulty. He took not the slightest interest in the party programme, nor had he any reverence for Hitler and the other party leaders. He had joined the SS simply in order to get some fighting and he had actually managed, in spite of his age and war disability, to take part in the Polish cam-paign; then, to his disgust he had been classified 'Fit only for garrison duty at home' and had been sent to this camp. What he had seen in Poland, and since then, in the camp, had given him a furious hatred for everything to do with the Nazis, and unlike most Germans who always tried to excuse Hitler by saying that he did not know what was being done in his name, Odörfer was clear-sighted enough to place the whole blame upon him. What could you expect from a corporal? He liked his officers to be gentlemen, and if a man was not fitted to be an officer he was probably equally unsuitable as political leader of his country.

In spite of his inclination towards a life of violence Odörfer, from the very first and as long as he was with me, did everything that he could to help me and render my life as agreeable as possible. He considered that I had been unjustly treated, and that as I had been captured by a trick and not during an honest fight, it was his duty to help me to liberty. Almost daily he came out with some wonderful scheme for escape which he had worked out in the minutest detail; unfortunately, none carried us farther than the door of the Bunker and this we would only reach after we had slaughtered half a dozen warders and other officials—how we were to get out of the camp itself, for he intended to accompany me, was a problem for which he could find no solution. When telling me of his plans his enthusiasm was tremendous, and he had a way of puffing and snorting with excitement which made you expect to see flames issuing from his nostrils like a dragon of old.

Apart from entertaining me during my hours in the cell, Odörfer also introduced something which for many months was to render my hours of exercise much more interesting and agreeable than they had been before; this was skittles. Like most Bavarians he was a great skittle player, and when I told him that I had never played he felt that my education had been neglected and that it was his obvious duty to bring to me some knowledge of this greatest of games. As a start, he cut out with his pen-knife from some small billets of wood, a set of miniature nine-pins and a ball of roughly spherical outline, and we then started playing in my cell. This, however, aroused immediate protests as we made a devil of a noise and the paint at the bottom of the door which we used as a back stop soon showed signs of damage. Odörfer was, however, a very determined man and one of the next days he arrived looking singularly obese, and produced from under his tunic a full-sized skittle ball, saying: "Now we can play out of doors." I do not know by what barter he had acquired the ball which he said came from the officers' skittle alley, but it was certainly one that had seen better days, for it was nearly pear shaped and had such bias that one could almost bowl it in circles.

Out in the garden, we selected some approximately straight pine logs and cut these into lengths suitable for our purpose, and setting them up on the path, we began our game. The path was rough and uneven and with our crooked ball it was a pure matter of chance whether we could bowl anywhere near our skittles and scoring was very low, but we had started something and were soon to find co-operation from the Stevens and Elser corporations. One of Stevens's guards produced a really good ball and Elser manufactured a wooden base on which the skittles could stand. Not to be outdone, we then raided the wood shed and robbed it of three or four fine long planks. These we embedded in the path using a water level to get them perfectly true and very soon we found ourselves the owners of a first-rate skittle alley. From the end of May 1941 till the autumn of 1942 hardly a day passed without my playing skittles, and from my cell I could hear the balls rolling whenever Stevens or Elser were out. We got away with our constructional work because the warders also liked skittles and they soon began to play their own matches in the evenings after the prisoners had been put to bed. Gradually too they got into the habit of coming out to join in our games, as also did any guards who were off duty, and we soon had most exciting matches.

At first I was, of course, the rabbit of the party, but as my health and strength gradually improved through regular exercise I began to be able to hold my own and in the end was looked upon as a very promising player. The warders often got so keen on the game that they were disinclined to stop when my hour was up, and gradually I went in later and later, until it came to be recognized that I was entitled to stay out for an hour and a half.

I forgot to say that already in 1940 some attempt had been made to render the garden more attractive, and flower beds had been laid out on the west side of the main path; there were pansies, foxgloves, and marigolds, and I cannot express what a pleasure it was for me to look at them. In 1941 orders had been given that vegetables must be grown on every available plot of ground, so our garden had been devoted to cabbages except for the beds along the walls where tomatoes were planted. Between the wood shed and the building nothing had been done and the original waste land had been left untouched, but even this had its advantages, for one could build a couch of planks and lie on them in the sun. A couple of biggish piles of bricks had been erected here and to my delight two pairs of water wagtails nested and brought up their families in recesses which I had made by the removal of a few bricks. It was curious how very few birds ever visited us; only the two wagtail families who remained faithful throughout my entire stay, a pair of magpies and some crested larks. One year I occasionally saw a tit picking at the sunflower seeds and in the winter of 1944 after a heavy fall of snow a lot of sparrows turned up.

I scattered food and did everything I could think of to attract more birds but they seemed to sense that this was no place for creatures as free as they. When one is free one takes so many things for granted, and generally one is not even conscious of the pleasure one derives from the presence of the graceful gifts of nature around one. In prison, everything in me seemed to revolt against the ugliness of my surroundings and I felt a real hunger for beautiful scenes; I derived a pleasure which I had never known before, simply by looking at a flower or by seeing a bird fluttering about. I often wish that I could recapture something of the emotions which filled me then, for in ordinary life one is apt to see too much of ugly things and to neglect the beautiful frame of nature in which they are set whilst then, flowers, birds, and even insects shone out like jewels against the monotonous drabness of their surroundings.

On the 8th May there was that curious feeling which Germans describe as 'Dicke Luft', which may be paraphrased "as the shadow which coming events cast before them"; something abnormal was in the air. When the time came for my exercise, I was told that I would have to wait as the garden was not free. I heard a lot of movement near the entrance and the Heil Hitlering which always attended the arrival of important visitors, and then there was a lot of marching about and the sound of cell doors being opened and closed. I went out for exercise in the afternoon when everything seemed to have quietened down to normal. The only thing of interest was that I was told of a rumour that there was to be war between Germany and Russia, and that there had been big troop movements towards the Eastern Frontier. Next day one of my guards, I forget which, told me that there must have been a big row in the party as some very important prisoners, all men associated with Rudolf Hess, including his adjutant, were in the Bunker, and there was much speculation as to whether Hess had tried to start something like the Roehm business in 1934. Of course we could not find out what was happening, but it was certainly startling to read in the paper on the 13th, that is five days later, that Hess had flown to England and a story that illness, a tumour in his brain, had rendered him no longer accountable for his actions. Something wrong here. Had he flown from Germany after the arrest of his entourage to avoid a similar fate, or had he been sent on a mission and his people interned in the interests of secrecy. I don't even now know what is the true story, and can only go by the entries in my diary for 9th and 13th May, 1941.

During the weeks that followed, rumours about a war with Russia multiplied and became more positive, so it was no surprise to anyone when on 21st June the radio blared out the news of the German invasion. Ettlinger came in in high glee to tell me the news: "In six weeks we shall have finished off Russia and then our hands will be free for the final reckoning with England." Yes, six weeks. That is what Hitler said too. I did not see any signs of elation elsewhere and my Berliner guards told me that the news had been received in fear and depression. No one in Germany had ever really liked the *entente* with Russia, but war on two fronts, that was worse still—it was too much like the memories of the last war. To every German the idea of the limitless expanse of Russia is something horrifying—fear of the East is, as it were, a national bogey. Even though the Russians had accepted the volte-face in Soviet foreign policy which resulted in the *entente* between Molotov and Ribbentrop, this had never gone down with the Germans, for most of whom Hitler's greatest merit was that he had saved the country from communism. From the moment that the non-aggression pact with Russia was signed Hitler lost the support of that section of the population which, without joining his party, had voted for him in 1933, and administered a severe shock to many of his most stalwart followers.

I do not think that it has been sufficiently realized how much the start of the war in the East shook people's confidence in the political wisdom of the Führer, for it was an admission that the agreement with Russia had been made on false premises. Hitler had always said that the Communists were not to be trusted; why then had he trusted them, and on the basis of their lying promises involved the country in war with the West? No matter what the news was from the Russian front, nor how spectacular were the reported successes, I never saw the slightest sign of enthusiasm on the part of any German with whom I came in contact, whilst the old soldiers, those who had fought in Russia in the

First World War, expressed their view of the situation by the proverb: "Viele Hunde sind des Hasen Tod" (With enough dogs the hare will be killed)—there were so many Russians that the loss of a few million scarcely mattered.

I hope that I may be forgiven for this excursion into the field of politics, for my intention is merely to tell the story of my own experiences. It must be understood though, that throughout my imprisonment my real life consisted in active mental participation in every event of the war. All the time I was trying to obtain by deduction some vestiges of truth out of the fog of German propaganda. I can in fact truthfully say that the only thing from which I really suffered was the deprivation of news; news from my wife and news of the war. Although on the whole I was inclined to discount German stories about the havoc caused by their bombing of England, accidents can always happen, and having absolutely no idea where May was I could never quite divest myself of my fears for her safety. Of the general course of the war I knew only what I read in the German papers, and during 1940 and 1941 there was indeed little news from which one could derive any comfort. My only consolation came from the fact that there had been no attempt at invasion and from my certainty that we should never give in. Of course when Russia entered the war I became much more confident, for if Hitler had not succeeded in overcoming us when we stood alone, how much less chance he had of doing so when faced with heavy commitments on the East. What a prisoner needs most is hope. Really, the material hardships mean so little to him and as long as he can feel that his country will emerge victorious he is unlikely himself to lose courage.

People often ask me questions about my experiences in Germany, generally adding: "If you don't mind talking about them. I suppose you want to forget all about it." Prison is an experience that you cannot forget and one which you cannot explain. In life you may be forced to do many things which are distasteful to you, but all have some purpose; as a soldier you have to give blind obedience to orders, you may suffer great dangers and privations, and you will certainly be moved about in a way that often seems purposeless, yet always with you is the feeling that you are engaged in an enterprise which must be carried through and that, however stupid some orders may appear, there must be reason at the back of them. As a prisoner, everything that happens to you is the result of a force with which you are at enmity; you resent every order which your instinct tells you to disobey—the fact that you cannot, fills you with a horrible feeling of impotence and uselessness. You feel fit and energetic, anxious to play your part in life, and find yourself merely a number condemned to live an absolutely sterile existence. When at last liberation comes you enter a world that is strange to you and in which, except amongst those closest to you, there seems to be no place for you—you are supernumerary to the establishment. You have also become slightly queer, for there are many ideas and prejudices common to your friends which you can no longer share—you do not judge others by what they appear to be but imagine what showing they would make as prisoners, deprived of all the make believe and flummery of what we call normal life. I know that I cannot put into words the things that I feel, and all that I can really say is that prison robs you of many things which you believed essential but at the same time gives you a new understanding of your fellow men, a feeling of greater warmth in your relation to them, so that on the whole I think that you gain on balance.

There were quite a lot of R.A.F. raids on Berlin during the spring and summer of 1941, but from all that I could learn very little damage was done to the city. The defences had been greatly built up and the volume of flak fire was, it seemed to me, far greater than when in 1943 the really big raids started. I could see nothing of what went on, of course, and simply had to lie in my bed and hope for the best. There is something slightly disconcerting in the knowledge that you are chained to a wall and that should any-thing happen it is most unlikely that you could be freed. Quite a number of bombs were dropped fairly close to the camp, and there were also casualties from dud flak shells which were far from infre-quent. On the 4th September there was rather an amusing event. Suddenly I heard the whine of bombs and next moment explosions in the woods just the other side of the prison wall; this was followed by the sound of planes diving and machine-gunning some ground target. It was not until some five or ten minutes later that the alert was sounded and the flak started a barrage.

Next day the story went round that this had been a Russian raid with German Heinckel planes supplied to the Soviet Govern-ment and which had consequently not been recognized as hostile. I don't know whether there was any truth in the story but it raised quite a scare, especially, when a few days later (on the 7th), there was a really big British raid which seemed to have caused serious damage in Berlin. The idea that they might now have to face bombing from both East and West had a depressing effect, even on Ettlinger who still pretended to believe that the war with Russia would be a walk-over.

The 27th October was for me a red-letter day for Eccarius came in the morning and brought me my first real letter from May. She was well and living at Chagford in Devon. Although I did not know exactly where Chagford was the postmark on the envelope was Newton Abbot so that I knew that she must be in the Dart-moor district which was probably safe from German bombs. From what she said it was clear that she had been writing regularly. Some of her previous letters I had seen in a Gestapo file. I have never had such a complete change of spirit as this letter brought me; everything seemed bright and easy, and I was really a bit off my head with excitement. I managed to get hold of a sheet of paper and wrote her a long letter which I gave to the commandant next day, who assured me that it would be sent off at once. Then the Gestapo put in some very dirty work. Just a month later, when I was hoping that perhaps May would soon have my letter, it was brought back to me with a message from Gestapo Headquarters that it had not been sent on because it was written in English—both my wife and I might only correspond in German.

I immediately wrote another letter, this time in German, taking great pains to write nothing which might be considered undesirable. This letter was supposed to have gone off on the 25th November, but on 31st December it was brought back again; it had not been sent because I had put the name of the camp at the top and this was forbidden. An absolutely absurd excuse for it had been reported in the British Press that I was at Sachsenhausen and May's letter had been addressed to me there. Well, on 5th January, 1942, I wrote a third letter and this she actually received on the 3rd March; the first news she had had from me since the 9th November, 1939. Although she had received assurances that I was alive and well it was not until my letter came that all her fears for my safety were really allayed. I feel it very difficult to forgive the Gestapo, and particularly Schellenberg, who I later heard was responsible for this cowardly example of petty cruelty.

At the beginning of December Stevens left the camp, as I later heard, for Dachau. I spotted this at first because two of his guards, Deckert and Lenkeit, were wished on to me, and after a day or two the latter told me what had happened. I did not mind having Lenkeit who was a silly old fool and might be useful, but I was determined not to have anything to do with Deckert, who was, I knew, a thorough-going Nazi and a most unreliable customer. He was stupid enough to pretend that he knew nothing about me and that he was a stranger to the Bunker, and when he asked me some questions about myself, something that was strictly forbidden, I seized on the opportunity and reported him at once. He lasted just three days with me after having spied on poor Stevens for nearly two years; he got a bad telling off for his indiscretion and was sent to Buchenwald, where he had to do sentry duty instead of sitting in a comfortable, warm cell.

The year 1941 came to an end and after two years of prison I had become pretty well accustomed to the life. I had news of May and there were some gleams of light in what I could gather from German war reports. The word 'Vergeltung' (retaliation) seemed to be taking the place of 'Sieg' (victory), and it was obvious that the Germans were not having it all their own way. It was towards the end of 1941 that I first heard the mention of new secret weapons, and particularly of a rocket carrying three tons of explosive and having a range of nearly 400 kilometers. As time went on stories about such secret weapons became more frequent and precise.

Although the food was excellent and the quantity more than sufficient, the fact that everything was cut up and prepared for me so that I could eat only with my fingers or a spoon was most annoying. There were some things for which I did not particularly care, and it would have made my diet much more agreeable if I could have accumulated things like butter, jam, and cheese, so that I could use them as and when I wished. I had made myself a couple of knives of beach wood, rather similar in pattern to those used by the Eskimos, and at the end of 1941 Paul König induced a new trusty, who did not yet know the regulations, to bring me my bread unbuttered and cold provisions in bulk as issued. In addition to making my meals much more to my liking this change afforded me valuable evidence that much of the food supplied for me was being stolen. Grothe had told me once that I must not think that I was being kept free of cost, for I should have to pay for my board and lodging at the end of the war; for every day, I was being charged ten marks; five for lodging and five for food. I happened to know that when guards were travelling to and from home they were given 2.50 marks a day in lieu of rations, so I said to Grothe that it was unfair that I should be charged as much as five marks. To this he answered, "Oh, but you are getting double SS rations and of course must also pay double rate."

I did not rise to this as it struck me at once that this information might come in useful some day. I was getting as much food and more than I could eat, but since I had a pretty good idea of what my guards received in the way of rations (they frequently brought them to eat in my cell) it was clear that I was not getting my double rations, and as they were certainly supplied by the kitchen, someone else was taking them. As long as my food was brought to me ready prepared to eat it was impossible for me to obtain definite evidence that I was being short changed, but as soon as I was given my rations as issued, I could compare them with those of my guards and prove that they were identical in quantity and weight.

It was not long before Ettlinger found out what the trusty, Schwartz, was doing and of course he made a hell of a row and gave orders that nothing was to be brought to me in bulk; he was quite bright enough to see where the danger lay, but I had succeeded in establishing a precedent and had not much difficulty in inducing Lieutenant Heydrich to revoke Ettlinger's order and permit me to carry on with my wooden knife spreading butter, cheese, and sausage, on my black bread at my own sweet will. I managed to find out, too, that there were at least another four prisoners in the building who were entitled to the double rations and that none of them got them, any surplus being a perquisite of the warders.

I knew of quite a number of other forms of graft on which the warders, in particular Ettlinger, were engaged, but at the time thought it better to keep my knowledge to myself and save it up for use on some suitable occasion. It was obviously of no use to complain to the commandant, for I knew perfectly well that his thieving was carried on on such a large scale that he was obliged to turn a blind eye to the petty peculations of his subordinates; besides, Ettlinger was one of his chief assistants, as his father-in-law, a Berlin butcher, was the link between the camp supplies and the Black Market. I felt, therefore, that my best policy was to wait for a suitable opportunity and then perhaps spring a mine which would remove not only Ettlinger, but the commandant as well. I was getting to know the ropes, and knew that my only hope of improving my position was to play off Gestapo against the camp authorities. But this was ticklish work and I needed to play my cards very carefully. I was, though, very hopeful that ultimately I should succeed in gaining a certain ascendancy in my prison and indeed, it would have been strange had I failed; after all, I was dealing with a lot of uneducated men, and my greater knowledge and experience must give me a great advantage.

The winter of 1941–2 was not nearly so cold as that of 1939–40, but we had a great deal of snow, and as I had taken upon myself the task of keeping the paths passable I got a lot of healthy exercise, and no little amusement, clearing them with a sort of miniature snow plough which I made out of some old boards. I had another letter from May in November 1941 and two in January, and my spirits were of the best.

After Drexl's dismissal the staff had been increased by two young warders, van Detzen and Saathof who, having nowhere to live, camped out in the Bunker where they had been given a vacant cell, and since they were in the building Ettlinger had quite given up doing night duty which made everything very much pleasanter. The two young men were nice fresh countrymen from near the Dutch border and enjoyed speaking their Low German to me, which so closely resembles Dutch that I could understand it without difficulty. They had both passed through Hitler Jugend and Labour Corps and were thus representative of the German youth educated to be worthy citizens of Hitler's third realm which was to last for the next thousand years. Myself, I saw no sign that the Nazi teaching with which they had been innoculated had taken with either of them. As is the case with most young people, they had merely suffered education because they had no other option, and now that they were free they thought no more about it, and were simply intent on enjoying themselves as much as they could. Both had fathers who held small offices in the party, and it was due to their influence that they had come to Sachsenhausen as warders instead of being drafted to the front.

Actually, van Detzen would far rather have joined the Wehrmacht; he was a big hefty fellow and found the life in the Bunker intensely boring; Saathof, on the other hand, had not the faintest wish to go anywhere near danger, and was in a panic when there was news of medical reclassification of men engaged on home duty. Eccarius was always careful to keep well within the letter of the law, and never failed to do his turn of night duty, and, as I have already said, he was always quiet and efficient and never made sudden inroads to my cell as Ettlinger was apt to do. Consequently I could feel free in the evenings to do anything which I felt inclined to undertake, without fear that I might be caught wielding a needle or some other sharp or pointed implement.

In February an epidemic of typhus started amongst Russian prisoners, of whom there were now a large number in the camp, and we even had a case in the Bunker. As a result, the whole building, wing by wing, was disinfected with prussic acid gas, and I was shifted out of my cell while this was done. I heard from one of the guards who came to me later, and who at that time was employed on sentry duty in the camp, that every hut occupied by Russians in which a case of typhus occurred was immediately surrounded by a fence of barbed wire, and sentries were stationed round it with orders to shoot down any prisoner who tried to leave the hut. The prisoners were given no medical attention of any kind, but every morning a couple of men of the Bible Student category came to fetch the dead and take them to the crematorium, after which they had to join the Russians in the hut, ostensibly to give them medical care. My informant told me that he had seen as many as thirty corpses taken away from a single hut.

At this time the treatment of the Russian prisoners must have been indescribably cruel, and as they were given much smaller rations than other prisoners a very large number starved to death. I was also told that when the first batch of Russians arrived in the autumn of 1941 they were forced to run the gauntlet between two rows of SS-regulars armed with oaken cudgels; it was said that half a dozen men were killed. This seems to have been done without the knowledge or approval of the commandant, for two or three of the ringleaders were punished for their participation by a few days in the cells.

In March Himmler visited the camp for the first time since I had been there. For days before we had known that something was up, for there had been a most thorough clean up and new uniforms had been issued to guards and trusties alike, and my cell having been inspected by the commandant and his adjutant, orders were given that all the cobwebs which festooned the corners must be removed. On the morning of the great day, Eccarius came to

my cell and removed the guards' ash tray and warned them not
to smoke. It seems, such was Himmler's stupidity, that he really
believed that because he himself disapproved of smoking no SS
man would dream of indulging in such a vice. The great man came,
but he did not honour me with a call, and I heard that the object
of his visit was to consult a homeopath, a certain Dr. Schmidt,
who was one of the men of Hess's entourage imprisoned in the
Bunker. Shortly afterwards arrangements were made for this man
to return to Berlin and carry on his practice there; not as a free
man but as what was called an 'Ehrenhäftling' (prisoner of honour)
accompanied by an SS guard wherever he went. Ebert, one of
my old guards, was one of the men chosen for this duty, and he
told me the story some months later when he returned to the
Bunker.

Himmler did, however, pay another visit to the camp and this
time came to see me. This was on the 30th June, 1942. There had
been the same days of prior excitement and the same drill with
ash trays. At about eleven o'clock there were the noises without
which always heralded important visitors; the great man had
arrived. I heard him with his bodyguard pass my door to a cell
farther along the passage and after an interval, repass; I was just
about to say to my guard that it was now safe for us to smoke
when the tramping feet stopped and then moved back again
towards my cell. The door opened a bit and a hand beckoned
to the guard who went out hurriedly, then the door was thrown
wide open and I saw the passage full of officers, but only one
entered and the door was gently closed behind him. He advanced
the regulation three paces and, raising his hand only the level of
his chin said, "Heil Hitler!" To which I responded with "Grüss
Gott, Reichsführer," for of course it was Heinrich Himmler. A little
sandy coloured man with wobbly glasses on his nose and an absolutely expressionless face. "I am sorry, Herr Best, to see a man
like you under such circumstances, but it is war and we are trying
to do our best for your comfort. Have you any complaints?"

"No, Reichsführer, treatment and everything else is splendid,"
(Tadellos)! Experience had taught me that complaint was useless
and only brought grief in its train.

"Have you any wishes? Do you lack anything?"

"No! Reichsführer."

"Well, Mr. Best, you have now spent several months in this
notorious camp of Sachsenhausen, and you have certainly been
able to ascertain for yourself that all the stories of atrocities
(Greuelgeschichten) in the British White Book were nothing but
lies, Jewish inventions."

"I am sorry, Reichsführer, but from what I have seen and heard
since I came here I believe that conditions are even worse than
as pictured in the White Book."

Heinrich Himmler turned on his heel without a word and went out leaving me to muse on the possibility that he might have taken my words in ill part, and perhaps dock me of my tobacco or have me shot at dawn. Noises without and their cessation indicated the departure of our august visitor; tobacco smoke and peace again filled the cell.

Not long afterwards Ettlinger came in and asked: "What has happened?" "Why?" I asked in turn. "The Reichsführer went straight out of the building after he left you and looked quite disturbed." "Look here, if the Hauptschar-Führer wants to know anything about a private talk between the Reichsführer and myself, he had better ask the Reichsführer to tell him." In German, to speak to a man in the third person singular, addressing him as 'he' and continuing to speak of him as though he were not present is a particularly contemptuous mode of address which has completely fallen out of current use. I, however, frequently used it when speaking to Ettlinger or anyone else who annoyed me as, however much it irritated them, there was no way in which they could get back at me for, even if archaic, this way of addressing an inferior was perfectly correct and I was quite entitled to employ it if I chose. Frederick the Great always spoke to subjects in this way, and I thought what was good enough for him was good enough for me.

Later, on the same day, the commandant came to see me. This was quite contrary to his usual habits as I had never known him to visit the Bunker except in the morning, also, what he had never done before, he told my guard to leave the cell. Then he started off. "The Reichsführer is furious. It will cost you your life. I am expecting orders for your execution any minute. . . . What did you say to the Reichsführer?"

"I'm very sorry, Oberführer, but you will understand that it would be most incorrect of me to repeat anything which the Reichsführer discussed with me privately. Anyhow, I am sure that when you get your orders for my execution you will also learn with what I am charged." The Oberführer looked as though he would like to spit in my face but contented himself with making the sort of noise with which, in old melodramas, the villain received the news that the hero had paid off the mortgage on the old homestead and that his plot to get the girl had been foiled, then, exit Oberführer.

Well, I was not shot and nothing happened at all. If anything, I was treated with even more consideration than before. Since the beginning of the year Eccarius had taken over the job of providing me with cigarettes or anything else which I needed. Instead of having to beg Ettlinger every time I wanted some cigarettes, and then getting them doled out to me six at a time, Eccarius had been bringing me a box of a hundred every Monday; quite good cigarettes they were too, they were called Ibar and came from Yugo-slavia. Not long after Himmler's visit I ran a bit short one week and asked him if I could have a few cigarettes in advance, and to my surprise he answered: "Certainly, you can have as many as you like. You only have to ask." I felt that wonders never cease. Letters were coming pretty regularly from May and I knew that my own were reaching her; I was feeling well, the weather was glorious, and I seemed to be able to stay out and sun-bathe for two hours or more without anything being said; my food was much more satisfactory as I could always manage to save up sufficient butter, jam and cheese to tide me over when something I didn't like appeared on the menu; and now it seemed that I could smoke as much as I liked. I was really beginning to enjoy myself.

Rumours reached me that a general stocktaking was being carried out in the camp, and soon the cells in my wing were filled with higher camp officials who, it was said, were to be charged with theft. Stock was even taken of all the things which I had in my cell, and I was surprised to find that I had succeeded in accumulating no less than fourteen blankets most of which found their use as cushions, rugs, or tablecloths. I also heard that General Glücks, the Inspector of Concentration Camps, had appointed a commission to inquire into conditions in the camp and that the most unusual, indeed, revolutionary procedure had been adopted, of taking evidence from camp prisoners. Theoretically, the moment anyone was brought to the camp he ceased to be a human being and became merely Häftling number so and so (it was in fact a punishable offence to speak of a prisoner as a 'Mensch' (human being). As a camp prisoner he ceased to possess that quality 'Ehre' which is so everlastingly in the mouths of Germans and which, although translated by the word 'honour' is so different to anything that we mean by it. Anyhow, a man who has no 'Ehre' cannot take an oath nor can any reliance be placed on anything he says; he is a moral outlaw. If a prisoner was accused of an offence he could not defend himself, but must take whatever came to him by way of punishment. It will therefore be understood how the decision to take evidence from prisoners caused something like a panic, and that SS officials felt as though their world had come to an end.

There were other signs, visible even to me, that strange things were happening. Some time before, the commandant had had his yacht brought into the prison grounds and a sort of shed had been built over it which was directly under my window; a great nuisance it was, too, for whenever it rained I was disturbed by the noise made by the drops beating on the corrugated iron roof which was just on the level of my window. A gang of prisoners came one day and removed shed and yacht. I was told that a valuation of the yacht was being made and all costs would be charged up to the commandant. A few days later more men came, broke up the wood shed in my garden, and took all the timber away; they even removed the planks of my skittle alley.

On the 22nd August the commandant came to my cell bringing with him a wee little man with big round glasses who looked a bit like Mr. Pickwick, and introduced him to me as Obersturmban-führer Kaindl, the new commandant: "I am leaving you; I have been promoted to Chief of Police in Norway," he said. I should say here that the commandant had always been very courteous and correct in introducing to me any new officer who came on duty at the camp, so the fact that he introduced the new com-mandant to me was just a matter of customary routine, but it was obvious that something big was happening, and afterwards there was a lot of talk about the matter. It was said that Glücks had wanted the old commandant arrested and put on trial, but Himmler had intervened and had given him the new job in Norway. Curiously enough, never afterwards did I come across mention of his name in the papers, nor could anyone else tell me what became of him. As a prisoner, one has a rooted objection to change, even change for the better, but I could not feel sorry that Lohritz was going, and I certainly liked the look of the new man. Well, time would show.

Ettlinger had been away from duty for a couple of months on sick leave; he had some trouble with his tonsils though rumour placed an unkinder construction on his indisposition. He returned to duty on 2nd November and that evening came in at eight o'clock and wanted to chain me up for the night; he brought my own bracelet too, instead of Stevens's old one, which I had been wearing for some time past. Of course I refused to be chained up at that hour and said he would have to return at ten-thirty. He was extremely angry and said: "This sort of thing will have to be changed, I am not going to stay up for the convenience of a 'Häftling'." Got you, I thought, for I knew that strict orders had been given by the Gestapo that no suggestion might be made that I was considered as a 'Häftling'. Next morning Ettlinger roused me at five when, for a long time past, I had only been getting up at eight. On the two following days, when duty was taken in turn by van Detzen and Saathof, there was the same business of coming in to chain me up at eight and the early wash at five in the morning. Then came Eccarius's turn and as soon as he came on duty I had him in and told him what had happened, and that I understood from what Ettlinger said that I must now consider myself to be a 'Häftling'. Eccarius went white as a sheet and asked, "He didn't say that, did he?" "Ask Paul König," I replied, "he was in the room." Eccarius promised faithfully that everything should be as it was and that Ettlinger must be mad to try to make changes without authority.

I heard nothing more about alterations in my bedtime or hour of rising, but next time that Ettlinger was on duty he sent the trusty Schwartz round with bracelet and padlock with instructions that my guard should lock me up. Of course I refused and when Ettlinger turned up in shirt sleeves I gave him a first-class 'snort' (Anschnauzer), and he had to go back and put on full uniform and equipment before I would permit him to chain me. A few days later, on two occasions, I noticed that all my belongings had been searched whilst I was in the lavatory, and when Ettlinger or one of the two young warders was on duty the door of my cell was suddenly opened at night on several occasions, ostensibly for the warder on duty to check whether the guard was awake; there were other annoying intrusions into my privacy and interference with my established customs. I had Eccarius in again who said he was very sorry, but Ettlinger would not listen to him and the things which he had done recently to annoy me were all strictly in accordance with regulations, he therefore advised me to ask the commandant to come and see me: "Don't forget though that I have always done my best for you and have tried to make you comfortable."

"Right," I said, "give the commandant my compliments and say that I should like to see him."

That day and the next there was no sign of the commandant and I had plenty of time to think things over. I knew perfectly well that in the circles in which I now found myself, complaint to a higher authority was very apt to boomerang and that I might easily come in for the harder knock. I had liked the look of the new commandant and my intuition told me that he was a man who could be trusted. Should I go nap on this hunch and speak out openly to him? It was very difficult for me to make up my mind.

On the morning of 25th November the commandant came in accompanied by Eccarius. The guard was sent out and the commandant said, "You wish to speak to me, Herr Best? Here I am, in what can I be of service?"

"I am sorry to have troubled you, Obersturmbanführer, but might I perhaps speak to you 'unter vier Augen' " (alone).

Eccarius looked deeply shocked and very anxious, but the commandant waved to him to go away and then turning to me said, "What are your troubles? Don't be afraid, you can talk to me quite frankly as man to man."

I suppose as a result of the many months of imprisonment behind me my nerve suddenly gave way, or rather, I should say, my physical nerves, for my determination to go ahead and spill the beans was unchanged. I began to tremble so much that I could no longer stand but had to sit down on a chair. The commandant said, "A good idea, Herr Best, why should we stand. With your permission I will sit down too, and we can have a comfortable chat. Now don't worry, for I know all about you, and everyone admires you for your 'Tadellose Haltung'; I was coming to ask for your help in any case, for you made some remarks to the Reichsführer which I should like you to explain. I have been given the task of cleaning up this camp and clean it up I shall."

He was such a nice little man, he can't have been much over five feet, and he twinkled at me in such a friendly fashion through his large round spectacles that I gradually became quite calm and started off telling him about life in the Bunker. I told him about the hazing of prisoners by Ettlinger, and how he often went from cell to cell making prisoners stand to attention and then knocking them down—this was an amusement in which he was joined by van Detzen and which they called their morning exercises. I told him what I knew about the thieving in which Ettlinger was involved. For weeks past Paul König had been ferreting about, finding out everything that he could about camp scandals, and particularly the misdeeds of our warders, so I had no lack of material for my story to the commandant. His reaction though was to say that all this was relatively unimportant, for theft was so general in the camp that he was surprised that even the prisoners had not been taken away. What he wanted to know from me were two things, could I mention any specific case of ill-treatment of a prisoner since he became commandant and, secondly, had I been deprived of anything which should have come to me.

I then told him that two days previously, after his adjutant had been in the building interrogating one of the prisoners, Ettlinger had gone to the man's cell and beaten him up; as the cell was only a few doors away from mine, I had been able to hear him tell the prisoner that if he did not want more beatings he had better not say that he had been badly treated; next time he did so he would be beaten till he was as limp as a rag (Windelweich). Next, I said that I had reason to believe that I was entitled to double SS rations, but that so far I had not been receiving even full single rations. The commandant then got up and said that he would come and see me later, but that I must not worry as everything would be all right.

Late in the afternoon he came to see me again and told me that he had looked into things and that he was very grateful to me for my information. "You will not see Ettlinger again as I am moving him before his next turn of duty, I am also transferring Saathof, as Eccarius tells me that he is very careless and inefficient, but now I should like to know what you think about van Detzen and Eccarius."

This was something of a poser, for although I could have made out a very good case against both men, I did not like the idea of a complete change of all officials, as this might very well prove to be a leap from the frying-pan into the fire; I therefore said to the commandant: "From everything that I have observed I should say that you would find it difficult to get a more suitable man than Eccarius for the job here. It is true that he is not a strong character and that he was quite unable to cope with a man of such dominating personality as Ettlinger, but he certainly knows how things should be done, and whenever he is on duty it is quite remarkable how smoothly everything runs and how little fuss there is. To me he has always behaved absolutely correctly, and I have never heard anything which would suggest that he had treated any prisoners with unnecessary harshness. Of course, he certainly knew what Ettlinger was doing and should have taken steps to exercise more control over his actions though this was made difficult for him by Oberführer Lohritz's obvious partiality for Ettlinger."

"As for van Detzen, when he first came here he was a nice unspoilt lad, and if latterly he has rather gone off the rails, I think that Ettlinger is solely to blame; given a chance, I should think that he might become quite a useful official. What I would suggest is that you should leave these two here, but instead of appointing any more regulars, you should give Eccarius two elderly reservists. He would be able to control them more easily and the danger of friction would be much reduced."

The commandant had listened very attentively to my long speech and then said: "I am grateful to you that you have spoken so frankly, and I agree with what you say, for it accords with the conclusions I had already reached. Since our talk this morning, I have learnt a lot more about Ettlinger and he is certainly a bad lot (Volksschädling); I shall not, however, take any steps to have him brought to justice now, for were I to report the matter to the law officers (SS-Gerichtsoffizier) there would certainly be a lot of inquiries made and you might be called upon to give evidence. This might be bad for you as your reputation with the Gestapo is none too good, and I have seen several reports about difficulties you have made since you came here, most of which came from Ettlinger. You won't see him again here, for he has orders to report to me in the morning, when I shall get him to apply for transfer to a different post. I don't expect to have any difficulty with him. As regards your food, you were quite right, and from tomorrow you will receive the full double rations which are due to you. Now, don't worry about things. I think that I can promise you that you will find your life here much pleasanter in the future than it has been in the past."

I felt pretty well all in by the time that the commandant left me. I really think that this conversation was about the most difficult experience of my whole life, for my vitality was at low ebb, and if I had guessed wrongly in my estimate of the commandant as a man whom I could trust, I could with certainty look forward to some pretty unpleasant treatment from the prison officials. But I have never regretted taking the chance.

It was a very pale and shaky Eccarius who came in to chain me up that night. I had heard something of the storm that had burst over his head that afternoon, and had wondered how so small a man as Kaindl could produce such formidable bellows and yells. I said to Eccarius, "Well, I took your advice and spoke frankly to the commandant." "Didn't he just have me on the mat? (Was habe ich eine grosse Zigarre bekommen; aber so was!)" was his only reply. I told him that I had really done all that I could to help him and that it was his own fault if he now found himself in difficulties. As he was supposed to be the head man in the building, naturally the commandant blamed him if things went wrong but, I consoled him, " 'The soup is never eaten as hot as it is cooked,' and I believe that you will find that everything will blow over as far as you are concerned, but be careful. I could have told the commandant where you got the material for that uniform and the leather for those smart riding boots." Eccarius spluttered protests that these materials had been given to him by Ettlinger. "Yes, but Ettlinger stole them and you knew that he had. Don't interfere with me and don't make trouble with the trusties or with my guards. We have always got on well together, and I hope that we shall do so in the future, but believe me, if we fall out, I know enough to blow you sky high whenever I choose."

Although after this our relations were a little strained for a time this soon passed and, since I continued to support Eccarius whenever I had occasion to talk to the commandant, he came to rely on my advice and help whenever he was faced with any difficulties, and in turn did everything he could to meet my wishes.

Three days later the commandant came to see me again and told me that he hoped soon to be able to find more comfortable accommodation for me, and also that he had arranged for me to spend more time out of doors. I took the opportunity to show him my chain attached to the ring in the wall. He asked me what on earth this was for and when I told him he was greatly shocked and said: "Such things aren't done where I am" (bei mir gibt es so was nicht) and went straight away saying that he would be back shortly. After about ten minutes he came in again and said, "I have telephoned to Gruppenführer Müller and he has authorized me to stop this stupid business if I take responsibility for your security. This I have done, and I am sure that I can rely on you not to let me down." After he left me Eccarius came in and asked me to go to the interrogation room for a few minutes, and when I returned to the cell the only sign left of my fetters was a patch of wet plaster on the wall where the ring had been.

By this time, after three years constant wear, my clothes had reached the stage where holes appeared faster than I could mend them. Of my shirt, little remained of the original material except collar and cuffs; all the rest had gradually been used to cover and re-cover the essential visible portions, having been replaced by pieces of sheet or towel which I had managed to purloin. My tie was mere artistic patchwork and my suit was a threadbare façade. May had written to me that she had been obliged to leave all my clothes at our house at The Hague but that our housekeeper, who had remained there, was looking after them. I had, therefore, sometime previously, applied to the Gestapo to have some of my things brought to me, but had received no reply to my request. I mentioned this matter to the commandant who said that he would make inquiries. Next day Eccarius came to my cell with two of the trusties carrying a really splendid wardrobe which, since I possessed nothing with which to fill it, seemed a bit of a white elephant; but I had my hopes.

Sure enough, the following week I was called to the interrogation room and there was Grothe with a couple of enormous parcels. What a delight it was to unpack them and to find clothes and linen, books, soap, and dozens of other things for which I had longed. As soon as I got back to my cell I stripped and cast aside everything in the way of clothing that I had on me, or in my cell, and then dressed myself in fresh things from top to toe. One can say what one will, but it makes a lot of difference to one's morale to feel that one is clean and tidy in one's dress; at all events it does to me.

Three days later the commandant came to see me again, bringing me this time my monocle, pen-knife, and other of my belongings which I had so far not been allowed to have; he also told me that in future I would be supplied with knife and fork for my meals and that, if I wished, I could order wine or beer to be brought to me from the canteen.

On the 10th December I was again called to the interrogation room where I found a certain Kriminalrat, Dr. Clemens. I had known for some time that this man had been appointed by the Gestapo to act, as it were, as my guardian, but so far I had never set eyes on him as he had left everything to his assistant Grothe. He told me that he had come to see me now because it was he who had fetched my belongings from Holland, and who had seen my sister-in-law and our housekeeper there. The latter, he said, wished to be relieved of the responsibility of looking after my belongings, and he had therefore arranged to have everything which she had in her keeping sent out to me. He considered that it was better that this should be done as, otherwise, there was danger that the occupation authorities might take it into their heads to requisition my things as enemy property. He also gave me letters from my sister-in-law and the housekeeper, and told me that if I wished to write to them he would see that my letters reached them.

On the 24th December I was again visited by the commandant, who had with him Eccarius who was carrying a small Xmas tree, two bottles of wine, and a large Xmas cake, a sort of current bun. These the commandant handed to me with his best Xmas wishes and again assured me that I should find the coming year much pleasanter than those which had gone before. I appreciated his kindness even though all these gifts were later charged up to me and I had to sign for them.

So the year drew to its close and at its end I wrote in my diary:

1942 has on the whole passed quite pleasantly. May's letters have been the greatest comfort and help. The old feeling that I was a helpless prisoner, forgotten by everyone, has quite gone, and I feel myself again to be a civilized person with a right to lead a civilized life.

CHAPTER VI

THE year 1943 started auspiciously, with news through Paul, that the position at Stalingrad was pretty well hopeless and that the Russians were proving everywhere too strong. Of course the *Völkische Beobachter*, the O.K.W. reports, and the broadcast commentaries of Ditmar and Fritsche, still brought news of German successes on all fronts, but it was impossible not to notice the gradual damping of the spirits of the camp officials and the growth of optimism and confidence amongst the prisoners. For my own part I felt on the top of the world and really began to believe that this might prove to be the last year of the war; indeed, from what my Berlin guards told me, there seemed to be a pretty general idea that the beginning of December would see the end for, by then, the war would have lasted just as long as the previous one. At this period of the war there was still something in the way of public opinion left and people could still discuss the situation with friends, listen to B.B.C. broadcasts, and pass on rumours, in spite of all the repressive efforts of the Gestapo.

Of course it may be said that my opinions are valueless, formed as they were in the strict seclusion of my prison cell, but throughout the war the camp reflected events outside with an accuracy which often astonished me, so that I often felt that I was like a man in a well-heated room who, by looking through the window at a thermometer, could measure the cold outside.

As far as I, myself, was concerned, I felt that I was out of the wood and could look forward to spending the remainder of my internment in comparative comfort, and all that I had to fear was a possible breakdown in my health, or some sudden decision by the Nazi bosses who controlled my fate which might bring about my liquidation. I was on the whole, though, very well satisfied. True, I had not yet got everything exactly to my liking, but if my estimate of Kaindl's character were correct, it would not be long before I did, and anyhow I rather enjoyed the struggle to improve my position. Since the removal of Ettlinger and Saathof, Eccarius's attitude towards me had been most submissive and, at least for the moment, there was no fight left in him. Rather to my surprise, Kaindl had followed my advice in almost every detail; he had left Eccarius as head man, with van Detzen as his deputy, and in the place of Ettlinger and Saathof he had sent two reservists, Robert Luchs and Hans Schmidt, both holding the rank of Unter-scharführer (sergeant), who seemed quiet and inoffensive fellows.

Eccarius had been relieved of routine work involving regular turns of duty, and had been made responsible for the smooth running of the building; the other three men did two days' duty on and one day off, so that day and night there were always two of them on guard. Eccarius spent the whole day in the building, and although he was permitted to spend his nights at home, frequently paid surprise visits. Since the commandant too had the habit of turning up when he was least expected the men were kept constantly on tip-toes to the great benefit of all prisoners.

Lohritz, our old commandant, as I said previously, liked pomp and ceremony and never entered the camp without a train of officers. As he preferred to be properly received wherever he went he had no objection to advance notice being given of his intention to carry out an inspection, and so he never saw anything which had not been prepared for his approval. Kaindl's system was the direct reverse. One of the first things that he did on taking command was to obtain master keys to every lock in the camp. Then he appointed a clerkly young fellow named Wessels his adjutant, and handed over to him every detail of administrative work with which he was not compelled to deal himself and, wearing shoes with thick rubber soles, started wandering about the camp seeing things for himself. At first one or two people gave telephoned advice to quarters towards which his footsteps seemed to be directed, but he soon put a stop to this by monitoring all telephone calls at the central camp switchboard. At the beginning, his rule over his SS guards and officials was severe in the extreme, and for the smallest offence the punishment was always three weeks cells on bread and water followed by transfer according to the age of the offender, either to a unit destined for the front, or to a concentration camp in one of the occupied territories.

Towards the prisoners he was benevolent and immediately scrapped beatings and confinement in dark cells as punishments, substituting longer or shorter terms in the punishment squad which, nevertheless, under his rule was always far smaller than it had been in Lohritz's day, or at the most two days on bread and water in a light cell. Most of the men were crimed for stealing from each other or for bullying. On one occasion, having discovered that most of the room bosses were bullies, he put the whole lot of them in the punishment squad for three weeks and let them carry forty pounds on their backs during a daily march of twenty-four miles. This effectually put a stop to one of the worst features of camp life under which the non-criminal element had suffered. Many times I was told by our trusties that under Kaindl's administration prisoners said that, in comparison with the past, the camp was more like a sanatorium (Erholungsheim) than a concentration camp.

In our building everything was being repainted and redecorated and I heard wonderful stories about cells of which the walls were distempered in colour instead of the usual whitewash, and it was not long before Eccarius let out the secret that soon I should move to a much better cell on the front and sunny side of the building. It was even said that the new cells were comfortably furnished with large tables, arm-chairs, and beds with spring mattresses, so my guards and I were equally hopeful and excited. Then, on the 8th January Kriminalrat Clemens paid me another visit, and told me that he had been to Holland and had brought back with him all my belongings there which he had been able to find; everything would be sent on to me as soon as transport was available.

On the 25th January I heard that the German troops before Stalingrad had been cut off, and two days later I moved to my new cell, No. 43. What a difference! The walls were distempered with a rolled pattern of pink on a cream base; everything looked clean and fresh, and the sun was shining in brightly; after my cell with its dirty greyish walls and cold north light it seemed to me like a palace. My guards and I got to work bringing in all my possessions, and it was a real joy to arrange everything and take possession of my new home. Kaindl came in when we had just about finished our labours, and with him, Eccarius bringing a magnificent hydrangea in a pot, which was formally presented to me with good wishes for my happiness and for a speedy return home. When I moved into the new cell Eccarius had said that in future the door of my cell would have to be bolted, so I took the opportunity to ask the commandant what was the reason for this change. He did not seem to know anything about it, and when I told him that so far I had never been locked in, he asked Eccarius what the devil he meant by making changes without orders, and told him that he had better remember for the future that there was only one commandant in the camp, then, turning to me, he said: "Remember, Herr Best, if at any time there is anything you want to ask me you need only tell the head warder and I will be along right away."

I have never really understood what was Kaindl's motive in saying a thing like this for he must have known that he was placing a most formidable weapon in my hands, but I like to flatter myself that he realized that I should not be so stupid as to misuse it and, indeed, there was only one occasion after this when I actually asked for his help in a matter which concerned the behaviour of Eccarius. One day, some time later, I said to him: "Commandant, you treat me almost as though I were your deputy here." He twinkled at me for a moment through his big round glasses and said: "Ach, Herr Best, it seems to work all right so why need we define our relations in words."

Two days later I was called by Eccarius to the interrogation room, and found that two enormous bales had come for me which contained everything in the way of clothes which I possessed; most of them things which were not of the slightest use to me in prison. What was I to do with all the paraphernalia for formal afternoon and evening wear, with stiff white shirts and black silk socks? Things which I could have used, such as day shirts and thick tweeds, were not there, and indeed to this day their disappearance has remained a mystery. I collected a few things which I could use, gave some things as presents, and consigned the rest for safe keeping to the cloak room from which, as far as I was concerned, they never again emerged. The following day Grothe turned up bringing with him a suit-case of mine which did contain some articles which were to me of the greatest value. One was the typewriter on which I wrote this story, and the other my electric shaver.

Since the middle of 1940 we had enjoyed the amenity of a barbers' shop in the building, and every morning I went there to be shaved. Although this was a great improvement to shaving with the dull, wornout razor blades with which I had previously had to cope, I have for some reason always had a great dislike to being shaved by anyone else. In any case, I had for some time before the war become a convert to the use of an electric razor, and I do not think that anyone who has once mastered the art of using such an appliance would ever willingly return to the messy business of brush and shaving soap. From that day, until the end of my imprisonment, my morning ablutions became a pleasure and when later, under orders from above, I was forced to leave my cell for shelter during air raids, there were three things that I always took with me: the letters from my wife, my typewriter, and my electric shaver.

My life during 1943 and 1944 was really about as agreeable as any prisoner could desire, and gradually I lost all of the feeling of strain and anxiety of the previous three years. Letters from May reached me with very fair regularity and with the knowledge which they brought me that she was well and happy and had found good friends, I had really nothing to worry about.

When I took up residence in cell No. 43 my first delight was somewhat tempered by a terrific noise of hammering which went on day and night from the direction of the end of our passage, and it was not long before I heard that a suite consisting of sitting-room, three bedrooms, and lavatory was being constructed to accommodate some extremely distinguished visitors. One of the cells in question, No. 38, was the double cell which had previously housed Stevens and where, until a day or two previously, an English officer had been imprisoned about whom, all that I had succeeded in finding out, was that he was probably a general and wore a red hat. It was two years and more before I met him at Dachau and learnt to know him as Lieutenant-Colonel John McGrath, R.A. It soon became obvious that the new occupants of the No. 38 suite must be of superlative importance, for we heard of carpets being laid, of curtains to the windows, and pictures hung on the wall; special furniture too was brought in, civilian beds and upholstered easy-chairs. The access to the suite was blocked by brickwork and a real front door complete with bell and knocker. When building and refitting operations had been completed there was an official inspection by the Director of Concentration Camps, Obergruppenführer Pohle, and a few days later the new guests arrived and were christened by me 'The Bears' and their home, 'The Bear Pit', both names soon being used by everybody. Who they were and what the reason of their imprisonment I was never able to discover; all that my guards could find out was that the party consisted of a Roumanian prince, his secretary, and his valet.

At about the same time a considerable number of other distinguished strangers took up residence with us, amongst them several Frenchmen, said to be ex-ministers of the pre-occupation government. One of them I saw by chance at the barbers, when the warder on duty had carelessly omitted to find out whether it was disengaged, and I am practically certain that this gentleman was M. Mandel. More and more the atmosphere of the bunker became that of a select boarding house rather than that of a prison; instead of the groans and shrieks of tortured prisoners one heard obsequious warders hurrying to answer the call of cell bells, and the jingle of cups and saucers as the trusties carried dainty trays of food to one V.I.P. after another. Gone were the old aluminium bowls and mugs in which for the previous three years all our food had been served, and gleaming white plates, cups and saucers, and stainless steel cutlery was the order of the day. The dark cells which housed prisoners from the camp had been cleaned and redecorated, and the windows of those which faced my garden instead of being boarded up now had ground glass screens which, whilst admitting light and air, were designed to prevent the occupants from seeing V.I.P.s of the highest class, such as the Bears and myself, when we went out for exercise. There were, it is true, some slum quarters, mostly on the opposite side of my own passage, which were occupied by SS prisoners awaiting trial for serious offences; generally for stealing gold, but they were a quiet, well-behaved lot, and their presence was hardly noticeable except when morning and evening they went with their well-closed sanitary pails to the lavatory, and at meal times when they drew their rations.

Prisoners fell into three main groups; those who were permitted to see each other but not to talk together, those who during exercise and when visiting the lavatory could associate freely, and those, like myself, who were segregated from all association with other prisoners. The first class took their exercise together, but under supervision of guards had to march round and round separated from each other by an interval of some twelve feet, instead of being permitted to pass their hour of freedom in the fresh air as they pleased. For the last category arrangements had to be made that their visits to garden and lavatory were solitary and unobserved. Luckily there were not more than about a dozen of us, and while the west garden was reserved for the Bears, Elser, and myself, the others had to take their turn in the east in the intervals between the mass exodus of the vulgar herd. Gradually, by dint of a little give and take, everything was sorted out and everyone had his fixed hours for the morning wash, for baths, and for exercise, and soon it was my task to prepare the roster required for the smooth running of the establishment. Naturally, I looked after myself first and so succeeded in arranging my hours of exercise to suit my own convenience and to give me the maximum amount of sunlight. I usually went out from ten-thirty to one in the morning, and in the summer again from 6 p.m. till bedtime; so far had I travelled since the days when my exercise was limited to one hour daily.

Although the whole building had been painted and decorated, and really everything looked bright and clean, there was one blemish which for over a year was a constant source of discomfort; a plague of cockroaches which infested the boiler room and lavatory. Although, of course, I had heard of these beasties it had so far never fallen to me to live with them and so I had no idea of the speed with which they multiplied, nor how all pervading they could become. I was lucky, for only an occasional bachelor wandered sufficiently far to reach my cell, but I know of others who lived closer to the main nursery whose life at night became an absolute torment through the mass infestation of their cells. My trouble was limited to the fact that before I could take a shower bath I had to spend some ten minutes washing a space clear on which I could stand, and that when on one occasion I wished to go to the lavatory at night I found on opening the door that the entire floor was so thickly carpeted with cockroaches that not an inch of it was uncovered. From that moment I also kept a pail in my cell.

Everything that could be thought of was done to combat the plague, but it was not until the lavatory and boiler room had their walls stripped of plaster and were then gassed for twenty-four hours that the attempts were crowned with victory.

The cockroach was not the only insect with which I became closely acquainted in prison for there was also the cricket. Probably through youthful memories of Charles Dickens I had always carried with me a certain sentimental regard for this animal, which I looked upon as a sort of domesticated grasshopper who imparted an air of old-world romance to the fireplaces in Elizabethan houses. In fact, I can remember as a child being told by some old lady that if I were a good little boy and would keep very still, the dear little cricket would come and sing to me. Well, there may be crickets whose chirps are of such dulcet tone that they are desirable housemates, but they must belong to a very different species from those who carried on their courting during the first two years of my stay at Sachsenhausen. These were obtrusive vulgarians who lived on the pipes of the central heating system along which they could travel as though they were broad motor roads. They were disgusting looking beasts, a dull grey colour and apparently about the shape and size of a medium frog, though they could pass without difficulty through the smallest crevice. The noise which they made was terrific and, since the whole building acted like a sounding board, I was forced every night to listen to the love songs of some hundreds of courting couples. Worse than this, for often some lovelorn male would sit on one of the pipes leading to the radiator of my cell and sing of his blighted affections the long night through; there would be pauses when I would hope that he had gone, but always, just as I was on the point of sleep, he would start his monotonous plaint anew.

Hofmann, the guard whom I mentioned earlier, became an enthusiastic cricket hunter and would crouch at night for hours at the foot of the radiator with cap in hand ready to knock off its perch any insect that ventured to leave the safety of its recess in the wall. Unfortunately, a cricket knocked to the ground was not a cricket killed for the beasts would not only run like greased lightning but as jumpers looked upon fleas as tiros. There would be a sudden burst of violent movement; the cricket jumping lightly and easily and Hofmann making ungainly leaps in his heavy jack boots, in vain endeavour at a synchronization which would bring his boots into contact with a cricket on the floor. Then I would make my protest at the disturbance, Hofmann would return to his chair, and the cricket soon sang with renewed vigour from the radiator. The cyanide gassing which protected us from typhus infection at the beginning of 1942 put an end to every cricket in the place, and as far as I am concerned, I shall be happy if I have heard their song for the last time.

My life during 1943 can best be described as comfortable monotony. I had become used to prison life and there was neither conscious impatience nor revolt, but throughout there must have been a deep subconscious resistance which ate constantly into my nerves and from whose effects I am not yet fully recovered. Imprisonment is such an affront to every human instinct that in its effects it causes just as severe a disability as the loss of an arm or a leg, for the memory of having been treated as an animal to be driven about and fettered or tethered at one's keeper's will is not one that time seems able to eradicate. I always fought hard to retain my sense of humour and to maintain a reasonable outlook on all matters connected with my daily life; I tried to make allowances for everything which seemed to me unnecessary or unjust and to make myself believe that I was even happy during the last years when my material circumstances could justly be considered comfortable, but somehow or other I feel almost more resentment in regard to this period than I do for the far worse years which preceded it when I was, in a measure, forced to fight for my very existence. The more one has the more one wants, and the more comfortable one is the more one is surrounded by temptation.

I was like someone suffering from an agonizing cancer of which the worst pain was dulled by the constant administration of hypnotics. The conditions of my life were really just about as comfortable as they could be in prison; my cell was bright, warm and comfortable; I had access to a very good library of some 6,000 books; my hours out of doors were restricted only by the arrangements made with Eccarius to permit other prisoners also to have a spell of fresh air; food was really excellent both in quantity and quality; I had as guards four men in whom I could place complete trust and to whom it seemed to be a pleasure to serve, and indeed spoil, me in every possible way. But I was too well off and events which took place outside my little realm gradually lost their reality for me, and like some monk my life was nothing more than existence governed by routine. I tried to make each day as much like its predecessor as possible, doing the same things at exactly the same minute day after day, for when they resembled each other closely enough they became as one and the sense of time was lost.

Letters from May were the only welcome interruptions in my even passage towards freedom or execution and when, as sometimes happened, several months passed without any reaching me life became an utter blank when I could neither eat, sleep, nor settle down to anything. Yet when the time came once a month when it was my turn to write, I experienced the greatest difficulty in making up my mind to make the breach in my accustomed routine and really get down to writing. My letters had to be artificial for I was not permitted to say anything which would convey any concrete idea of the actual circumstances of my life. I must not say where I was, that I was confined to a cell, or that my imprison-ment was solitary. I had to write cheerfully, for I did not want May to worry. Then too, all my letters had to be typed and written in German, which introduced another degree of unnatural restraint. I would read her letters over and over again trying to discover in them hidden meanings, just as she did with mine. Ours is a very happy marriage and never before had we been separated for more than a week at a time; even then, as we still do now, we wrote to each other every day and shared every incident and thought. There seemed no possible end to our separation; or, at all events, I was unable to imagine one and I often felt that I was enmeshed in a web from which there could be no escape.

I suffered neither from depression, boredom, nor self-pity, but my active participation in life was confined to the four walls of my prison and the present moment. I was always busy and, as I hope, apparently in the best of spirits; at all events the warders and my guards always came to me to tell of their troubles and never seemed to think that I had any of my own. I said that I was busy; indeed, the day always seemed too short for all that I had to do. Having managed to get hold of some tools I became watch and clock repairer; having learnt something of the art of leather work from my guard, Johann Braun, a saddler, I made purses, pocket books, and tobacco pouches, then there was the mending of my clothes often involving ambitious alterations and reconstructions; as I succeeded in obtaining books on the subject I devoted more and more of my time to exploration of the realm of higher mathematics—I really got to the point when I understood quite a bit though I seem to have forgotten it all now.

Gradually I took over the garden, buying my own seeds and plants, laying out paths, and planning my circumscribed landscape to my pleasure. Previously I had never taken the slightest interest in gardening and had, indeed, looked upon those who could find no better way of spending their leisure than digging and weeding with a certain contempt. Then I discovered how delightful it is to prepare the ground, to sow tiny seeds, watch them sprout and tend their growth fending off all approach of inimical weeds. It seems that I have green fingers, for whatever I planted grew and flourished even on the bare sand of a prison yard. The ground was in fact pure sea sand and manure was unobtainable. Paul, though, had a bright idea. He heard that at the beginning of 1943 Kaindl had given orders that all the straw mattresses in the camp were to be refilled with clean straw; something which had probably not taken place since the camp was first opened. Well, Paul managed to lay hands on the filthy stinking straw which came out of these mattresses and this we dug in two spits deep and, as for the result, stable manure simply wasn't in it. Then I got hold of a big water vat into which the contents of the prisoners buckets were emptied and after this had stood and weathered for some time it gave me a supply of liquid manure which was so appreciated by my tomato plants that they gave me seventy and more fruits each.

In the main I grew vegetables, for only on this condition could I have run the garden, but on certain beds and along the edge of others I found plenty of room for flowers and, to my eyes at least, my garden was very beautiful. At first I had a little difficulty about the disposal of my harvest as, according to regulations, this had to be turned over to the camp kitchen, but in the end Kaindl allowed me to deal with it as I liked so that I could give my guards such things as potatoes and cabbages and distribute the more dainty produce such as tomatoes, cucumbers, and radishes as an addition to the diet of the other prisoners in the building. Of course, when I say that I did all this I am scarcely being fair to my guards who not only gave me advice and taught me the primary elements of the craft, but also took much of the hardest work off my shoulders; indeed, they became such keen gardeners that it was sometimes difficult to prevent them from doing all the work.

When I moved from Wing C to Wing B, I was translated into another and much more interesting environment, for most of the more prominent prisoners were housed on Wings A and B, down both of which I could look and, on occasion, catch fleeting glimpses of fellow prisoners. There was one, No. 7, who had the freedom of the house and was never locked in his cell. He was a tall, thin, white-haired man of feeble gait whom I had at first put down as nearly eighty years of age, though later on I learnt that he was only forty-eight. He was a Dr. Luther and had held a fairly high post at the Foreign Office with the rank of Brigadeführer in the SS. One day he had had the temerity to query some items in an expense account of Ribbentrop's and had been consigned to the Bunker as what was called an Ehrenhäftling (honourable prisoner) to meditate on his sins. At first he was always assuring everyone that he was only 'in' for a short spell and orders would soon come for his release, but time went on and no one came near him. One of his sons fell in action and the other was taken prisoner at Stalingrad; his house in Berlin was destroyed by bombs and his wife became a nervous wreck. Gradually, he too, after one or two vain attempts at suicide became the ghostly aged man whom I came to know so well, who wandered about the passages, noticing no one, and engaged in interminable conversation with himself.

In the cells next to mine there was in No. 44 a Lettish ex-minister and in No. 42 a French Roman Catholic bishop, both of whom took their exercise in front of my window. The first had been taken prisoner during the German advance because of his supposed communist opinions, whilst his wife, parents and children had been 'transferred' by the Russians. I have never seen a man who wore such a look of hopeless desperation. He had an insatiable appetite and although the trusties always gave him especially large helpings, if he saw me looking out of the window he always made signs pointing to his mouth and his stomach. I often put some cheese or other food on my window-sill which he took with every sign of gratitude. No. 42's trouble was lack of smokes for he was rationed to three cigarettes a day. He would start his exercise with one cigarette in his mouth and the other two held between his fingers, ready to light when the first was finished. He was not, of course, allowed to have matches, but I managed to throw some to him and later gave him a tinder lighter. I then threw him lighted cigarettes to smoke during his exercise so that he could save his own to smoke surreptitiously in his cell. Both men vanished after a few months and what happened to them I do not know; after they left none of the prisoners took their exercise where I could see them except a young lad in uniform whom I later discovered to be a Russian flying officer and a nephew of Mr. Molotov. At a later stage I was to get to know him very well, though even while we were in the Bunker we became in a way friends without ever having spoken to each other.

On several occasions when one of my guards was away unexpectedly, owing to illness or because of some casualty in his family, one of the men doing duty with Georg Elser in Cell No. 13 would come to me for a time. Most of Elser's guards were youngish men, and it was not long before I had made friends with some of them and so established a link with my fellow prisoner in whom I was deeply interested owing to the manner in which our names had been associated in the German Press. He was not at all popular with his guards for he went out of his way to make their duty as difficult as possible by causing them all manner of petty annoyances and in particular robbing them of opportunities to rest during their off-duty hours. Unlike my guards who had a cell of their own, where they slept and to which they could retire when off duty, his men simply had a bed in his cell on which one could rest while two of them were supposed to be awake and on guard day and night. Obviously, they got little undisturbed sleep at night and wished to make up for it by day, but this Elser would not allow, and as soon as one of them lay down to rest he would at once begin to hammer, saw, or do other work which occasioned the maximum of noise. At one time he even did this at night but other prisoners objected and it was stopped.

Of course if Elser himself wished to sleep his guards had to be still as mice, as if anything or anyone annoyed him he promptly went on hunger strike. Orders had apparently been given that he was to be kept in safety and in good health, and as he was far from robust his failure to eat had to be reported to the commandant with trouble for all concerned. In some respects his guards were quite fond of him as he could be very good company if he liked, but he was firmly convinced that he was doomed to execution and took pleasure in, as it were, daring people to get on with it.

It was a puzzle to everyone why he had never been brought to trial, and what was behind his story that he had planted the bomb in the Bürgerbraukeller at my behest, and that I had bribed him to do this by a promise of forty thousand Swiss francs. He told this story to all his guards though none of them who knew me believed a word of it, and I had never noticed anything since my arrival at Sachsenhausen which indicated that I was suspected of collaboration in an attempt on Hitler's life, so the whole business was very much of a mystery to me. Why should this little German workman who had been pilloried in the Press as a traitor, who had not only attempted to assassinate Hitler, but had also caused the death of a number of his associates be treated as one of the most privileged prisoners in the building?

Like myself, Elser was a chain smoker. After a bad attack of bronchitis he was for some time limited, on doctor's orders, to three cigarettes a day, and as I was then in enjoyment of almost unlimited supplies of tobacco I often sent him presents of cigarette paper and tobacco through one of his guards. In return he made various things for me, a parallel ruler, a darning mushroom, etc., and gradually he seemed to form a sort of affection for me and to look upon me as his friend. At the end of March 1943 Eccarius brought me some bookshelves for which I had asked and as these lacked a flat top which I needed for my big Stieler's Atlas I arranged with him that Elser should make one. When I came in from exercise a few days later I found that this had been done and that I had now a space where my atlas could lie open for ready reference. I was surprised though to find that the shelf which Elser had made did not seem to be quite true but was inclined to wobble, so I took it off and immediately noticed that there was some tightly folded paper wedged under one side which, when I opened it, turned out to be a long and closely written letter. In this Elser gave me an account of his early life and the main events leading to the so-called 'Bürgerbraukeller Bomb Plot' of 8th November, 1939, and his adventures since that date.

The letter was badly worded, the writing was minute and very difficult to read, as he had used an indelible pencil which was rather faint, but when I succeeded in making out most of what he had written I was astounded and deeply interested. This was only the first of many letters which we were able to exchange during the following twelve months as one of the trusties agreed to help us. During this time I did everything I could to obtain all the information possible from Elser, and I believe that the following account is as close to the true facts as we shall ever be able to get. Several people have written about this matter before but I can safely say that no one besides myself heard the story from the

Self portrait by Marie 'May' Payne Best, the author's wife.

I was in a car with an extremely nice officer in uniform (Hauptmann) the same Tho, in mufti, had lead the raiding party which captured us. He told me that Klop was not badly wounded, a shot through the arm & a glancing shot on the head, and that he had recovered consciousness. Many months later Grothe told me that Klop's wounds had proved much more serious than was at first thought & that he was then still seriously ill. I was not allowed to wear my glasses. Smoking was also forbidden but the officer very kindly gave me two or three cigarettes. Although a halt was made for lunch no food was provided for me, but after we had got going again the officer gave me two apples.

We were quite a procession of cars going to Berlin. Stevens & Lemmens were presumably each in separate cars & then my own car also came

along with us. We arrived at Berlin after dark & when we reached the Gestapo H.Q. it was black night. We drove into a sort of courtyard & when we stopped a voice asked whether I was handcuffed & whether my feet were free. Then some one tore off my hat and thrust a sort of sack of black stuff over my head. I was then seized by two men & roughly dragged out of the car which, as I was still handcuffed was rather a painful operation, wrenching my wrists badly. I was then marched by these two men, each holding me by the wrist into a building & upstairs & downstairs and along long passages until, owing to the obstruction to breathing occasioned by the hood over my head, I was quite breathless. At last I was taken into a brightly lighted room & was pushed on to a soft seat - that I later found was a sofa. Then my feet were tightly strapped together & a voice

Pages from one of the author's diaries, showing part of an account of his capture written about a month later.

said: "you can remove the hood". It took me some time to recover my wind as I was completely pumped. In the meantime I look round & took note of my surroundings. I sat on a sofa & next to me a very tall man - later one of my guards. There was also present another man (Hoffmann) who remained with me as guard. Sitting on a chair opposite me was an extremely intelligent looking man of sympathetic appearance & manner (Dr Max Schönbacher) & next to him, sitting at a table with type-writer, a stoutish middle aged woman — Frau Rudolf. Also in the room was a fat man in jersey & trousers of prize fighter type who was apparently one of the two men who had dragged me from the car and up & down the stairs. He was, as I later discovered the head jailor of the H.Q. prison & really a most pleasant creature - we became quite

good friends during the course of my stay at H.Q.

The room in which I found myself (No 315) was apparently someone's private office which had been prepared for my reception by the addition of a bedstead to its normal equipment. Immediately I had recovered my breath I made violent protest to Dr Max as to the way in which I had been treated since I had left the car and the fact that I had been fettered. Dr Max obviously felt the justice of my complaint & did not like the situation. He said in defence that they had only taken a leaf out of Scotland Yard's book and, as beginners, had copied English practice. I strongly protested against the suggestion that such behaviour was possible in England & then put that was: that my fetters were removed on the understanding that I would neither attempt suicide nor escape.

chief actor himself, whilst information which I later received from other sources all tended to bear out the truth of what Elser told me.

He was born in Munich and when he was quite small his mother died in giving birth to a dead sister, and his father was killed in action shortly afterwards. An uncle, the only relative of whom he had ever heard, a railway guard and a childless widower, had taken charge of him and brought him up in a rough and ready fashion. Young Elser must have run pretty wild for he had one or two clashes with the police which nearly ended in his being sent to the German equivalent of a Borstal establishment. He seems though, to have given evidence at school of having brains above the average and one of the masters, the only person of whom he wrote with any affection, helped him to escape punishment. This man seems to have been the teacher of handicrafts and endeavoured to induce Elser to continue his studies after he left school at a technical college.

When he was fifteen or sixteen his uncle died leaving him only a small sum, quite insufficient to pay for further schooling, and he was placed in charge of the Munich municipal children's officer. He was apprenticed to a joiner who took him to live in his house and generally acted as his guardian. Here too, his insubordination was a frequent cause of trouble but his intelligence and aptitude for his work soon made him a valuable assistant and after the end of his apprenticeship his master tried to induce him to remain in his service. As soon though as young Elser was free, nothing would hold him and with his tools and other few possessions in a bag on his back he set off on the traditional wanderings of the German journeyman.

His travels took him through most of south Germany and even into Switzerland and at first he had little trouble in finding work. For a time he said, he had a responsible job as model maker at one of the biggest Bavarian engineering firms, the manufacturers of the B.M.W. cars, but from what he wrote, all his jobs seemed to end with a row with his immediate superiors and in the autumn of 1937 he found himself back in Munich without a penny in his pocket, his tools sold or pawned, and with but faint hope of finding further employment. By that time the Nazis had such a firm grip on all matters connected with labour organization that it was practically impossible for a man who would not at least pay lip service to the party to obtain employment; above all things, Elser hated the Nazis. As was natural under the circumstances he drifted into the society of other out-of-works like himself and got mixed up with a band of Communists. Somehow or other these men were always able to get hold of funds and although he never joined their party, he did help in the printing and distribution of leaflets and so was tacitly accepted as one of the group. He really enjoyed this life with its element of danger and the feeling that he was

I

actively engaged in a fight against authority, and all went well until one evening the café where he and his friends used to congregate was surrounded in a police raid, and the whole lot of them were bundled into a police van and taken to the 'station'. Although no definite evidence was found against any of them, as none was usefully employed, they were labelled 'anti-social and work-shy' and taken off to the concentration camp at Dachau for re-education.

The first months which Elser spent here always remained for him the most horrible experience of his life. Not, as far as I could gather, because of any ill-treatment which he suffered, nor because of atrocities which he witnessed, but merely because for the first time in his life he felt the full naked force of irresponsible authority which crushed out every trace of individuality and illusion of freedom. At first he had to labour with pick and shovel like all other newcomers, but very soon his talent as a carpenter and joiner was discovered and he was set to work in the camp furniture-making factory.

Elser was very far from being of the ordinary run of workmen for he was really something of an artist who worked best from his own designs. I was often shown cabinets and other articles of furniture which he made at Sachsenhausen for the commandant and the warders, and really I have never seen their like except in museums. Amongst other things, while he was at Sachsenhausen he made a full-sized lathe cutting all gears and making all parts by hand; I also saw a length of chain that he made cut out of a single rod of wood with every link as perfectly finished as if it had been machine made from metal.

He had not been long employed in the Dachau carpenter's shop before something attracted the commandant's attention to his work, and from then on he was exclusively employed in making articles of furniture for him and his friends. As time passed he was granted many privileges including freedom from attendance at the morning and evening roll calls and eventually he was put on the SS ration strength and so received good food as well. I imagine that while he had work he was about as happy as it was his nature to be, though in his letters he kept saying how much he had hated his life at Dachau and how intense was his longing for freedom. As far as I could make out, freedom for him meant 'girls', for he was a man who suffered intensely from the forced continence of prison.

One day early in October 1939 he was called to the Kommandantur where he was interviewed by two men who asked him a number of questions about his antecedents, and in particular about the names of former associates and relations. As for the latter he had none as far as he knew and friends, well he knew them as Paul, Heinz, or Karl, just as they knew him as the little Georg—surnames were not much used in the circles he had frequented.

A week or two later he was again called for and again met the same two men. On the first occasion he had been questioned while standing at attention, but this time he was taken into another office, was told to sit down, and was given a cigarette. The men were extremely friendly, told him that the commandant had shown them some of his work and that really it was a shame that so good a workman should be wasting his life in a concentration camp. Would he not like to regain his freedom? To this suggestion Elser expressed cordial agreement. Well, this could easily be arranged if he would only be absolutely discreet and obey orders without question; all that they wanted from him was that he should do a little job in his own line, and when this was finished he would be handsomely rewarded and sent to Switzerland where he would be free to live as he liked and hold whatever opinions he pleased. As Elser put it: "What else could I do but say yes. If I had refused, I should certainly have gone up the chimney that evening." This was the expression used by the inmates of concentration camps to describe the process of execution and cremation.

I do not know whether it was on this or on a later occasion that he was told the story of a plot against Hitler in which some of his closest associates were involved. Hitler was to speak at the Bürgerbraukeller in Munich on 8th November in commemoration of his comrades who fell during the 1923 Putsch, when he made his first attempt to overthrow the government. After Hitler had finished speaking it was his custom to stay a while talking to his old associates, and certain scoundrelly traitors had conceived the plan of hustling him to one side and shooting him. Although the names of the people involved in the plot were known it was not considered advisable to arrest them, as this would occasion a big scandal which, now, in war-time, must be avoided, and it was therefore intended to adopt other measures to liquidate the traitors. The idea was to build an infernal machine in one of the pillars in the cellar which could be exploded immediately the Führer left the building, which he would do directly his speech was finished; in this way all the conspirators would be exterminated, lock, stock, and barrel, and no one need hear anything more about their plot.

Elser was not such a fool really to believe that after he had been told so much he would be set free or even left alive, but since it was a question of certain immediate death or liquidation at some uncertain future date, he naturally promised to do what was required of him.

After this interview Elser was not allowed to return to his old quarters in the camp, but was put in a comfortable cell in a building used to house important political prisoners. Here, instead of his striped prison garb, he was given civilian clothes, and he was also brought good food and as many cigarettes as he wished. Next day, as he expressed a desire to finish some work which he had on hand, a carpenters' bench was brought to a large cell in the building and he was given his tools.

In the first week of November 1939 Elser was on two occasions fetched at nightfall by the same two men and taken by car to the Bürgerbraukeller where he was shown the pillar into which the bomb was to be built. This pillar was covered with an ornamental wood panelling over bricks, so all that he had to do was remove part of the panelling and extract a couple of bricks. Into the recess thus formed, he inserted the explosive, which was of a putty-like nature, the inside of an alarm clock, and a fuse. From the fuse he was instructed to make an electric lead to a push button in an alcove near the street level entrance to the building. The whole job was to him mere child's play and he was at a loss to understand why such a fuss had been made about it.

I took a great deal of trouble to get from Elser the clearest possible description of the bomb, and from what he wrote it was quite clear that the clock, which he called an ordinary Swiss alarm, had nothing to do with the fuse which could only be actuated by electric current applied from outside.

Elser's comfortable life at Dachau continued for yet a few days; he had been told that he would have to wait for his release until it had been proved that he had carried out his task properly. He was not afraid of any failure here, though he had little faith in the promise made him of freedom and reward.

On the 9th or 10th November the two men called for him again and when he got into a car which was waiting, they told him that he was now on the way to Switzerland and a life of liberty. They took the road leading to the Swiss frontier near Bregenz at the eastern end of the Lake of Constance which Elser knew well since for a time he had worked at St. Gallen just across the frontier, so at all events he could check the direction of his journey. When they reached a point about a quarter of a mile from the frontier customs post the car stopped and he was told that he would have to make his way farther on foot. He was handed an envelope which, as far as he could see, contained a large sum in German and Swiss notes; he was also given a picture postcard which illustrated the Bürgerbraukeller and on which the pillar into which he had built the bomb was marked with a cross. He was told that if he showed this to the frontier guards they would know who he was and would let him through without asking him for his papers; everything had been arranged.

He did as he was told, but neither frontier guard nor customs seemed to know anything about him or to understand the meaning of the postcard. He was asked a lot of questions and, as he had no passport or other papers, he was searched. The envelope containing the money was found and he was immediately marched off and put into jail on a charge of currency smuggling. Presumably, if the pretended ignorance of the men at the frontier was real, someone who saw the marked postcard became suspicious and, having heard of the bomb outrage at Munich, reported the arrest of Elser to a higher quarter. Anyhow, next day Elser was taken, handcuffed and heavily guarded, by prison van to an airfield and flown to Berlin. On arrival, still handcuffed, he was put into a cell and later was interrogated, being badly beaten up in the process. He was, however, wise, and said nothing about the trick which had resulted in his capture. He admitted that he had built the bomb into the pillar, but denied that he had had accomplices, stating that his action was the result of his own political opinions and his hatred of Nazi domination. His interrogation continued until deep into the night, but nothing more could be got out of him.

Next morning he was taken by lift to one of the upper floors where, in a room to which the jailer took him, he found the two men with whom all his previous arrangements had been made. They were most friendly and sympathetic and told him that his arrest at the frontier was entirely due to the unfortunate fact that the guard who had instructions to let him through had suddenly been taken ill and was therefore not on duty when he reached the frontier; he was not to worry though, everything would come all right in the end. Unfortunately, he could not be liberated at once as his photograph had been circulated to the police throughout the country and had also appeared in the Press; everyone thought that he had been guilty of an attempt on the Führer's life, and if he were to show his nose anywhere he would simply be torn to pieces for, as he could well imagine, everyone in Germany was overcome with fury at the dastardly outrage which had so nearly succeeded. For the time being he would have to remain safely under cover but he need fear no more ill-treatment, everything possible would be done to make him comfortable, and as soon as the first excitement had blown over steps would be taken to get him to Switzerland as had been promised. He was then taken to a big room on the top floor of the building which, as he later discovered was the Gestapo Headquarters in the Prinz Albrechtstrasse, where he found a bed, a carpenter's bench and the tools which he had used at Dachau. Two men remained with him as guards and from that moment he was never left alone for a moment. He was not, however, interfered with and was well fed; having been given suitable wood he set to work and made himself a zither; he could not play it but it had always been his ambition to learn.

He remained here undisturbed for about a fortnight when he was again visited by his two friends who took him down to one of the corridors where he was told to sit on a bench. He was told that an Englishman would be brought along past him, and he must look at him carefully so that he would be sure to recognize him if he saw him again. A tall dark man followed by two others passed him twice, apparently on his way to and from the lavatory. A few days later he was taken to the same place again and shown the same man. After this he was taken to an office where there was a high-ranking officer of the SS in uniform and another man, obviously an ex-student, as his face was covered with duelling scars. This man now talked to him and asked him whether he understood that his life was forfeit, and that he was nothing more than a candidate for death. This phrase was often used. He had already admitted to the police that he had built the bomb into the pillar of the cellar, and the whole German people was eagerly awaiting news of his trial and execution. He had, however, been promised life and freedom and the Gestapo always kept its word; he must though do something more to earn his security. He was then told the following story:

The German Army had already proved in Poland that it was invincible, and nothing now could save England from defeat. When that country was occupied by the victorious German Army he would have to appear as witness at a trial of the British Secret Service chiefs who, as all the world knew, were a gang of murderers and gangsters, and through their false information were really responsible for the whole war. At this trial one of the chief defendants would be the Englishman whom he had just seen; a certain Captain Best who had been captured a short time ago while attempting to leave Germany where he had been spying.

Elser would have to declare at the trial that for a long time he had been in relation with Otto Strasser in Switzerland and had acted for him as courier to and from Germany. In December 1938, Strasser had called him to Zürich where, at the Hotel Bauer au Lac, he had introduced him to the Englishman Best, telling him that in future he wished him to work for the British who were determined to get rid of Hitler and who could certainly do more than he could himself. Elser was therefore to take his orders from Captain Best who lived in Holland, and arrangements were made so that they could communicate with each other via the Dutch frontier. The Englishman handed Elser a thousand Swiss francs in notes as earnest money.

During the months that followed he had maintained regular contact with Captain Best, and had acted as courier between him and other agents in Germany; in this way the British Intelligence had received valuable information regarding German rearmament, and for his work he had been very well paid. In October 1939 he had met Captain Best at a place in Holland called Venlo, and there he had been given instructions about planting a bomb in the Bürgerbräukeller at Munich with the promise that if he did so he would receive a sum of 40,000 Swiss francs as reward. At first he had refused to have anything to do with this but Best put pressure on him and left him no choice but to do as he was told

or be denounced to the Gestapo as a British agent. In the end
he had agreed to do what was required of him and he was given
an address in Germany where he would receive his final instructions
and be given the infernal machine. He was then to tell in his
evidence how he went to the Bürgerbraukeller some four weeks
before the date fixed for the explosion and had little difficulty in
concealing himself there so that he could do his work during the
night. He built the bomb into one of the pillars as he had been
instructed, but did not wind up the clock which actuated the fuse
as this could only be set to work a maximum of ten days later.
He was therefore obliged to pay a second visit to the cellar at the
end of October in order to wind and set the clock. He had no
difficulty in doing so as he went in the afternoon when the place
was quite deserted.

Elser was given a typewritten copy of this story which contained a lot of further details about the work he was supposed to
have done for Strasser and me, and this he was told to learn by
heart. Subsequently he was several times examined to see whether
he was word perfect.

The story certainly seemed very strange and really I was unable
at that time to make head or tail of it. What on earth was the
object of a fictitious attempt to assassinate Hitler which resulted,
from what I had heard, in the death of quite a number of the
people who came to hear his speech? I could have understood if
it had been followed by a purge in the party such as took place
in June 1934, but as a matter of fact very little publicity seemed
to have been given to the whole thing in the German Press, and
although I had seen illustrated papers in which the photographs
of Stevens and myself were placed next to that of Elser nothing
which occurred during my interrogation, except a few questions
to establish that I had visited Switzerland in December 1938, tied
up with Elser's story in any way. To go to all this trouble merely
to bring an accusation against me seemed very much a case of
using a whale to catch a sprat. Anyhow, in spite of repeated
inquiries, Elser could tell me nothing more, and so I had to leave
it at that.

Until Kaindl came as commandant Elser had always been
provided with plenty of good wood, as he was constantly employed
making articles of furniture for the commandant and for the
warders, and the latter could always abstract any special wood
which was needed from the commandant's private store in the
wood sheds in my garden. Kaindl, however, put a stop to all this
and all that he allowed Elser was some deal and other inferior
timber. Elser too, had been promised by the previous commandant
that he should have an electric motor for the operation of the
lathe which he had made, but this was also turned down by
Kaindl. As a result, life became purposeless to Elser who gradually

sank into a state of profound depression, refusing to take any exercise
and eating hardly enough to keep body and soul together. Early
in 1944 Obergruppenführer Müller came to see him and, seeing
how ill he looked, gave instructions that he was to be given sufficient
wood to keep him occupied, and also arranged that he should be
permitted to visit the camp brothel twice weekly.

I only saw Elser once, to my knowledge, for I did not notice
him at all on the occasions when he said I passed close to him at
Gestapo Headquarters. One day while I was having a shower in
the lavatory he suddenly rushed in followed by two extremely
agitated guards to whom he had given the slip; he later let me
know that he had wanted to make sure whether I was indeed the
same person he had seen at Berlin. He was a thin, pallid little
fellow with very bright eyes and a shock of unbrushed dark hair;
his clothes hung loosely upon him as though he had lost a lot of
flesh.

At the end of August 1944 his guards were taken from him,
and thenceforward he was locked in alone in his cell. At the
beginning of February 1945 I heard that he had suddenly received
orders to pack up and had been taken away, whether to some other
place or for execution no one could say.

CHAPTER VII

FOR me, the highlights in 1943, apart from increasing good news
of the progress of the war, were a visit to an oculist in Berlin and
the receipt of a wireless set, both of which events occurred within
a few days of each other in July.

Quite a number of people, including Elser and the Bears, had
wireless sets in their cells, but I never liked asking for anything
and so had not been given one. At the beginning of July, though,
a number of loudspeakers were erected all over the camp and I
was again in the unfortunate position of receiving the noise from
two different sources which failed to synchronize. I therefore asked
the commandant whether I could perhaps have a set so that I
could at least have some means of drowning the noise of these
loudspeakers which was really driving me frantic. At the same time
I mentioned that my sight was getting so bad that I could scarcely
read, a perfectly normal development at my age. He promised to
attend to both matters and sure enough on 28th July Eccarius
brought a really magnificent looking set. Other prisoners I knew
had only the small so-called 'People's Receivers', sets with which
reception of local stations only could be obtained. Eccarius warned
me that I must on no account attempt to listen to any foreign

broadcasts and also that I must not tamper with the set, the back of which was sealed. I fixed up a length of wire to act as an indoor aerial and found that although I got good reception on long and medium waves the short waveband was dead.

Of course I broke the seals and the same evening investigated the source of this trouble. I discovered that the short-wave coil had been bent so that it was shorted and very soon put this to rights. It would have been quite impossible for me to have attempted to listen in to English broadcasts on the medium or long waves, as these were jammed by a wailing note sent out from Berlin which was far louder than the reception from the English station; anyone trying to listen to the B.B.C. could not fail to let the whole neighbourhood know that he was doing so. The short waveband was a different proposition and to my delight that same evening at 10.30 p.m. I got clear reception of the B.B.C. German broadcast on the forty-nine metre band. For nearly four years I had been cut off from direct immediate contact with my own country, and deprived of news of what was happening there, for May's letters reached me with a delay of five to six weeks and, of course, she could write of none of the things which I wanted to know; so perhaps it will be understood what my wireless meant to me.

Two days later Grothe turned up to take me to an oculist in Berlin. He had a car with a driver and another man whom I had met before in Berlin and who had always been very pleasant. They had come far earlier than needed so as to lengthen for me this brief glimpse of freedom, and on our way they stopped the car in a small wood so that we could go for a walk there. I have never seen the world look so beautiful. It was wonderful to see girls in light summer frocks tripping along the road, indeed, to see people of any kind not dressed in uniform. It was a beautiful, hot day, and the air seemed to me scented with summer flowers, so totally different to the vitiated air of the camp. Grothe parked the car by the side of the road and we went for a walk in some woods—everything seemed so lovely that it drew tears to my eyes, and I could hardly bear the thought that very soon I must leave it all and return to my cage. I saw little of destruction on the road we took nor indeed, at Spandau, the suburb of Berlin where the oculist lived. The oculist was an unpleasant fellow, dressed in the uniform of an SS captain and very military in his manners. He examined my eyes and gave me a prescription which, owing to his writing a plus instead of a minus turned out to be useless. Eventually, I went to see one of the prison doctors, a Paris oculist, who put things right.

This man told me that he was on his feet from 5 a.m. till 10 p.m. almost without a break, for he was the only oculist in the camp. He asked me how old I thought he was; he looked at least seventy-five, but to encourage him I said sixty-five. It turned out that that day was his fifty-first birthday. Although there was an official SS camp doctor, his duties were confined to supervision, and the prisoners were attended by doctors who like themselves were also prisoners. The equipment of the camp hospital was first class and the SS doctors generally gave their prisoner colleagues every assistance and support, but their numbers were never enough to give really adequate attention to all the sick amongst the large population which inhabited the camp; phthisis was rampant at all times but nothing could be done for sufferers from this disease. Life in a concentration camp was always horrible, but it was not impossible for those who had the stamina to stand up to it, and there were thousands of men who had endured this life for ten years or more and looked little the worse for it.

My greatest sympathy always went to those prisoners who through some physical weakness, or lack of a certain hard streak in their characters, were destined to pass to the oblivion of the camp crematorium, just numbers struck off a list. It is a funny thing that one should have this innate dislike for unrecorded death as though, however insignificant one's life, one wished to make one last bid for recognition. I have always been so busy living that I have never troubled to think much of death beyond accepting it as inevitable. In prison I was often so close to it that I could not help sometimes considering my own attitude towards any sudden demise, and came to the conclusion that for myself I did not really care one way or the other except in so far as my death would affect my wife; my strongest feeling was the wish to be able to let her know what had happened and to assure her that there was no cause for sorrow or pity. After all, we had been separated for some years and whether this separation continued only for a limited time or for ever was really immaterial; yet I did not like the idea of dying merely as Herr Wolf, or as No. 43, so that possibly at the end of the war nothing would ever be found out about my end and I should merely join the ranks of the 'missing'.

As regards my material circumstances, I was really not to be pitied, for I was better fed and better housed than thousands in England, and I escaped all the hardships and dangers of war. It must not be thought because I write about my imprisonment that it is an incident of which I am in any way proud or that I am seeking sympathy. All that I am trying to do is to give a truthful account of my experiences which were in a measure unusual owing to the length of time that I was deprived intercourse with my fellows and so thrown entirely on my own resources. I had read many stories of imprisonment, but none of them seemed to me to convey any clear idea of the need for readjustment with which I found myself faced after my capture, nor gave me any hint how this was to be accomplished. I had to work out everything for myself by trial and error, and so achieved a vast improvement in my material circumstances, only to discover that this meant nothing to me in the end, since without freedom everything else was valueless.

My cell in 1943 and 1944 made a very different picture to that in the previous years. The walls were a soft pinkish shade and on them hung two self portraits that May had painted and sent me, and a sketch of the farmhouse where she was living at Chagford. These had been framed, very nicely too, at the camp workshops. On the right as one entered was the small table at which my guard sat, and next to it my own large table with my wooden arm-chair. On the left of the table was my wireless set, before me my type-writer, books, papers, or whatever else engaged my attention. On my right stood a table lamp, a most valuable acquisition since its light could be properly shaded at night so that I could be in dark-ness whilst my guard could still see to read. On a stool to my left stood my electric cooker for which Elser had made me an asbestos-lined cover which enabled me to keep food warm for long periods. Next to the table was a large double wardrobe which contained not only my clothes, but in a special glass-lined cupboard, my reserves of provisions. On the other side of the cell came first the radiator and next to this a three-shelved bookcase with on top of it my large atlas. Then came my bed, in the daytime covered with a rug and with a large blanket-covered bolster which I had made, against which I could lean if I wished to lie on my bed and read. The tables and stools were all covered with blue and white checked covers, I usually had a bowl of flowers or a growing plant so that, especially in summer with wide open window, the general effect was bright and cheerful.

Until the middle of 1943, whenever I wanted anything I had to ask Eccarius who, if he felt so inclined, might get it for· me. He entered up the cost in a cash book which I had to sign. In July of that year I was told that in future I was to receive officer's pay at the rate of ninety-six marks (£10) per month, and that I was free to buy anything I wanted either at the canteen or, through my guards, in Berlin or elsewhere. I was particularly told that no restrictions were placed on what I might buy except that I must enter every purchase in an account book which would be open to inspection. As regards anything in the way of drink which I needed from the canteen, I was not, like the SS, subject to ration but could buy any quantity I liked. Eccarius was a thirsty soul, and when he told me this I could see from the gleam in his eyes that he felt there were happy days ahead and indeed, I did not disappoint him.

The food was excellent, and as I received double SS rations, more than ample. Through a wangle with the doctor I had got them divided into one ordinary military ration and one so-called special diet which entitled me to eggs, milk puddings and an extra butter allowance. Breakfast consisted of *ersatz* coffee with butter, jam, or margarine, and the weekly ration of the two former was so liberal that I never once ate margarine during my stay at Sachsenhausen. The midday meal consisted, except on two days when 'Eintopf', a sort of Irish stew, was obligatory for everyone in Germany, of soup, meat with potatoes and some green vegetable, and either a sweet or fruit. For the evening meal there was again butter or margarine with sausage, tinned fish, cheese, or something similar; once a week there was generally a hot supper such as sausages and mashed. In the evening I received my bread ration for the next twenty-four hours, which consisted of a loaf and a quarter of excellent wheaten white bread weighing nearly $2\frac{1}{2}$ lb. At the midday and evening meal I also received a quart of some milk pudding or three or four fried eggs. Of such things as sausage or cheese my double ration had a weight of $\frac{1}{2}$ lb. or more and, for instance, I often received two whole Camembert cheeses, or two tins of pilchards. Besides this, there were many extras such as sweets, oranges, lemons, strawberries, caviare and other specialities of the occupied territories. To drink I could buy wine, beer, and spirits, though for my own use I bought by preference a quart of very good skimmed milk daily.

I am a small eater so that with my extra food I could supplement that of my guards, two of whom had insatiable appetites, and my alcoholic beverages were in great demand with Eccarius who was only happy when drunk. For a warder to accept presents from a prisoner was punishable with death, so Eccarius was very much under my thumb which was just as it should be. The important thing was that nothing that happened should be reported. I feel pretty sure that had the commandant come into my cell one day and found me listening to a B.B.C. broadcast he would have said nothing and behaved as though he had not noticed. If, however, some chance passer-by had heard one of these broadcasts through the window of my cell and had reported this to Eccarius or one of the other warders the matter could not have been hushed up, but would have had to pass through the usual channels until it reached the commandant and, as a result, I should have lost my wireless set. So it was with everything, and I became so expert that although I had one or two narrow escapes I got through without any of my misdeeds forming the subject of an official report. Only one of the warders was a bit of a problem, a zealous young man named Hackmann who was a school friend of the adjutant to whom he was inclined to toady in the hope of promotion. It was some time before I could get him to accept bribes, I mean, of course, gifts, but in the end he chose the better course and accepted odds and ends from my wardrobe; he had been bombed out and lost everything, so he was glad of my help in making a new start towards civilian life after the war.

Paul came back one day from Berlin in a state of great excitement for at the station he had met Ettlinger. Ettlinger told him that he had a splendid post at the concentration camp at Vugt in Holland, and that it was an absolute gold mine as many of the prisoners were well off and their relatives would pay anything to secure good treatment for them. With the money obtained in this way all manner of goods, unobtainable in Germany, could be bought and resold in Berlin at enormous profit. The camp commandant, as Ettlinger put it, was an intelligent man and had gone into the business with him, sending him to Germany almost weekly.

About three months later Paul came with fresh news. Ettlinger, the camp commandant, and his adjutant from Vugt were all prisoners at the Kommandatur, awaiting trial before an SS court charged with stealing from prisoners and of misappropriating government property. Early in 1944 I heard that the commandant had been sentenced to seven years penal servitude, his adjutant to five, and Ettlinger to three and a half years, and the three men were sent wearing the badge marking them as habitual criminals to the Dachau concentration camp. I was really delighted with this news and the justice of a sentence which would condemn Ettlinger to similar treatment to that which he had delighted on inflicting on the helpless prisoners in our building. Probably though this sentence was the best thing that could have happened to him for, to the best of my knowledge, in common with other prisoners at the camp, he was liberated by the American advance, and I have heard nothing to indicate that he was ever brought to trial as a war criminal as he certainly would have been had he remained with us. Kaindl and Eccarius, on the other hand, according to a report published in the German press were condemned by a Russian court in 1947 to life imprisonment in a labour camp; curiously enough, one of the crimes to which they confessed in court was complicity in the murder of Major Stevens and myself in the winter of 1941, though at this time Kaindl had not even been near the Sachsenhausen camp.

During the earlier part of 1943 there had been several pretty heavy raids on Berlin, but for me, and I believe for most people in the city, the real war from the air started with five terrific R.A.F. raids on consecutive nights starting with the 22nd of November. From that time on my own life and that of everyone in Germany seemed to be governed by the sound of the sirens and the weighty remorseless passage of masses of heavy bombers overhead. The camp was on the direct approach route for planes coming from the northwest and was just within the outer flak girdle. There was a second line of flak batteries and searchlights between us and the city, whilst Berlin itself could develop a terrific volume of fire in which I could distinguish the strings of red beads of the short range guns.

From my window I could look clear over to Berlin and had a splendid view of everything which took place between us and the city. In course of time I drew a quadrant direction indicator, based on the observation of former raids and the information received as to the localities bombed, and by means of this I could estimate very closely which area was being attacked. When the Pathfinder system was introduced, red flares, they looked like strings of coloured balloons and had the popular name of Xmas trees, were dropped to mark the four corners of the camp and these always gave me a wonderful feeling of security, then in the distance the green and white Xmas trees would make their appearance over the appointed target just before the faint sounds of distant flak heralded the approach of our planes.

From the moment that the sirens sounded the alert a curious hush came over the camp, and even in my cell I noticed that we spoke to each other in whispers as though afraid our voices could be heard from the air. Before the alert there had been a sudden bustle, the trusties running along the passages turning out the lights in the cells, and I pitied all the unfortunates locked in their dark cages for, of course, I had a proper blackout and my light was left on. Then came the crescendo of the approaching planes till their roar directly overhead seemed to make everything, even ones body quiver, and the noise of the flak barrage sank beside it to insignificance—no sound that I have ever heard has left such a tense memory as this passage of the R.A.F., creaking and groaning along and forming an apparently solid ceiling overhead. The later American daylight raids were spectacular, but because they were flown at great heights lacked much of the blind horror of the terror by night.

Those five great November raids were a magnificent, a terrible sight. The German defences of Berlin were at their highest pitch of perfection and neither searchlights, flak, nor fighters were lacking. For the last there were at least three lanes of the approaches to Berlin in which they could operate; a fighter would fire a red and green, two red, or two green star shells, the code varied from day to day, and immediately the exploding flak shells would disappear from that area and soon tracer bullets would show that battle with one of our planes had been started. A plane would be caught in the beam of a searchlight, which would be quickly joined by a number of others, soon the beams of most of them would move away to continue their ceaseless search of the skies leaving three to hold the silver moth in the clutch of their crossed beams. The flak would be terrific at that spot and in these early raids far too often a yellowish spot would show, standing out sharply from the prevailing silver tones, would grow, turn red and the plane would veer out of the embrace of the searchlight arms developing a comet-like tail of fire. There would be a bright flash somewhere in the distance and then a long, long time afterwards the sound of a plane diving at unearthly speed followed by a bang which would shake the building. In those November raids our casualties must have been very heavy; I have myself seen on one occasion as many as five of our planes falling in flames at the same time but, no matter what the opposition, there was, as far as I could see, no evasive action and all planes followed their appointed path and bombed their targets without fail.

We, of course, in the camp ran no danger from bombs, but there was always the possibility of a dud German shell, of which there were many, coming through the roof; also several planes fell, shot down fairly close to us. The pilot of one, who landed in a nearby wood and was captured by one of Elser's guards, attributed his bad landing and a broken leg to the fact that he had waited to bail out until there was no danger of his plane falling on the camp. This officer spent the night in the cell opposite mine and great trouble seemed to be taken by the commandant and the doctor to make him comfortable. It made me very miserable to know that a countryman was so close and that I could do nothing for him. Where he was taken next day and what happened to him, I do not know. Later several men landed with parachutes in the camp, one of them, whom I saw plainly, on the roof of the barrack opposite my window.

I held then, and I still believe that this is true, that German morale was at its lowest ebb in the autumn of 1943. Then, as the Allies demand for unconditional surrender became generally known and German towns were smashed by strategic bombing there was a gradual hardening in people's temper. The working man who lost his home and his painfully gathered household effects saw in German victory his only prospect of compensation and rehabilitation. Homeless and ruined, what could peace bring him except destitution and misery; no, far better fight on, and gladly he allowed himself to believe the promises of Goebbels that victory was not only possible but certain, that Hitler had terrible new secret weapons which would turn the tide of allied success into the bitterness of defeat. It was in those days, I believe, that Hitler, although in fact already nearing madness, became for the masses a god; even my own guards, men who had never been Nazis, and who were almost entirely under my influence, became infected with mystical blind faith that what the Führer said must be true. From everything that I have seen I think that the idea that the morale of a civilian population can be destroyed by physical means such as shells or bombs is entirely false; in fact, I believe that the power of resistance of civilians living in their own familiar surroundings is even tougher than that of troops in the field. As regards the latter it is, I think, true to say that they will show greater stubbornness in the defence of a position in which they have spent some time and which they know than if their surroundings are unfamiliar. The instinct to stick to 'home' and to defend it to the last seems to enable all but the very weakest and most cowardly to find courage to withstand the most brutal efforts to evict them.

The blitz never broke the courage of the British, nor did the far more severe 'strategic' bombing break that of the Germans, who I am convinced never feared our planes with anything approaching the dread they felt for the Gestapo. Air raids and bombs were concrete facts and dangers limited in time; you became a casualty or you didn't, and when the all clear was sounded you could carry on as usual till the next time. The Gestapo with its spies and informers was always there, and at any moment you, or some member of your family, might disappear, and do what they would, no one could find out what had happened. It was a creeping terror against which there was no safeguard.

Two of my guards were Berliners, one living near the Tempelhof Airfield, an obvious target area, and of the other two, one came from Köslin, a small town in Pomerania, and the other from a lonely village on the slopes of the Schneekoppe, the highest mountain in the Sudeten. The two last, their homes being in no particular danger, bothered little about the bombing and accepted it as a matter of course. The Berliners, who from my window could see their town being bombed and possibly their homes destroyed were in a terrible state of nerves, especially if, as sometimes happened, they had to wait for a couple of days before they had news of their families. When, however, raids came on when they were off duty and at home, they turned up next day cheerful and in good spirits, full of praise for the measures taken to protect the lives and property of the inhabitants of Berlin. The raid had not shaken their morale but rather had toughened it and made them feel more united with their fellow countrymen in the fight against an invader; I understand that the reaction of Londoners to the blitz was identical.

In sharp contrast to the courage shown by the people in their own homes was their fear of being caught in a raid while travelling by road or by rail, and when later on really widespread attacks were made by fighters on traffic of all kinds, and as it was said, even on single pedestrians and people working in fields, the effect seemed to be far greater than any mass bombing. Warning could be given of the approach of bombers, but the path of individual raiding fighters was unpredictable, and in time they came to be the terror of the entire population and people became afraid to move except under cover of darkness.

To avoid too great disturbance to the life of the city the Germans introduced two forms of alert; a small alarm consisting of only three up and down shrieks from the sirens, and the full alarm when the sirens continued their wailing for two minutes. In the case of the small alarms work was not stopped at factories and people were free to remain at their homes and air raid precautions only came into force for the full-scale alert. The Berlin population had been

Colonel-General Franz Halder, late Chief of the German General Staff and (*below*) with his wife after their liberation.

(*Lower right*)

Major J. B. 'Johnny' Dodge, D.S.O., D.S.C., M.C. A photo taken while a prisoner of war in Germany when he was usually known as 'The Dodger'.

General Alexander Baron von Falkenhausen, Commander-in-Chief in
Belgium after the German occupation. Imprisoned by the Gestapo after
the July 20th attempt on Hitler's life.

well trained for the latter, knew exactly what to do, and had the feeling that they were being looked after; in the case of the small alarms they were thrown on their own resources, they felt naked and unprotected, and lacked the cohesion which came from facing common danger in a crowded air raid shelter. When later our Mosquitoes came over in groups of sixty and a hundred, sirens sounded the full alert, the population went under cover and everything followed the accustomed routine, and I heard no more grumbling about those accursed Mosquitoes with their aerial torpedoes which had been so greatly dreaded.

I was very accurately informed as to the results achieved by different raids as Paul always managed to find out exactly what damage had been done, and information received later from other sources showed that his reports were correct. The Germans would then claim to have shot down their usual sixty or seventy planes, and the B.B.C. would report the dropping of several thousand tons of bombs on Berlin and the destruction of specific buildings there which every Berliner knew were untouched—I can't remember how many times the destruction of the Potzdammer Bahnhof was claimed; about as often as the Germans said they had destroyed Waterloo Station, I should say.

From my observation post at the receiving end I concluded that if we had wished to achieve the biggest possible results from our air offensive, we should have concentrated on making as many small raids as possible, six planes or so, during day and night, dropping not only bombs, but also forged ration cards and propaganda leaflets. It was always easy to tell when either of the latter had been dropped. Normally, an alert lasted only as long as hostile planes were over the city and when, later in 1944, concentrated attacks were made and all bombs were dropped during a period of fifteen minutes or so, the all clear often sounded within half an hour of the alert. Occasionally though it was greatly delayed and as much as two hours passed before it was sounded. Everybody knew what this meant. Ration cards or leaflets had been dropped and the whole life of the city remained at a standstill whilst air wardens, police, and Gestapo sought for and collected them. The Nazis feared nothing so much as that people might hear the truth, and the death penalty was rigorously imposed in cases where people had been guilty of picking up allied leaflets, or of disseminating news heard in B.B.C. broadcasts.

For me the raids on Berlin were a wonderful spectacle, and I must confess that during 1944 the progress of our air offensive was the most absorbing interest of my life. The German authorities seemed to have come to the conclusion that it was better to give the people the longest possible warning of probable or possible danger from the air instead of subjecting them to the sudden shock of wailing sirens. Early in 1944 a system was started by which

K

telephone subscribers in Berlin, and also in certain other cities, could hear reports broadcast from the local air command post (Gefechtsstand Berlin) by making a connection from a certain point on their telephone receiver to the aerial terminal of their radio set. The results obtained by this system of pre-warning must have been satisfactory, for shortly afterwards these broadcasts could also be heard on any radio set by tuning in the usual Berlin station, which ceased transmitting its normal programme during raids.

Still later, in the late spring of 1944, a special station started operating, which gave reports of enemy air activity for the whole country. At first the position of raiding planes was indicated by map references which gave a general district indication, and then the exact area by letter groups indicating the north-south and east-west limits; I did not find it at all difficult to plot out the different areas by checking up the code numbers given with the subsequent reports of places raided as reported in the war bulletins, and when later I was given a map on which the references were indicated I found that for the area round Berlin and the northern route from the coast I was only very little out in my estimates. As air activity increased after 'D' Day the position of invading planes was broadcast in plain, and one had the most detailed information about all air activity over Germany, including not only reports on large formations engaged on strategic bombing, but also on tactical operations, on the movement of reconnaissance machines, those engaged on mine laying in the North Sea and Baltic, and even of single low-flying fighters engaged in the disturbance of road and rail traffic.

This news was broadcast throughout the day and as the war in the west developed the frequency with which hostile planes were present increased until there was practically no intermittence. The announcer was generally a girl, and however sensational the news, it came in a monotonous expressionless voice in clipped carefully enunciated phrases. She would tell how the red raiders were on such and such a course, the blue, the green, the yellow, sometimes almost running out of colours to specify fresh invaders, were taking other courses; she would give details of approximate numbers, their height and, every now and again, an urgent warning to some particular town which might possibly be one of the chosen targets. Then there were district warnings of the approach of low-flying fighters, and speculations about the purpose of small groups or single planes; whether they were bombers or reconnaissance machines. It was fascinating to follow all these movements on my map and to mark the positions of the various groups with counters, and to note the often devious routes by which targets were approached. In the winter of 1944-5 planes which appeared to threaten some town like Magdeburg or Leipzig would suddenly make an unexpected swerve and almost before the alert could be sounded bombs would be falling on Berlin.

Then we had the cuckoo. Tired of listening to everlasting air raid reports I would turn on Berlin or the Deutschland station to listen to a concert; suddenly the music would be broken off, interrupted by a noisy and extremely agitated cuckoo repeating his call without stop for about a minute. Then the station would go dead and one knew that one was in for something really big. There would be the usual sound of running feet in the building and the camp outside, followed by an unearthly hush broken only by the sirens sounding the full alarm, and shortly afterwards the noise of the approaching planes to the accompanyment of flak which, as 1944 drew to its close, grew less and less until it practically ceased. I stood on my bed, my guard next to me on a stool, prepared to follow every detail of the impending attack.

On one such occasion, on 22nd March, 1944, I was standing at my window watching a big daylight raid on Berlin. I heard the sound of a returning bomber which seemed to be in difficulties and losing height. Suddenly there was a loud plop and the barrack opposite me on the other side of the wall seemed to erupt flame like a volcano. Then followed the sound of bombs rushing down on to us and several other plops. I smelt burning wool and, looking down, I saw spots of flame on my bed caused by drops of phosphorus which had splashed in through the window. I bundled the blanket up and shoved it in my pail, and then went to the door to see what was happening, for I could hear a lot of shouting and people rushing about. It seemed that a bomber carrying phosphorus incendiaries had been badly hit and, before trying to make a forced landing, had jettisoned its load of bombs and no less than seven fell in our garden, of which two neatly straddled my cell falling twelve yards in front of it and about the same distance behind.

After this exciting event there was a sudden rise in British stock; "You don't know what may happen with these damned Yankees. What do they know about geography? Why, they may mistake us for the Heinckel works next time and unload all their bombs on us." The warders became very martial and all guards off duty were ordered to report back at the building immediately an alert was sounded. Then a large gang of prisoners invaded the garden and dug an enormous hole which swallowed up one of my most cherished flower beds. In this a shelter was built of prefabricated hollow 'L'-shaped concrete blocks which interlocked in such a way that no mortar or cementing was required. It was said that shelters built in this way had proved better than more solid structures as they were resilient and could give better to the shock of explosions. I was extremely annoyed at the result of this work, for one day there was a high wind which laid sand inches thick on all parts of my garden. When the shelter was completed I was informed I must go to earth there whenever the alert sounded, and until the all clear, might not even show my nose above ground. It was a beastly dark, dank place, which I promptly christened the mass grave of Katyn. I went there both for day and night raids at first but stood on the steps leading to the entrance so that I could watch what was going on, and only took cover when there was a heavy fall of flak splinters from directly overhead.

I soon gave up going there for night raids as I got a better view from my window, but I maintained the theory that I did so during daylight raids as otherwise I might have been surprised in my cell by the commandant, and in any case, the progress of these raids could be followed much better from outside. For sheer beauty it would be difficult to beat the sight offered by one of the big American raids of some thousand machines on a fine summer day. The planes flew at great heights and looked like tiny silver fish each followed by a gleaming wake of foam. They kept perfect formation and moved in great curves leaving the sky patterned by the fine network of their exhausts. Over Berlin smoke flares had been dropped, which formed gigantic figures reminiscent of the symbols used on flags and badges to denote the SS. When the bomb carpets were laid one felt rather than heard them by a curious tremor of the ground under one's feet. Then over Berlin a black cloud would form compounded of smoke from the flak bursts and that from fires on the ground; slowly it would grow and gather denseness until nothing would remain of our fine summer's day which, more often than not, ended in rain.

Through my visits to the shelter I got to know the Bears by sight as they also took cover there. They were always there when I arrived and, as it was very dark and they never came outside, I was unable to distinguish more than that they were three smallish men; more interesting was the fact that some six to eight SS men also came to the shelter, and through them I discovered the existence of a small military prisoner of war camp within the walls of the concentration camp, in which some British officers were imprisoned. These SS men were normally on guard duty at this camp but, during raids, all those who were off duty at the time had to come to the Bunker to reinforce our own warders. They were a very decent lot of fellows, and as they saw that I was on most intimate terms with my guards and seemed to know a lot about what was going on, they soon got used to my presence and talked quite freely. It was in this way that I learnt of an attempt to escape made towards the end of September by a number of prisoners, some of whom were British. I was to meet most of them later and learnt then that the party consisted of Wing Commander ('Wings') Day, Lieutenant Colonel Churchill, Major Dodge, Flight Lieutenants James and Dowse, and four British N.C.O.s and men; also with them were five Russian officers and the Italian naval, military, and air attachés from the Berlin Embassy.

When I heard about the affair it was said that all the men

had been recaptured within twenty-four hours, and that most of them had been brought to the Bunker, but I subsequently learnt that this was not quite correct, for one officer, Major Johnny Dodge, D.S.C., D.S.O., M.C., succeeded in escaping capture for about a month, having managed to reach some French slave workers who had concealed him. Without money or food and knowing no German it was impossible for him to get very far afield, and in the end he was discovered by a search party and brought back to spend the rest of his imprisonment in our Bunker. Dodge, Wings Day, Jimmy James, and Sydney Dowse were specialists in escaping, and no camp had yet been found strong enough to hold them. They had all taken part in the famous mass escape from Stalag Luft III when fifty of their comrades were murdered after their recapture on orders from Hitler. Undaunted by this evidence of the risk that they ran, no sooner had they arrived at the special camp at Sachsenhausen than they started preparations for a fresh escape and, in spite of insuperable difficulties, tunnelled their way out. To me it is a great consolation and a vindication of my having stayed 'put' for so many years that, when these doughties were at last imprisoned in the Bunker, they found themselves in a cage proof against even their superlative ingenuity.

On the 6th November, 1944, while I was working in the garden I heard someone in cell No. 67 whistle the 'British Grenadiers'— funny how every Englishman at once thinks of this tune if he wants to make his nationality known. One of the warders happened to be in the garden that day and, as he was standing not far from me, I could not make any response at the moment. Next day though as I passed the window I whistled the same tune which was immediately taken up from the cell. I could not loiter there for long as I had been working on a bed at the other side of the garden, but as it was not far from where I kept my garden tools I managed to pass near the window once or twice more. On the first occasion I pretended to be singing and said: "My name is Best, sixty years old, five years here, and still going strong." When I next passed I could see a vague figure through the ground glass screen of window and a voice said: "I am Flight Lieutenant Sydney Dowse, R.A.F., and there are a lot of us here. We escaped. You are Best, I know all about you, but there were two of you, what happened to the other?" "Stevens," I said, "he's at Dachau, been there three years." "Oh, so he wasn't shot. We had heard that he was dead." "Oh no, the last I heard he was alive and kicking." I warned him to be careful and not to get caught talking to me through his window as I knew that there was a most untrustworthy fellow in the next cell. We wished each other luck and arranged to try to have another chat next day, but when I then whistled the 'British Grenadiers' there was no response, and I later found out that he and all the other British prisoners had been moved to cells in Wing 'A'.

After this I tried hard to make contact with some of them but my guards had been specially warned to keep us apart and as, if I had succeeded in inducing them to help me, I should have been risking their lives I did not feel justified in trying. I had about thirty English books which had come with my gear from Holland and, as I knew that there were none in the library, I handed over the whole lot to Eccarius and asked him to lend them to any British prisoners who might be in the camp. I had carefully erased my name from all of them and although Eccarius hummed and hawed a good deal, in the end he agreed to do what I asked, and I later heard that he had been as good as his word. Really, I grew to be quite fond of Eccarius. True, he was a weak drunken fellow, a coward, and a lickspittle, but there was something good-natured and kindly about him, and after the five years we had been together there was little with which I could reproach him, and in many ways he showed genuine affection for me; whenever he brought me a letter from May, or had any other news for me that was good, his face used to light up in a way which showed that he shared my pleasure.

The knowledge that there were other Englishmen in the building obsessed all my thoughts, and the fact that I could not meet them made me realize how intensely lonely I was, and how much I longed for a chance to speak freely to someone who felt and thought as I did. Later I heard that they too had tried to reach me through the little barber, Max. Unfortunately, whenever I went to him one of my guards was always with me, and he, of course, was far too much afraid of their uniform to dare to say anything compromising in their presence; they in turn were afraid of him, for he was a great favourite of the warders, and they could not be sure of his discretion. There was only one thing which I could do to help my fellow countrymen. I learned that they were being docked of their exercise, especially on Saturdays and Sundays, because Eccarius had no one available to guard them. I therefore suggested to him, after first having obtained their consent, that my guards might help him out when they were off duty and to this he agreed. Later, as this became too much of a tie for my men, I arranged that Karl Böning should be transferred to this duty and that my remaining three guards would manage without him.

At this time all short leave had been suspended and my Berliners could no longer go home on their off days; it was therefore no great sacrifice to them to increase the number of hours which they spent in my cell where, I am sure, they found life almost pleasanter than elsewhere. Karl Böning was a good-natured fellow and I knew that I could rely upon him to interfere with his charges as little as possible, and he would certainly never have given them away if they committed any small breach of regulations.

It was about this time that I had a talk with Eccarius which amused me very much, and which I think is typical of the German attitude towards obedience to orders. The papers had been full of threats of severe penalties to be imposed on any Germans who assisted escaping prisoners of war, and Hitler's general attitude towards allied prisoners of war was one of 'Hang the lot'. So I asked Eccarius one day what he would do if he were given orders to shoot me.

"I would have to shoot you, of course."

"I don't see any 'of course' about it, we have always been very good friends, and I think that it would be a very dirty action if you were to shoot me."

"Of course, Herr Best, I should hate doing so, and should never be easy in my mind again, but if it were an order and I disobeyed, I would be shot myself."

"But, my dear friend, you are a brave fellow I know, surely you would not do something which you knew was wrong, simply to save your own life."

"Ach, Herr Best, it isn't that at all. You don't understand. If I were shot for disobeying an order I should be disgraced, while if I shot you, you would die a hero's death."

I am thankful that the occasion never arose, for I am sure that he would have been so nervous that he would have made an awful mess of the job. To me the principle of punishing Germans in subordinate positions for acts committed under order has always seemed to me unjustified. For generations the idea has been drilled into them that obedience is the most sacred virtue and that orders given by a superior demand unquestioning obedience. Even with us, I can hardly imagine that personal responsibility would be imposed, and punishment enacted, on any soldier who performed an illegal action on direct orders from a superior. If, in fact, Eccarius had received orders to shoot me, or to subject me to ill-treatment, I am sure that he would have hated doing so, and for my part I should certainly not have borne him malice. My own experi-ence during all the years of my imprisonment was that the vast majority of men whose duty brought them in close contact with prisoners had no inclination to treat them cruelly, but on the contrary sympathized with them and did what they could to help them; rough manners were frequently merely a façade which concealed reluctance to perform duties which the man could not avoid.

When I first came to Sachsenhausen the general tone there was very rough and all the warders spoke to prisoners as though they were animals, giving them brief orders in a harsh voice. For my part, I never reacted to this lack of manners except by an almost exaggerated courtesy. I always said good morning and good night, and thanked the warders when they told me that I could go for exercise, when they brought my meals, and even when they chained me for the night. At first they looked at me as though I were crazy, but one day the plug-ugly Drexl replied rather shyly to my good night with "A pleasant rest", and this became a sort of personal contact between us, which developed to the point that he would come in for a chat in the evening. Then Eccarius joined in with a response to my morning and evening wishes and started saying please, and asking me whether I would do this or that instead of giving me a curt order.

It was a very slow process but in the end a normal friendly spirit developed, and the standard of politeness which I had introduced came to be generally accepted as correct; in fact, the degree in which everyone struggled towards good manners was sometimes quite amusing. In the morning we all shook hands when we met for the first time, and whenever on my way to the lavatory or to the garden I passed a warder he stood to attention and saluted; not a Nazi salute, oh no, that I had suppressed as vulgar long ago, but a proper military salute worthy of the Reichswehr. As a matter of fact, all these fellows were eager to learn how to behave themselves, and as soon as I had convinced them that I was not pulling their legs, or laughing at them I found them, most willing pupils. Anyhow, their newly acquired knowledge of social behaviour was most useful to them when our building was turned into a fashionable boarding house inhabited by important foreigners. Of course occasionally there were instances of a return to primeval sin, but whenever I heard the sound of shouting I always called Eccarius up short, had him in, and told him that such practices must cease.

Letters from May reached me with very fair regularity and I even received three of the seventy-three parcels containing tobacco and cigarettes which she sent me, and four of the Red Cross food parcels which I should have received fortnightly. At first I frequently inquired about parcels which I knew had been sent and which I had not received, but in the end it became clear to me that the Gestapo had only very few prisoners of war directly in their charge, and it was hopeless to expect that they would forego such an opportunity of increasing their supplies of tobacco and food. I am sure that I scored by ceasing to make complaints, for I noticed that I no longer had difficulty in getting as much to smoke as I wanted, and in many other ways it was evident that my forbearance was appreciated. Yes, I got plenty to smoke, but what stuff it was!

There is a tobacco produced in Russia called Machorka which has always been the smoke of the moujiks. It consists of the stems and the ribs of the tobacco plants from which all the leaf has been rubbed off for use in cigarette manufacture. This detritus is then passed through a chaff cutter, or similar instrument, until it is reduced to small fragments varying in size from about a quarter of an inch diameter to a coarse powder resembling post-war ration tea. The Russians, I am told, smoke it by pouring it into a funnel-shaped twist of newspaper which must be kept upright by holding the head well back, and it is possible that the newspaper may to some extent disguise its natural flavour, which to me tasted like burning rubber and smelt like a bonfire on a refuse heap. I made the discovery, however, that if Machorka were steamed for three-quarters of an hour, and then dried, something which really reminded one of tobacco, indeed more so than the mixture of home-grown herbs of which German cigarettes were made, could be obtained.

I manufactured a linen bag in which I put the tobacco and suspended this in a deep enamel jug which I placed on my electric cooker and when this had been done, the window was opened wide and my guard and I fled to the garden. The stench which came from my cell was indescribable, and newcomers to the building often jumped to the conclusion that it arose from some horrible Nazi torture such as burning a prisoner's feet. After a lapse of three-quarters of an hour one of my guards would pop into my cell and switch off the cooker and when, after a decent interval, I returned, I would find my Machorka gleaming a beautiful golden colour and smelling quite fragrantly. After drying it I sieved it by shaking it about in a cardboard box, in which I had substituted for the bottom a network of quarter-inch mesh made of sewing cotton. I had an awful job making it, but it proved its value. That portion which passed the sieve I kept for myself as cigarette tobacco and the remainder I gave to my guards to smoke in their pipes, which, as the tobacco allowance had been reduced to three cigarettes a day, was very much appreciated. In the end I really got to like this stuff and on the few occasions when I got some of the English tobacco sent me by May it tasted quite tame by comparison; but all the time I suffered agonies from stomach ache which nothing that the doctors could do, although they did everything they could think of, could alleviate. Page after page in my diary tell of my sufferings, of special diets and numerous medicines which the doctors prescribed, but neither I nor anyone else diagnosed the true cause, Machorka poisoning. When circumstances forced me to stop smoking Machorka, my digestion returned to me as good as new.

Somehow or other time passed and the passage of the weeks was marked for me by my Wednesday visit to the barbers for a haircut and shampoo, by the arrival of my clean linen from the laundry, and by the scrubbing out of my cell; I had managed to acquire an entirely new set of household linen, beautiful linen sheets and blue and white bed-spreads, a dozen towels, and an equal number of pillow cases and dusters, all of which went to the laundry in my own bag and were returned each week. I had accumulated all sorts of cooking utensils, tools, and, I must confess, a mass of useless junk. From the day of my arrival I had picked up and kept everything that I could lay my hands on; old nails, bits of wire and string, rusty razor blades, in short the biggest collection of rubbish that one could imagine. This collecting habit is a real prisoner's psychosis.

The passage of my days was very regular and indeed, timed to the minute. I got up at six-thirty, stripped to the buff and did exercises before my open window. Dressed in my warm dressing-gown I ate my breakfast at eight o'clock, always the same, four slices of bread which I toasted with butter and jam. At eight-thirty I went to wash and on my return shaved, and with the help of my guard made my bed and swept out the cell— in this, my duties were confined to supervision, for my guards were deeply offended if I tried to do such things for myself. I did some mending or read until ten-thirty when I went out, staying in the garden till twelve-thirty in the summer or for an hour or so in the winter. When I came back I had my lunch which had been keeping warm for me on my electric cooker, and after this I had a nap until three o'clock. At three o'clock I took down the German war bulletin which at this hour was given at dictation speed, and to this I added comments derived from B.B.C. broadcasts. After this I warmed up some coffee and ate a couple of slices of bread and jam and then struggled with mathematics, did crossword puzzles, or tried my hand at chess problems until my supper came at about five. I ate another four slices of bread with cheese, sausage or whatever else was on the menu, and then went out; in the summer to water my garden and to stay out until about ten o'clock, in the winter for a brisk walk. At ten o'clock I had a shower bath and then I settled down to try to get the B.B.C.

With all respect to the B.B.C. who certainly saved me from desperation and put out some wonderful broadcasts, I do not think that they had much success in rendering news available to the general public in Germany. No one could, of course, listen to the medium and long-wave broadcasts unless he could shut himself up in a soundproof cell, for the whining noise which the German stations superimposed on British wave-lengths was so much louder than the speech that it could be heard from a distance. I dared only listen to the short-wave stations, but my set, like most in use in Germany was a straight circuit with reaction, and no matter how carefully I manipulated the latter I could not avoid, when trying to keep the volume so that I could hear what was said, occasionally starting my set generating, which of course, was picked up on other receivers in the building.

Although Eccarius knew perfectly well that I was listening in to England, Hackmann, one of the other warders, was constantly trying to catch me out, and often listened outside my door. In the summer I got good reception at night on the fifty-metre band, but in the winter the only time when I could get England was in the afternoon on the thirty-metre band, and at this time lots of people passed under my window and I had to be very careful. As a rule, I depended in the winter for my news on the Swiss station which gave both the German and the British *communiqués*. News was like dope to me and on days when for some reason I had been unable to get anything I felt absolutely miserable; worse than I did when I had nothing to smoke.

I could, of course, only listen to the broadcasts in German for, even when the actual words could not be heard, anyone listening outside my cell would almost certainly notice the different rhythm of a foreign language. In this connection I discovered a curious thing about the talks given in German by English broadcasters; my guards could not understand what they said and would not even believe that they were speaking German. Although we make no claim to be linguists, in common with the French we have the ability of understanding our own language, however incorrectly it is spoken, and whatever the accent of the speaker; in effect, we understand a large number of languages which are lumped together under the name of English. We have, I believe, acquired this faculty as a result of our refusal to learn languages, which has forced foreigners who wish to communicate with us to use some variety of 'English as she is spoke', and ourselves to understand them. English people and French are so used to hearing their languages spoken badly that they have little difficulty in understanding foreigners, but Germans seldom hear their language spoken with foreign accent, rhythm, and intonation, and their ears are not attuned to such variations. At the best of times great attention is required to follow and understand a broadcast talk, especially when the volume is small and subject to fading, so I am really not surprised that my men could not distinguish the German words through the veil of the Oxford accents in which they were enveloped.

After the failure of the attempt on Hitler's life of 20th July, 1944, things became very jittery for a time in our building, and it often seemed as though the lives of all political prisoners, including my own, hung by very slender threads. Almost daily new people were brought in; from what I heard most of them were German officers of high rank, who after a very short stay were taken out at night for execution. All the Germans with whom I had any personal contact expressed the greatest horror at the attempted outrage, and were really bloodthirsty in their wish that all connected with it should be exterminated. Hitler's escape seemed indeed so miraculous that the growing belief in his Godhead was immensely strengthened. My men were all anti-Nazis and had not a good word to say for any of the head men in the party. But Hitler, he was Führer. He was omniscient except that he knew nothing about the bad things done in his name by the Nazi bosses—"The Führer is good. He never wanted war and he has time and again tried to make peace. It is all the fault of the Jews and the plutocrats in England and America who grow rich on the sufferings of the people"—in this way the propaganda of Joseph Goebbels bore some fruit although his broadcasts were listened to with derision.

No one had any real hope of a German victory and yet, buoyed up by the repeated reassurances in press and radio, no one could yet envisage defeat—Hitler must be right when he said that never again would there be a German capitulation, and the Allies demand for unconditional surrender—of course, this could not be considered for a moment. I have often wondered had any offer of peace approximating to Wilson's fourteen points of 1918 been made, whether even Hitler, Himmler, and the Gestapo, could have continued the war in face of the hopeless weariness of the people.

It was obvious to every sane person that German defeat could not long be deferred, and one would have thought that prisoners would be hopeful and more cheerful than ever before. Curiously enough though, at no time were there so many attempts at suicide amongst them, and during the latter half of 1944 at least a dozen prisoners tried to cut their veins or hang themselves. The little Russian to whom I have referred, after making one attempt to cut the artery of his wrist with the glass of his spectacles, was put in a cell with another Russian lieutenant in the hope that company might cheer him up. One night when the alert sounded he climbed down from his top bunk intending to look out of the window, and stepped into something wet, warm and sticky. He said that the whole cell smelt of blood and he started shrieking wildly; even from my cell, quite a long distance away, I heard his desperate yells. A warder came and found a pool of blood on the floor, and the Russian officer apparently lifeless with deep cuts in both wrists which he had made with a secreted razor blade. The doctor came at once and gave him a blood transfusion, and I was told that he recovered in the end, but my little Russian never really got over the shock and to the end remained terribly nervous and depressed.

He was only twenty-two and had been dropped by parachute behind the German lines to organize a party of Russian partisans. Owing to failure to supply them with food and munitions from the air, and after suffering great privations from cold and starvation, they had been rounded up and my young friend, being a nephew of Molotov, was not murdered with the rest of the party but had been fairly well treated. At the time of his capture he was suffering badly from frost-bite, and as a result the toes of both his feet had been amputated. For a time he had been in the special prisoner of war camp at Sachsenhausen about which I spoke earlier, but at the beginning of 1943 he had made an attempt to escape together with a son of Stalin's who was also in the same camp. They had been caught almost immediately, having been hunted with dogs, and after this my young friend had been imprisoned in our building whilst young Stalin remained at the special P.O.W. camp.

After the shock of the attempted suicide of his friend he became so morbid and depressed that Eccarius did not know what to do with him, so I suggested that he should put him in one of the cells next to mine so that my guards could keep an eye on him. As I said earlier, he had for some time taken his exercise on the road in front of my window, and we had established a sort of distant friendship. I gave him tobacco and cigarettes and kept him posted with news of the front by writing brief details of Russian successes on paper which I held up to the window so that he could read it. Eccarius put him in cell No. 42, and he really did seem happier there, as if he were lonely or wanted anything he could rap on the wall and my guard would go and see what he wanted. He was also very fond of light music, and when there was anything cheerful on the wireless I would turn my set on full so that he could hear. Poor little fellow, I really became very fond of him, especially when later I got to know him personally.

I had become quite good friends with the dentist, Gussow, and as he appreciated that my walks to and from his surgery were the only escapes which I had from the monotony of my prison he helped me by spinning out my treatment as long as possible. Gradually all my teeth were removed one by one after quite unnecessary visits for X-ray photos. After each tooth was gone my denture had to be altered or a new one made—three complete sets of dentures were made for me during my stay and, as under the National Health Service, free of charge. He was a very good dentist and never caused me the slightest pain. Once though I was really a bit nervous for when I came in I saw that he was looking rather downcast and so asked him whether he was ill; "No," he said, "but my wife has just telephoned to tell me that your country-folk bombed my house last night, and everything I possess has been burnt." When I sat on the chair, opened my mouth 'wider, please', and he started work with the forceps, I wondered whether this time he had really injected an anaesthetic. He was a good conscientious dentist and I felt no twinge of pain. I don't know whether, had I been in his place, I should have resisted the temptation to practise a little of that retaliation so vehemently pleaded by Goebbels. A popular joke at the time was that Hitler had sent an ultimatum to Churchill that if the bombing of Berlin did not cease, Goebbels would broadcast retaliation for an hour daily.

On my walk of about 300 yards from the Bunker to the dentist, I always tried to see as much as I could of the life in the camp. Generally, at the hours when I went to the dentist, there were only a few prisoners about as most of them had their work outside, but on three occasions I passed through the square at a time when all the prisoners were lined up for the evening roll call. Until about October 1944 nearly all the men looked fit and well nourished. Since the arrival of Kaindl they no longer wore the old striped camp uniform nor had their heads cropped; instead, they were dressed in civilian clothes taken from the store of effects belonging to dead prisoners. Squares, triangles, or stars of contrasting material were sewn into the backs of their coats, and on their trousers they bore their number and the coloured triangle denoting the class to which they belonged. Taken by and large though, they looked much like any other crowd of men engaged on manual labour, and as I passed their ranks I got many a grin and rude personal remark. Curiously enough the old camp uniform was now affected by the camp dudes, the men holding as trusty some privileged position, and any one of these who could get hold of a clean and new uniform wore it with an air of conscious superiority. Some of these men, who were allowed to wear their own underclothing, had got their uniforms specially tailored to fit them and really looked quite smart compared to the prisoners in old, ill-fitting civvies.

The usual sights on my walk were, first, the punishment squad engaged on its interminable march round and round the square and, secondly, the line-up of new arrivals. My walk led me first about 200 yards in a continuation of the line of the wing of my prison with, on my left, the camp wall and, on my right, the large prison square. Then I turned left through a gateway which led to the Kommandantura, and in front of this gate all the new arrivals were lined up waiting to be registered and to be allotted their quarters. During 1943 and until the autumn of 1944 these had consisted of civilians of all classes, some well dressed and with expensive suit cases at their feet, men who looked like important company directors or successful professional men, others, shabbily dressed workmen; men of all ages and kinds awaiting their turn to be reduced to the lowest common multiple of a concentration camp. There they stood, often from the early hours of the morning until late at night, having their first lesson that they were no longer 'men' (Menschen), but prisoners. They would be under the charge of a big burly trusty who could be relied upon to see that they stood at attention and did not try to squat on the ground and, being Germans, they did their best to look military.

About October 1944 an entirely new class of arrivals appeared. Men, if one could call them such, mere living skeletons wrapped in the rags of what had once been prison uniform, their faces and hands covered with sores, and with strange little pot-bellies which grew like tubers from their naked bones. They stood there in their hundreds, sometimes I should judge a thousand or more, and always there were some lying on their backs or their faces on the ground, unconscious or dead. As I passed them, glassy eyes stared through me without interest or recognition—gleaming eyes set in fleshless sockets supported by jutting cheekbones—noses so wasted that one could see the outline of the bones. I have never seen, nor can I imagine, any more horrible sight, and it is something which, once seen, remains with one for ever after. Who were they? They were the prisoners evacuated from the camps in Poland and elsewhere on the line of the Russian advance. I don't know how many of them came to Sachsenhausen, but I was told that the quarters intended to house eighty prisoners, at the end of January 1945, had to accommodate 400.

After the beginning of October 1944 conditions became increasingly bad at the camp, for the simple reason that it was quite impossible to cater for its vast population. Food began to run short and, as refugees poured in to the Berlin area from the north-eastern provinces, there was such general scarcity that there was no source from which it could be replenished. All prisoners were put on short commons and the SS rations became insufficient even for my small appetite, while Paul complained that the skin of his tummy was hanging down in loose folds like a curtain. Kaindl had not been to see me for several months, and when at last he paid me a visit at Xmas 1944, I hardly recognized him, a tired, broken man. He sat with me for a while and said, "Ach Herr Best, you know I tried to make this camp fit to live in, I tried to look after everyone, but it is too big, one man can do nothing—it is a pigsty (Ein Saustall)."

There was yet another class of new arrivals. These were men whose faces were marked criss-cross with lines which seemed to have been made with a giant indelible pencil. These, I learnt, were men caught looting during the blackout. To prevent their escape during the excitement after a raid, when it was a case of all hands turning to rescue work, the air wardens were provided with a gentian violet dye with which they marked the faces and hands of looters, and for a man thus marked there was no asylum for everybody was his enemy. One day as I passed along I saw a group of people standing in the middle of the square, and a line of men dressed only in shirts which flapped in the wind around their bare legs. They were standing in a long row, and I then saw that two of them were being hung from small gallows, which looked like two high gymnasium horizontal bars side by side. I did not see anything in the nature of a platform from which the men could be dropped, and a man in prison garb was holding up the feet of one of the men as he hung by the rope; the other man was partly hidden from me by a group of guards. All the men in the row had the pencil-striped faces, and the man hanging showed gleaming white teeth and eyes which stood out sharply from his blue-striped face which, from the distance, was almost invisible. I could only take a quick glance as the warder who had accompanied me to and from the dentist hurried me along as fast as he could.

I later heard that a number of such executions invariably followed every raid on Berlin, and that in spite of the death penalty looting during the blackout and during air raids was increasing. Such executions had nothing to do with ordinary camp routine, nor did they fall under the jurisdiction of the commandant. Sachsenhausen was conveniently situated close to Berlin, and almost daily people were brought in by the Security Service for interrogation and subsequent liquidation.

From the moment that Himmler was appointed Commander-in-Chief of the Home Forces after the 20th July plot, great efforts were made to induce political prisoners in the camp to volunteer for military service, and intense pressure was exercised on the conscientious objectors, Bible Students, etc., who were threatened with severe treatment if they continued their refusal to join up. The latter remained immovable and in the end nothing happened to them, but a considerable number of political prisoners, including most of those of German nationality, did join up in the hope of being able to desert if sent to the front. There were also many comb-outs of SS men employed in the camp, most of whom were passed fit for active service and sent back to their units. Amongst them were three of Elser's guards, who were not replaced, so that from that time, 12th August, 1944, he was left solitary. There was also talk that my guards might also be taken from me, but when I asked the commandant he assured me that as long as he was in charge I need fear no change.

Elser's three guards, who had all at times done duty with me and who often came out to the garden when I was there, came to see me to say good-bye, and each of them asked me to give him a little note stating that he had always behaved well and had been guilty of no ill-treatment of prisoners, saying that he intended to desert at the first opportunity. I did not give them anything in writing but told them that they could use my name as a recommendation. Elser, I heard, was very low, for he rightly considered that the loss of his guards was a sign that he had lost his value to the authorities, and might soon expect to lose his life as well.

On the 24th August the Bears suddenly left, being fetched by Obergruppenführer Pohle. As this coincided with the fall of the Antonescu regime in Roumania, and they were almost certainly members of the opposition against him, their evacuation immediately after his fall did not seem to augur well for their future safety. They left in such a hurry that almost all their luggage remained behind; a few days later Eccarius received orders for it to be sent on to Berlin, and it was rumoured that the Bears had been taken to the Gestapo prison in the Prinz Albrechtstrasse.

One day in September I noticed curious circular marks on the paths in my garden for which at first I could not account; then, it dawned upon me that they could only be the imprints of a lady's high-heeled shoes, but how on earth could a woman have got into our exclusively masculine home? A few days later when the door was opened for me to go into the garden I caught a glimpse of a gentleman and lady who were already there, before I was hurriedly pulled back and the door shut. It was not long before I discovered that they occupied cell No. 80, and that they were a Dr. and Mrs. Vermehren, the parents of Dr. Erich Vermehren, a member of the German Intelligence Service in Sofia, who with his wife had succeeded in escaping to Turkey and thence to England. His brother was also in the building, his sister was at Ravensbruck, and his father-in-law, Count Plettenberg, with his daughter, had also been arrested. This was throughout, the Gestapo's strongest suit in combating any dissidence to Nazi rule; if the offender himself could not be found, then all members of his family were at once imprisoned. Whilst there were always enough men in the opposition who feared no danger for themselves, few could face the prospect of involving their womenfolk in their fate.

The year 1944 rang out with an exhausted Germany, in much the same military position as that of Great Britain after Dunkirk, but without her popular determination to achieve victory. The Press, Goebbels and Fritzsche could rant as they pleased about secret weapons and Germany's inevitable victory; no one believed it, and even Ditmar could not bring himself to paint rosy coloured pictures of the military position, and went sick. Himmler had started the Volkssturm in imitation of our Home Guard, and all old men and boys were being trained in the use of the 'Panzerfaust'. Even my old guards had to attend shooting exercises, and every week there were political pep talks by specialists from the Propaganda Ministry, which all guards and other officials in the camp except those engaged on essential guard duties were forced to attend. At this time only a small minority of men on duty in the camp were Germans and most were 'Volks Deutscher', or as they were generally called in derision: 'Hilfs Germanen'; they were Balts, Hungarians, Roumanians, and Russians, who because of German ancestry had been brought into Germany and pressed into the Waffen-SS. Only few could speak German, and in spirit they were far more in accord with the prisoners than with their officers—the German officials seriously feared that if the prisoners tried to revolt, these men might make common cause with them. Defeat was in the air and in the grossly overcrowded conditions in the camp, and not only there, but also in our building, where many prisoners were sleeping five men to a cell, effective control of the prisoners was a thing of the past. When I walked to the dentist with my guard, prisoners made no attempt to salute or stand to attention, but deliberately jostled

L

against us as we passed. SS men did not dare to walk through the camp alone but went in pairs with their pistols cocked.

The defences of Berlin against air attack grew visibly weaker day by day, and by the end of January 1945 allied planes were free to fly in whenever they listed without a single shot being fired, and often with hardly a searchlight to be seen. In a big attack on the 3rd February the Americans pretty well destroyed all that remained of the centre of Berlin, and for days after the city was cut off from the rest of Germany by rail, post, and cable. My Berlin guards were absolutely desperate with anxiety about their wives and families, but no one was allowed to leave the camp, and not even the daily paper reached us. By the end of February, whenever the wind blew from the east, the sound of gunfire on the Oder Front could be clearly heard, and all prisoners were wondering how soon a renewed Russian advance would bring them release, and what form this would take. Reading only German newspapers it was impossible to view the idea of falling into the hands of the Russians with complete confidence, and I was told that many of the prisoners, particularly the Poles, were panic stricken.

I was greatly worried myself on account of my guards, four of the best and kindest men I have ever known. What would happen to them? Would they be treated as Nazis because, against their will, they had been thrust into SS uniforms? Of Paul König and Karl Böning I have already spoken, for both had been with me since 1940. Besides them I had had many others, good, indifferent and bad, but since the beginning of 1943 I had found two others who matched up with Paul and Karl; they were Max Plath and Johannes Braun. The former was a hunchback with the shrewd mind, bitter tongue, and kind heart which occasionally accompanies this deformity. Early in the movement he had joined the Nazi Party and had entered the SS. He was one of the numerous men who had believed in Hitler's promises and had followed him in all good faith, but like so many others, he was full of bitterness at the deceit practised, and he was the only one of my guards who really saw clearly that real responsibility for all the evil done in his name rested upon Hitler; Hitler was no god to him, but a cowardly swindler. His home was in Köslin, a little town in Pomerania, which at that time was threatened by the Russian advance; he had married late in life and was now full of fears for the safety of his wife.

The second, Johannes Braun, came from the Sudeten, and his home was on the slopes of the Schneekoppe, the highest mountain of the range. He was a quiet, sober man, who had never taken the slightest interest in politics, and who lived in a house which had been occupied by his family for over 400 years. He had been born an Austrian but had been quite content to become a Czechoslovak, indeed, he seemed to like the Czechs better than the Germans.

A saddler by trade, his occupation had been the manufacture and repair of ski straps and fittings for the visitors at the three big hotels on the Schneekoppe.

He was one of those men who seem to be dogged by ill-luck. He was fifty-five years of age and thus free from any obligation for military service, but the self-appointed Nazi headman of his village had sent in his name, with that of others, as a volunteer for the Waffen-SS. When he ignored notices calling him up he had been threatened with imprisonment and with the eviction of his family, so in the end he had given in and had been posted to Sachsenhausen. The sights and his experiences in the camp had made him absolutely ill, and he had become so desperate as to contemplate suicide; luckily the commandant had taken a liking to him and sent him to me, and from that time he clung to me as his saviour.

While he was with me he suffered one blow after another. First his grandson died and his daughter developed melancholia, then his wife died, and finally his only son was lost on board a submarine. He was a gentle creature and accepted everything that happened with submission upheld by his firm religious faith. For him the worst blow of all was the fact that SS men were not permitted to attend religious service, and he thus for months had been unable to go to mass or confession. The place where he lived formed part of the estates of Count Czerny, the father of Mrs. von Schuschnigg who, with her husband, the ex-Austrian Chancellor, lived in one of the special villas at the camp. Braun was deeply interested in them and so through him I was always informed as to all the circumstances of their prison life that he could find out. There were four of these houses just outside the camp wall, but within a wall of their own; one was occupied by the Schuschniggs, Fritz Thyssen and his wife lived in another, and the remaining two were occupied by members of the Bavarian royal family of Wittelsbach. On the 6th February he brought me news that all these people had been hurriedly evacuated, though he could not say where they had been taken.

Elser too had gone, taken away by two men from the Security Police, as we all supposed on his last journey. It is difficult to describe the general atmosphere of insecurity which surrounded us, and even I began to have my doubts as to my expectation of a long life. My five years' exclusion from contact with people of my own kind had, of course, left its mark on me, particularly the fact throughout these years I had spoken, read, written, and indeed, thought only in German. Through continual association with people in subordinate positions I had, I fear, become both conceited and domineering, and indeed, I was really beginning to feel myself one of the most important men in the country. My attitude to others was one of touchy benevolence; easy to get on with if I were allowed to have my own way, but liable to fly into a violent passion at the slightest provocation. I had plenty of good clothes and always took pains to be immaculately turned out; if I did not dress for dinner, I did change and put on a dark suit for the evening, and I am quite sure that the fact that I looked entirely different from the usual run of prisoners who, even if they had plenty of clothes, tended to be slovenly and let themselves go, had a great bearing on my standing with everyone from commandant downward. One day after I had asked the commandant whether it would be possible for me to be photographed so that I could give my wife some concrete proof that I was well, the adjutant, Captain Wessels, turned up with a camera and took some snaps of me. He came quite unexpectedly and I had not dressed up for him, but when May received the photograph which he had taken she was much surprised to see me looking so prosperous, and when I look at it now I cannot help feeling that my dress was rather out of place in my environment. Perhaps I was a little bit mad, but after all, even when things were at their best, my life was never free from strain, and at all times could be ended any day by an order from above.

CHAPTER VIII

THE 20th February, 1945, was warm and sunny, and for the first time since the autumn the ground seemed to be quite free from frost so that I could hope soon to start gardening again. The wind was from the east and the firing on the Oder Front could be heard very clearly; I wondered how long it would be before the Russians broke through the German lines again and made their next surge forwards. Really not much use bothering about my garden for it was clear that I should not see another harvest. I had really enjoyed this work so much that I felt quite sad at the thought of leaving it to revert to the wilderness which it had been when I first came to Sachsenhausen. The idea of leaving here seemed quite strange and I wondered how it would come about. While I was wandering round thinking in desultory fashion of the years that I had spent in my prison, and of what liberation would be like, I suddenly became aware that the commandant had come into the garden. It was quite a time since he had been to see me and his appearance now so fitted in with my thoughts that, following a friendly greeting, I asked him at once whether I was to be allowed to stay until the camp was occupied by the Russians or whether, like other prisoners, I would be evacuated away from the battle line.

"I have really no idea," said Kaindl. "About three weeks ago I

wrote to headquarters and asked to be relieved of responsibility
for some of my more important charges such as yourself, but up
to now I have had no answer of any kind. Anyhow, I don't think
that the situation is quite so bad as it was and even if we can't
drive the Russians back just yet, I certainly think that we can
hold them on our present line. We are not beaten yet. Don't forget
that we were as close to Leningrad and Moscow as the Russians
now are to Berlin. On the whole, I don't think that you will be
moved yet, though of course I really know nothing."

I suppose the poor man had to pretend that he did not know
that the game was up, even though for days past there had been
thick clouds of smoke arising from the Kommandantur, where all
camp records and other secret documents were being burned.
Kaindl was far too intelligent a man not to appreciate the position
and not to realize how precarious was his own future, and I really
felt very sorry for him. He had been a good and loyal friend to me,
and I am convinced that he had done everything in his power to
make life tolerable as possible for all prisoners under his care.

From what Kaindl had said, it was pretty clear that if there
were a sudden Russian advance, I should not be allowed to remain
at Sachsenhausen but, like others, would be evacuated. I could not
make up my mind whether to be glad or sorry. Of course the Russians
might recognize me as a British prisoner of war and treat me
accordingly, but there was also a possibility that they might consider me a worthless member of the bourgeois class who could best
be allowed to complete his disappearance. In any case, if the
Russian advance brought them close to the camp one could safely
reckon on a *sauve qui peut* on the part of all officials and guards,
and some pretty bad rioting by the camp inmates. There were
quite a number of SS prisoners in the Bunker, and it was to be
expected that there would be a raid on the building and in the
excitement it was improbable that great care would be taken in
separating the sheep from the goats—there were some pretty rough
customers in the camp who, if the opportunity arose, would think
far more of looting than of saving lives. The conclusion to which
I came was that I should prefer, when the time came, to be liberated
by one or other of the Western Allies, and so I hoped that I would
be evacuated in time.

That afternoon I had just settled down before my typewriter
to take down the German three o'clock war report when Eccarius
came in with a very disturbed look on his face and said: "Herr
Best, you are leaving us."

"What's that?" I said. "When?"

"Now, at once. The car is at the door waiting for you. You are
to pack up all your things as quickly as possible—within an hour
if you can manage it."

Even after my musings of the morning, this news came to me

as a great shock. I had been static for so long that I simply could not imagine what a change would be like nor how I was to set about packing and the rest. Paul, who was in the cell at the time, looked as though he might burst into tears at any moment, but Eccarius shooed him out and told him to get plenty of large card boxes so that I could start packing—I had only one suit-case which would hold but a fraction of my possessions. Paul came back with Max and Johannes, all carrying boxes, and we set to work. We filled my suit-case and five large cartons, but even then my wardrobe was far from empty. The clothes which I had given for safe keeping in the cloak-room could not be found, but it would in any case have been hopeless to attempt to take them with me also—what use to me anyhow were evening clothes on such a journey as I was probably undertaking?

Just as we had nearly finished packing Kaindl came in to bid me good-bye, and to assure me that when we had seen each other in the morning he had had no idea that I should be moved so soon. "It is better for you, Herr Best, and I wish you good luck and a safe return to your wife." I thanked him for all his kindness and we shook hands warmly. I was really fond of the little man and was very sad to leave him behind to face such treatment as would be accorded him as commandant of a notorious concentration camp. All, I think, were sorry to see me go, for they probably looked upon me as their only advocate when they fell into enemy hands.

Eccarius brought me my rations, including two loaves of white bread, which he said I had better take with me. I had quite a lot of cheese, butter, and jam which I had saved up and packed all my foodstuffs in a little handbag. Eccarius also brought me another pound of tobacco, so that I now had almost two pounds in all. Then the move was made with Paul, Max and Johann and the two trusties carrying my baggage. Near the entrance all the warders were drawn up to say good-bye, and really we were most of us near tears. Funny, but I felt quite attached to my old home. Waiting for me at the door was the stout jailer who had led me so gently into Gestapo Headquarters on my first arrival there on the 10th November, 1939. Then he had been a rough-looking man dressed in a sweater and flannel trousers, now he was a smartly dressed Obersturmführer. He was most friendly, and said how glad he was to find me looking so well: "I never thought, when you left us, that I should ever see you alive again. I can't tell you how surprised I was when I was ordered to go and fetch Herr Wolf from the camp."

We went out of the door together and to my horror I saw a German Black Maria, or as they call it, a 'Grüne Minna'. So far I had always been transported in private cars, and I felt it a great come down to be expected to travel by prison van. As far as I could see there was no one else in the van and there was plenty of room for all my luggage. Actually, there were two other passengers, the little Russian and the Englishman from No. 45, but they were shut in two little pens near the entrance of the van which I did not notice. A friendly Hauptscharführer who also remembered me from 1939, got in with me, and he was kind enough to leave door and window open so that I could see where we were going; he also told me that our destination was Berlin, but that he had heard I should only stay there for a day or two and would then travel farther south.

It was most interesting to me, after watching so many air raids on Berlin from a distance, to see something of the damage from close quarters. On the road between Oranienburg and Pankau we passed a fair number of burnt-out cars and lorries but most of the country houses seemed, as far as I could see, undamaged. As we entered the suburbs though, the picture rapidly changed until, as we approached the centre of Berlin, destruction seemed almost complete and nothing but rubble and gutted-out buildings were to be seen. Our van bumped crazily along a narrow pathway which had been cleared through the masses of rubble and it was often difficult to believe that I was passing through a great city. I saw an archway with a notice board 'Adlon' hanging crookedly from it; all that was left of the famous Hotel Adlon, then came the huge treasury building, fire-blackened walls standing amidst piles of bricks and stone.

Our car stopped before some ruins and I was told to get out. I was led through the remains of arches and past short stretches of walls about six feet high until we came to a hole in the ground from which some stone stairs took us into the basement prison of what had once been Gestapo Headquarters. I was booked in much as one is at an hotel, and taken to a cell about eight feet by four, in which there was nothing but a small table, a stool, and a bed folded up against the wall. I had been allowed to take with me my bag of food and other things which I needed for the night; the rest of my luggage remained at the reception desk. I was locked in and for the first time in five and a quarter years, I was alone. I didn't like the experience, indeed, I felt almost frightened.

There was no light in the cell and only a feeble glimmer through the fanlight over the door from an oil lamp in the passage, nor was the prison heated. The building above us had been bombed and gutted in a raid on 3rd February, and central heating plant, water supply and drainage had been put out of action. Although electric current was available there were no lamp bulbs to replace such as had been broken, of which that in my cell was one. As is so often the case after a fine winter's day the evening had turned very cold, and although I put on an overcoat and a thick dressing-gown I found it impossible to get warm. I made a meal from the provisions which I had brought with me, refusing the two unappetizing looking slices of bread and scrape which were offered me by a trusty, and accepting only a cup of peppermint tea. Then I decided to go to bed, all standing in the hope that I might find some warmth in sleep. I had only been lying down for a few minutes when a warder came to the door and said, "Don't undress. The Tommies are on their way, and when the alarm goes you will have to be ready to go to the air-raid shelter." Soon there were the customary three siren wails of the preliminary alert followed after some minutes by the cacophony of a full-dress alarm. The warder opened the door and told me to follow him. With him was the little Russian with whom I was able, when the warder turned aside, to shake hands for the first time. We had known each other for so long and lived together so much in thought that we really met now as dear friends after a long absence.

We were led along the passage in which was my cell and down some stairs which brought us to another similar row of cells. I was deeply sorry for the people who had to live in them, for the atmosphere at this lower level was absolutely poisonous and smelt like an open cesspool. From here we went through a number of passages whose roofs were heavily buttressed with pit poles, through a kitchen, out into a sort of court, and then by a zig-zag approach into a brightly lit concrete air-raid shelter. This seemed to house a number of offices and was probably the place where the remaining Gestapo officials worked. There was a largish square hall which was apparently open to the general public, for people, amongst them women and children, streamed in from outside. We had to stand in one of the passages leading to the offices where we were joined by Obersturmführer Gogalla, my stout warder friend of 1939. I took the opportunity to complain of my accommodation and of the lack of light and heat. "Don't blame us," he said, "it is your people who have done the damage. There are thousands of Berliners who have to live in cellars under the wreckage of their homes, who would be glad to be as well housed as you. You have no idea how horrible life is here. I have lost everything, and my wife went to take refuge with relations in East Prussia which has now been overrun by the Russians, and I have had no more news of her. You will be leaving here tomorrow or the day after and will soon be in more comfortable quarters. Obergruppenführer Müller has given orders that you should be well looked after."

No bombs fell in our neighbourhood and only a few Mosquitoes flew in on this occasion, so the all clear soon sounded and back we went to our cells. Three times that night this programme was repeated, and on one occasion a bomb fell near enough to rock our shelter, and when I got back to my cell I found my bed covered with splinters of glass from the window which had been blown in. In the morning there was a most unpleasant warder on duty who refused to let me out to wash and shave. We had quite a row which ended in my asking to see Obersturmführer Gogalla. The fact that I asked for him by name seemed to impress the warder, who changed his tone and began explaining that water had to be fetched from a stream some distance away, and that until it was brought no one could wash; he promised to let me know as soon as it arrived. It was after ten before I got out, and then I had another squabble before he would let me operate my electric razor from a light plug in the passage. I had a basin of clean water to wash in but was told not to let it run away as it would have to serve for another twenty prisoners. Of the w.c.s, the least said the better; it was merely a selection of the one which seemed slightly less full than the others—altogether, the whole thing was very beastly and not at all what I was used to. Back in my cell I spent a miserable cold day. I was brought some soup, which was just eatable, at noon, and for the rest just sat or lay on my bunk and shivered.

That night there were only two alerts. On one of these occasions when the warder unlocked the door of the cell next to mine a man, dressed in a leather jerkin and very thin-looking grey trousers, rushed out as though he were going to make a dash away from us along the passage. When we came to a better-lighted part of our route I saw that it was the Englishman from No. 45, of whom I had once caught sight as he came from his bath. We were held up on our way to the shelter in one of the passages and had opportunity to exchange a few words. He knew me right enough and told me that he was Squadron-Leader Falconer and that he had been captured three years before in Tunisia; since then he had had no news from home and his people probably thought that he had been shot. I was to see a lot of this gallant officer in the future, and shall always be grateful to him for the loyal way in which he always backed me up.

Generally when I went to the air-raid shelter I saw Gogalla who was always very friendly. He said he was sorry that it had been impossible to evacuate me earlier, but through the bombing everything was at sixes and sevens, and the senior officers were so busy seeking new and safer cover that it was almost impossible to find them. He believed that I was to go south, probably to Dachau, but so far no orders had reached him, and until they did he could do nothing. Next day there were two very pleasant young men on duty, both of whom remembered me from 1939, and welcomed me as an old friend. They were absolutely amazed that I should still be alive as they had been told when we left for Sachsenhausen that both Stevens and I had been beheaded; this had been officially reported in the SS paper *Schwartze Korps*. They were really very nice to me. One of them found a lamp bulb for my cell, so that at all events I could read, and in the evening they took me into the orderly room, where there was a big stove, so that I was able to have a thorough warm up. I was much amused at the way in which they turned on the B.B.C. ten o'clock news as though this were their regular habit; no secrecy about it and they let me listen in with them. There was another raid before midnight, but after that it was calm and I managed to get quite a good sleep.

The unpleasant warder was on duty again next morning and I had a real set-to with him before I could wash and shave; Gogalla came in shortly after to tell me that I should be leaving that evening so I complained to him about the warder's behaviour. After that I had no more difficulty, in fact, he became quite friendly and said that he had only been rude because he was so worried about his wife and children, who were in the area overrun by the Russians. I comforted him by telling him that he should not believe the reports of Russian brutality which were only propaganda and the usual Goebbels lies. He cheered up and after that could not do enough for me. I was genuinely sorry for these poor fellows for really, when one got to know them, it was obvious that they were more the victims of circumstance than the brutal sadists which they are commonly pictured to be. Once they felt that I listened to their stories with real sympathy they showed themselves in their true colours.

I know that I shall be classed as pro-German, but really the question of nationality does not enter into it at all. I am afraid that I completely lack the power of seeing people under some classification as Germans or Frenchmen, friends or enemies. They all seem to me to be so much alike once one knows them, and to me most of these Gestapo men were just ordinary German working men who had been put into uniform and taught that blind obedience to orders was a sacred law. It was a curious thing too, but through my long training as a prisoner I had reached a point where I felt completely sure of my ascendancy over these people. I think that it must be a similar conviction which enables a lion tamer to enter a cage of wild animals unscathed—when I look back I am really astounded at the risks which I took without at the time being in any way conscious that I was doing anything dangerous.

We were to have set forth on our further travels at 10 p.m., but there was another alert and it was nearly midnight before a move was made. When I emerged from the ruins I found another prison van waiting, and when I got in I was to my horror and disgust pushed into one of the cages near the entrance and the door was slammed to. The cage was about eighteen inches wide by two feet deep, with a six-inch ledge at the back to act as seat; at face level there was a small square of wire netting. Through this I could see Falconer and the little Russian in the two opposite cages. Both were considerably shorter than I and possibly were able to sit, but my long legs kept me tightly jammed between the front and back partitions and I could make no contact with the seat however much I twisted myself sideways. The idea of a long journey like this filled me with dread.

As soon as we started off though the guards, the same two men I had found so friendly the previous day, opened the door of my cage and I was able to sit on the floor and stretch out my legs. The other two poor fellows remained shut up for the entire journey, and I felt very guilty to be travelling in such comparative comfort; I was even able to get some sleep though every time I dozed off I was soon jolted awake as our van rolled over some scar left by bombs on the smooth surface of the Reichsautobahn. In the back part of the van where there was seating accommodation for eight people, I saw four of my fellow prisoners from Sachsenhausen whom I had already seen in the air-raid shelter at Berlin; they were the lady and gentleman who had occupied cell No. 38 after the Bears had left, the man, said to be a German general, from No. 9, and another lady who only reached the Bunker a few days before I was evacuated. I could not help envying their comparative comfort and tried to induce the guards to allow Falconer, the Russian, and me to join them, but there was nothing doing. The journey seemed interminable, especially as we could see nothing outside and had no idea what progress we were making; actually, I had a strange illusion that the car was travelling in circles.

At last we came to a stop and our guards opened the door and got out. The electric light was turned out and as the door opened fresh air and a gleam of sunlight brought us new life and hope. We were dirty and tired, filled with the wish to get out and go somewhere, anywhere, but for a long time nothing happened. We seemed to be near a concentration camp for a loudspeaker nearby was blaring out orders regarding the formation of working parties, and every now and again there was the sound of men tramping past us in wooden soled boots—a familiar sound to me. As time passed our guards became more and more agitated and both got out and became involved in argument with other voices. From what was said I gathered that our arrival was unheralded, the commandant could not be found, and in any case, there was no room for us. An agitated voice kept repeating: "Ausgeschlossen! Das gibt es nicht. Hier ist überhaupt kein Raum. Ihr müsst halt weiter." (Impossible! That can't be done. There is absolutely no room here. You will just have to go further.) To which our men protested that they had orders to come here, and that after they had unloaded they must return at once to Berlin.

Naturally we prisoners took advantage of the opportunity to get acquainted. I gave Falconer and the Russian cigarettes and then one of the ladies, the one from No. 38, came up and spoke to us. She was a Mrs. Heberlein who, with her husband, the late German Ambassador in Madrid, had been kidnapped by Gestapo agents whilst staying with relatives in Spain. She was Spanish but her mother was Irish. She told us that the other lady was the wife of General Halder, the late Chief of the German General Staff, and the man a General von Rabenau. The little Russian, Molotov's nephew, introduced himself as Wassilli Kokorin, flying officer in the Russian Air Force. Gradually we formed an animated group exchanging accounts of our experiences and our guards were by then so bewildered and agitated that they made no efforts to stop our fraternization. Falconer and Kokorin were still penned up in their cages and all that we could do for them was to stick lighted cigarettes through their wire gratings for them to smoke. As Falconer was bankrupt of tobacco I said that he could have about a quarter of a pound of mine which I had with me in a pouch.

After we had waited about like this for an hour or so the chief of our escort gave us the order to get out, and we were hustled through bright sunlight into the twilight of a whitewashed basement. All that I could see as I walked from the van—I was dazzled by the sudden change from our tenebrous van—was that we were entering a yellow-painted house of some five or six stories high. We were all lined up in a sort of cellar passage, our luggage was carried in by a couple of prisoners in camp uniform, and then a very stout, rather jolly looking man in the uniform of an SS-Oberführer came in accompanied by a Hauptsturmführer. The leader of our escort reported "Sieben Gefangene zur Stelle, Kommandant" (seven prisoners present, Commandant!) and the Oberführer then asked us in turn for our names. First Mrs. Halder was taken away, as I heard later, to another building, and then the Heberleins were ushered into a cell just behind where they had been standing. The commandant went in with them and we could hear Mrs. Heberlein protesting that the cell was far too small for two people, and the commandant apologizing and saying that unfortunately he had no alternative accommodation to offer. Then Falconer and Kokorin were taken to two nearby cells in the same row, Falconer cleverly abstracting my tobacco pouch from my pocket as he passed; then it was my turn.

I shouted, "Payne Best"—as a secret prisoner, one loses no opportunity of telling the world who one is—the commandant said "What?" looked again at a list which he was holding and said, "For us your name is Wolf." My answer was, "Yes, but I am such a very good wolf that people always call me Best." A feeble joke, I know, but it served to keep my spirits up. The commandant smiled and then personally showed me into a large whitewashed cell on the opposite side of the cellar, in a passage separated from the first by the central gangway through which we had entered.

After my miserable cell in Berlin and the discomforts of the journey this cell seemed large, bright and cheerful—I was very soon to learn how little this was the case. On this morning though both electric light and heating were on and it looked to me positively inviting, and I felt that I was in clover; it was more than twice the size of my Sachsenhausen cell. It was obviously occupied, for a large table was covered with books, framed photographs, papers, and toilet articles. I wondered whether I was to share it with someone and found the idea pleasing. Soon though, one of the trusties came in and began carrying out various things, and a tall man dressed in a dark suit but without a tie came in and began clearing up the things on the table; he was Dr. Pünder, a Secretary of State in the pre-Nazi governments and until recently Mayor of Münster. Whilst I was alone in the cell for a few minutes a tall, oldish man dressed in German hunting clothes slipped in cautiously, and asked my name and whether I had come from Berlin. Being new to the place and not wishing to start off with trouble through speaking to other prisoners I was rather short with him and asked by what right he questioned me; he mumbled something and slipped out of the cell again. He, too, I was to know quite well in the future; he was Werner Count von Alvensleben, a well-known figure in the sporting world. Two trusties came in carrying a bed—Pünder had apparently slept on a plank bunk hinged to the wall—but although I was given a bed, it consisted of a very thin mattress resting on hard planks. One of the trusties, a good-looking lad of about eighteen, said to me, "If you want anything out of your luggage, tell me, and I will try to get it for you." To this I answered, "Of course I want all my luggage brought into my cell; I have always had it with me." "You will find that everything is different here. They will never let you have it."

The only warder I had so far seen here was a rather pleasant-looking young fellow, Unterscharführer Sippach, a Saxon from Gera. When the men had finished tidying up my cell an older and bad-tempered-looking Oberscharführer came in and, without paying the slightest attention to me, looked round the place and started fingering the things which I had brought with me. I asked him whether I could have some coffee and something to eat, to which he answered that there was none; he then went out, slamming and bolting the door after him. I was so dead tired that I lay down on my bed and went to sleep almost at once. I was awakened by the Oberscharführer, Dittmann, was his name, unbolting the door of my cell. When he entered I at once asked him to have my luggage brought in to which, as to all my requests, his only answer was: "Gibts nicht" (nothing doing). At this I lost my temper and began to give him one of my famous Ausschnauzers, to which he retaliated in almost better voice so that we were soon in the middle of a first-class slanging match; he got so angry that he started fiddling with the pistol in his holster.

Sippach must have heard the row for he came along, edged Dittmann from the room and tried to pacify me, agreeing to everything that I asked for. Although the junior in rank, he told me that he was the head man in the building, and that if ever I wanted anything to ask him and not his colleague who was very nervous. He explained that this was really a place of detention for SS men, and that they had never before had any V.I.P.s, and Dittmann did not know how to behave. He was not really a bad fellow, but the constant air raids had got on his nerves and he could not control his temper. This may have been so, but I always found Dittmann a most unpleasant fellow; he was a cowardly bully and a swine who did everything he could to render the lives of those in his power as miserable as possible. We fought almost every time that we met and although he often threatened me with his pistol he was far too great a coward to be dangerous, and I always treated him like dirt.

In August 1944 the American Air Force made a daylight raid in which they very cleverly bombed all the buildings round the periphery of Buchenwald without damaging the camp itself at all. They were, at the time, probably ignorant of the fact that during the daytime there were seldom many prisoners in the camp, but that large numbers were employed at the Deutsche Ausrustungswerke and other buildings just outside the camp walls. The raid certainly destroyed the Kommandantur and the living quarters of the SS troops employed at the camp, but besides this resulted in the death of a very large number of prisoners, amongst whom were many V.I.P.s imprisoned in the Bunker. Amongst these were Breitscheid, the former leader of the Social Democratic Party, and Princess Mafalda of Italy, the wife of Prince Philip of Hesse. At the time the Germans announced that the Communist leader Thaelmann had also been killed in this raid, but from all that I could learn, this was not true, and actually he had been shot five weeks earlier at Flossenberg or Sachsenhausen.

The only buildings near the camp which had escaped destruction were five tenement houses used as married quarters for the camp officials, which were about half a mile away. These had since been evacuated by the original inhabitants and they now housed the Kommandantur and provided barracks for the troops. The building in which we were imprisoned was one of these houses of which the cellar had been reconstructed, half as prison and half as ammunition store. Very jolly indeed when you consider that one heard nothing from the warders except their certainty that soon or later we should be bombed again and none of us would escape alive. The two warders were absolutely panic-struck every time that the alert sounded and, after locking and bolting us in our cells, immediately fled to the cover of slit trenches in the fields nearby.

The first day did not on the whole pass too badly. I had got all my belongings in the cell and after tidying up a bit spent most of the time on my bed. There was a fairly good soup at midday, and in the evening a third of a two-pound loaf of bread, butter, and jam. There were two air raids in the evening during which all the lights in the camp were turned out at the main. Some bombs fell so close that I had hurriedly to remove all breakables from the table. In spite of the assurances of the warders I did not myself think that it was in the least likely that we should be bombed, and so these raids were merely an inconvenience which I could bear with equanimity, whilst it was really rather amusing to think of all the warders and guards lying shivering on their tummies in trenches outside. Not that I was warm, for I have never in my life been in a colder place than that cell. It was three-quarters underground and the only light came from a small window close to the ceiling which opened into a sort of brick chimney, so that only a mere glimmer came through. It was very damp, water ran down the wall in several places and daily I had to brush the beginnings of mildew from my clothes. There was no heating except that towards the end of my stay it was turned on twice for an hour; it was said that the coal stocks of the camp were exhausted.

Worst of all, after the first day there was practically no food; a thickish slice of bread per day and about two pints of tepid water in which some cabbage or a few carrots had been boiled. Sippach told me that the day after our arrival Obergruppenführer Pohle, the Director of Concentration Camps, had visited Buchenwald and had requisitioned all stocks of food and fuel for the use of the refugees who, for weeks past had been pouring into Thuringia from the east in advance of the Russian invasion. Fresh supplies should have been brought to the camp from the south and west, but by that time road and rail transport had been so completely disorganized by allied air raids that we were to all intents and purposes cut off from the rest of Germany. A few days after our arrival one of the warders from the Berlin prison came to bring some dispatches and orders to the commandant. He came to my cell to see me as he had a message from Kaindl to say that he was sending my old guards to me as he knew that I should be unhappy without them. This young man, one of the two who had travelled with us from Berlin, gave me a graphic account of the disorganization of communications. He said that it was no longer possible to phone or telegraph from Berlin and that letters, even if they arrived at all, took weeks to reach their destination. The railway was practically out of action as daily it was cut in several places whilst travel by road was only possible by night.

The day after my arrival at Buchenwald started off with another set-to with Dittmann, whom I found meddling with some of my things when I came back from washing. He claimed that he had the right to see what prisoners brought into the cells and wanted to take my typewriter and my table knife away. For a time it really looked as though he would get violent but he suddenly turned round, flounced out of the cell, and banged the door to with much ostentatious noise of bolting. About five minutes later he came back and told me that the Court-Martial Officer would come to see me in the afternoon and that he would report me to him. I said that, on the contrary, it was I who would report him, whereupon after some more argument we agreed that we would let bygones be bygones, and neither of us report the other, after which he became quite friendly and took me to the orderly room, where there was a light plug, so that I could shave. Shortly afterwards the Court-Martial Officer, Lieutenant Günther, turned up. He was friendly and polite but said 'no' to everything that I asked him. I could neither write nor receive letters as there were no facilities for dealing with them, nor was exercise out of doors possible, since the building was not in the camp and it would be impossible to guard prisoners properly; all that he could offer was that each prisoner could walk in the passage for half an hour daily. After he had gone I wrote a letter to the commandant making a strong complaint about the conditions of my imprisonment and requesting him to forward my letter to the Gestapo at Berlin.

Whilst I was at Buchenwald I wrote several similar letters to him but they had little or no effect; he never came to see me and the only tangible result was that he generally sent me some tobacco or cigarettes. When I look back on this time I am really surprised that I did not get into serious trouble for I was certainly a most exigent, troublesome prisoner. I had got so used to being top dog at Sachsenhausen that I expected the warders here, who knew nothing about me, to toe the line just as Eccarius had done; anyhow, my policy paid, for before long we were all doing pretty well what we liked, and the most that the warders could hope for was that we would behave ourselves and stay in our cells when any officer visited the building.

There were seventeen of us prisoners and if the warders had obeyed orders and let each of us out separately for half an hour's exercise they would have had no peace but would have been kept on the *qui vive* from morning to night. Since they much preferred to spend their hours of duty resting in the warm orderly room they soon began to let us out in bunches of half a dozen or more. At first each single person or each couple, in cases where cells were occupied by two people, were supposed to confine their promenade to separate passages, but very soon we all got together and talked with each other freely. By shifting the hour when I went out from day to day, I was gradually able to meet and talk to all my fellow prisoners. In the morning, too, all cell doors were unlocked at the same time, generally between 6 and 8 a.m., and we men forgathered in the lavatory while the trusties cleaned out the cells and made our beds.

It may make my story simpler to follow if I now give the names of my fellow prisoners, for most of them play a part in what I have

When we first arrived the place of Dr. Rascher was occupied by the chief medical officer of the camp, Dr. Hoven. I could never find out of what crime he had been guilty, but he was a very privileged prisoner who spent most of his day sitting with the warders in their room. Before the war he had had a clinic at Freiburg in Breisgau, which was apparently frequented by many well-known English people. Hoven was at some pains to curry favour with me, but he struck me as a shifty, cruel creature, and I was neither sorry nor surprised when, after the war, he was condemned to death and hanged by sentence of an allied court.

With the exception of the Heberlein's, Falconer, Kokorin, and myself, none of the prisoners possessed anything but the clothes in which they stood—they were provided weekly with clean underwear from the prison laundry. They had neither ties nor braces, and for those who had not been so lucky as to acquire a piece of string, hands in the pockets was the rule. I was far and away the best equipped, and so it was not long before almost everyone wore some article of clothing from my stock. I had also some books, a good atlas, two pocket chess sets, and patience cards, all of which I lent out to various people. Tobacco was the greatest problem. When I arrived I had about a pound and a half of Machorka with me, but this I distributed within a week and then we struck hard times. I had quite a lot of dried peppermint, and when things were at their worst we made cigarettes of this. The flavour was not at all bad, but the cigarettes had no pep at all and after one had smoked one, one wanted another immediately. One of the trusties was a Ukrainian and I became good friends with him. He was often sent on errands to the camp by the warders, and there he knew some Rumanians who still had tobacco which they had received in parcels from home. They charged black market prices for it, but luckily I had a couple of hundred marks left and so could buy enough to keep the wolf from the door. I shared everything that I got with the others, and although we were on very short rations, I don't think that there were more than two days when we were unable to get anything at all. I am sorry to harp so much on the subject of tobacco, but for me, the world is a sorry place when I cannot smoke to my heart's content. Actually, I believe that the conditions of prison life create an enhanced craving for tobacco, for nerves get on edge and there is nothing else with which to soothe them.

After the first two or three days my relations with the warders had so much improved that I managed to get out of my cell quite a lot, either sitting in the orderly room warming myself or, if any were about, talking to my fellow prisoners. Indeed, I got so far that when Sippach was on duty he would leave my cell door unbolted if no visitors of higher rank were expected. Sippach was a badly scared man, not so much frightened of bombs as of what

might happen to him if the camp were overrun by the Allies. I
don't know what he had done, but he seemed to be in the bad
books of the Russian prisoners, and he told me himself that they
would tear him limb from limb if they ever got hold of him. He had
been attacked before for he had a nasty scar on his throat which
he said had been caused when a Russian prisoner went for him
with a knife. When, towards the end of my stay at Buchenwald,
the Americans had advanced within a few miles of the camp he
told me that he was leaving as soon as we had gone, and later I
heard that he had done so.

When I first made contact with the other prisoners what struck
me most forcedly was the intense distrust of most of the Germans
of each other; almost every one of them warned me to be careful
of some other as he was a Gestapo spy. I paid no heed to these
warnings and just took people as I found them; later on we all
became good friends and none ever showed the least inclination
toward treachery. This atmosphere of suspicion was typical of
Nazi Germany, though it seemed to me strange that these people,
imprisoned by the Gestapo, had so little inclination to form a common front and pull together. Both then and later, most of the
German prisoners I met displayed an apathetic, I might say,
fatalistic resignation and, as I suppose they had done all their
lives, obeyed every order given to them without sign of unwillingness. I believe, that but for these two elements of mutual distrust
and subservience to authority, it would have been possible to
organize a mass escape in the company of our warders. These
men were so badly scared that it would have required very little
to convince them that their only hope of safety lay in helping us
to liberty, and in accompanying us to the American lines; I tried
hard to induce them to go off one night with Falconer, Kokorin,
and myself, but we were after all foreigners, and I could never
overcome their last instinctive distrust of us which only the whole-
hearted co-operation of the distinguished Germans of our party
could have perhaps done.

One of the first of my fellow prisoners whom I met was old
Count von Alvensleben, to whom I apologized for my rather brusque
behaviour when he spoke to me on my first arrival. He was a dear
old man, slightly senile although he was only just seventy; whenever he could he buttonholed me and told me interminable stories
about his hunting expeditions in Canada and his amatory successes
everywhere. His first words, whenever we met, related to the end
of the war, and with bated breath he would mention a date some
fortnight or three weeks later as though it had been communicated
to him from heaven. He had always opposed Hitler but, as he was
old and harmless, he had been left to live more or less in peace on
his estate in Westphalia. After the 20th July attempt on Hitler's
life he was, like so many others, suddenly arrested and taken to

Buchenwald, for although he had himself taken no part in the conspiracy many of those who had, amongst them Field-Marshall von Witzleben, were friends of his. No charge had been brought against him, and he had not even been interrogated; nevertheless about a fortnight after I reached Buchenwald he was informed that he had been sentenced to two years imprisonment, and was taken away to serve his sentence at the prison at Münster. He was highly delighted with this turn of events as Münster was close to his home and would certainly soon be in Allied hands.

General von Rabenau and his companion, Dietrich Bonnhöfer, were alike only in the fact that both were deeply religious. Von Rabenau, the author of *A Life of General von Seeckt*, had reached the rank of full general and had retired from the army in order to devote himself to religious study, having since taken degrees in both arts and divinity. He was a militant churchman who retained about him the authoritative bearing of the soldier and was, I imagine, inclined to expect unquestioning obedience to his religious opinions. Bonnhöfer, on the other hand, was all humility and sweetness; he always seemed to me to diffuse an atmosphere of happiness, of joy in every smallest event in life, and of deep gratitude for the mere fact that he was alive. There was something dog-like in the look of fidelity in his eyes and his gladness if you showed that you liked him. He was one of the very few men that I have ever met to whom his God was real and ever close to him. Yet both these men, each of them deeply religious in his own way, had played an active role in the plot to depose Hitler, which culminated in the events of 20th July, 1944. I do not know whether they were actually involved to the extent that they knew that Hitler's removal was to be effected by assassination, but they were in the confidence of all the main conspirators, and Bonnhöfer in particular had played an important role as messenger and connecting link between different parts of the country. Both men had been tried before a People's Court and both had heard the death sentence passed on them. Why execution had been postponed, and why they had instead been sent to Buchenwald, was something they could not understand.

Another active member in the 20th July plot was Captain Gehre. When he heard of the failure of the attempt on Hitler's life, realizing that his arrest was imminent, he shot his wife and tried to commit suicide, but succeeded only in blowing out his right eye. He had been nursed back to health by the Gestapo, had been tortured and interrogated, and finally condemned to death by a People's Court. He was a spare, dark, good-looking man of about thirty, and the absolute opposite of his room mate, Dr. Josef Müller, who, indeed, looked upon him, as he did on practically everyone with whom he came in contact, with the deepest suspicion. Müller was a very important man, and knew it. He was, next to Cardinal Faulhauber, probably the most influential representative of Roman Catholicism in Germany and Hitler's most bitter enemy. To look at he was just an ordinary stoutish little man with a florid complexion and drab fair hair cut *en brosse*, the sort of man whom you would not look at a second time if you met him anywhere and yet, one of the bravest and most determined men imaginable. He had spent some three years in the hands of the Gestapo, during which they had exhausted their arts in efforts to get him to talk, but in vain.

In revenge for their failure they had made his imprisonment as intolerable as possible. For two and a half years he had been confined in a small, dark, unheated underground cell, chained day and night. His hands were handcuffed together and his feet clamped to an iron bar one and a half yards long so that his feet were kept some two feet apart. His bunk was fixed to the wall and the bar was so long that it was impossible for him to rest both feet on the bed at once. The only occasion when these fetters were removed was once a month, when he bathed and changed his under-linen; for the rest, he wore them night and day and consequently could never remove his clothes. Add to this insufficient food of the coarsest possible kind and frequent beatings up about the head and face with rubber truncheons, and it will be understood that for him Buchenwald seemed like heaven, even though he had grown somewhat distrustful of his fellow men. Because I was English and because he remembered all details of my capture he accepted me at face value and eventually we became very good friends.

Of the Heberleins, the grey mare was undoubtedly the better horse. A mixture of Irish and Spanish blood cannot fail to produce something vivid and out of the ordinary. Margot Heberlein was all of this; indeed, she was so full of fire and energy that I had my work cut out to restrain her when in her impatience for action she interfered in delicate and difficult negotiations in which I was engaged with our jailers. She always wanted quite a lot of things, and she wanted them at once; she was as big a trial to her captors as two British prisoners, which is saying a lot. Her husband? A charming man, a diplomat of the old school, with impeccable manners and the impaired digestion of his class. Conversation was for him a screen designed to hide his feelings and thoughts from the world, and so much of his life had been passed in that atmosphere of make-believe which is called diplomacy, that I often doubted whether he really knew where he was and why. His wife tended him, shielded him, and was ready to fight for him.

Heberlein had been German Ambassador at Madrid and, as a professional diplomat, had carried on with his duties even though, as he declared, he was from the first an opponent of the Nazi regime. One day he went on leave and at its end did not return to his post, but continued to stay at the house of relatives of his wife. He was ordered to return and report at once to Berlin, but again disobeyed. This, of course, was more than the Gestapo could tolerate, so one night three or four men broke into the bedroom where the Heberleins were sleeping, laid Heberlein out with a blow on the head and bundled his wife up in the bed clothes. Both were then taken down a ladder, put into a car, driven to an airfield, and flown to Bordeaux, where they were imprisoned for some weeks. They were in their night clothes and were given nothing else to put on, so for warmth had to make shift with the blankets in which Mrs. Heberlein's cries had been stifled. They were then flown to Berlin where each was confined in a different prison until October 1944. Then, without warning, they were suddenly taken by car to Sachsenhausen, where they were conducted to what they called a magnificent and comfortably furnished suite, where they also found luggage containing clothes and other effects which had apparently been sent from Spain. Neither had ever been interrogated, and they were entirely ignorant of everything that had happened in the world since their capture, as they had seen no papers nor been allowed to receive or write letters; they had simply been forwarded from one place to another like parcels.

Dr. Pünder was a man who concealed a keen intelligence behind almost exaggerated politeness and good breeding. This formed rather a barrier to any intimacy between us, for after five years spent in the company of men of the working class my conversational style had become more graphic than polite, and I was, I fear, rather too much inclined to call a spade a bloody shovel. Our relations were, however, perfectly amicable, and I even succeeded in winning his gratitude by presenting him with my best tie, one of those delicate grey creations worn at weddings and other formal social functions, which certainly helped him to appear as well as to act as a one-time Secretary of State. His cell mate, Commander Franz Liedig, was a member of the staff of Admiral Canaris, the chief of the Germany counter-espionage organization, and had been stationed in Greece. Admiral Canaris, until his own arrest by the Gestapo, had been the influential hidden hand behind all plots against Hitler, and had used his organization to plant members of the opposition in key positions and to help others to escape arrest by fleeing the country.

I do not in the least know what had been Liedig's role, as it was not customary amongst prisoners to ask any questions, but it was obvious that at the time of which I am speaking he did not himself believe that he had much longer to live. Conversation with him was particularly interesting to me because he had such detailed knowledge of the German railway system, and could therefore estimate the possibility of any mass movement of troops from the north to what was already known as the Southern Redoubt. It was his opinion that even at this time, the beginning of March 1945, such a movement was no longer feasible, and that for all practical military purposes Germany had already been cut in half, into a northern and a southern zone. This was important, for rumours were already current that our final destination was the neighbourhood of Berchtesgaden, where Hitler intended to make his last stand, and that it was intended to use us as hostages to be bartered in exchange for the safety of important members of the Nazi hierarchy.

Colonel von Petersdorff, who later became a great friend of mine, was a wild adventurous fellow. In the First World War he had been wounded six times and already in 1914 had lost the use of his right arm. After the 1918 armistice he had joined one of the free corps operating in the Baltic, with which he had had a number of hair-breadth escapes. When the Nazi Party started he became one of the earliest members and, as a very wealthy man, a most valuable recruit. When Hitler rose to power in 1933 and showed that his reading of his election pledges was different from what they had generally been believed to mean, von Petersdorff immediately went into opposition and joined the party of dissidents in the S.A. under the leadership of Roehm, narrowly missing being one of the victims of the subsequent bloody purge. After this he went underground and came into association with most of those actively engaged in conspiracy against the Nazi regime. On the outbreak of war though he could not resist the call to arms and immediately volunteered for service. He took part in the Polish campaign and, in the invasion of France, commanded the armoured reconnaissance unit, which was the first to reach the coast on the English Channel near Abbeville. For this action he was awarded the Knight's Cross to the Iron Cross, being one of the first three men to receive this decoration. Very soon afterwards he was again in active opposition even though he continued to take part in the war, being wounded a further four times.

He had been involved in the 20th July plot and was one of the many hundreds of army officers arrested after its failure. Luckily, the Gestapo failed to find any proofs of his complicity, and although a case was made out against him and he was brought before a People's Court, he was acquitted. The Gestapo, as was often the case, did not agree with the verdict, and at once arrested von Petersdorff and consigned him to the prison in Laehrterstrasse, in Berlin. When this was destroyed by bombs on 3rd February, 1945, he was buried under debris in his cell, suffering injury to lungs and kidneys, for which he was given no treatment of any kind. When I met him he was obviously a very sick man, but his spirit was indomitable, and throughout the rest of our adventures as prisoners he never shirked danger or responsibility.

Of all the party at Buchenwald, the one whom I liked most and whom to this day I consider one of the finest men I have ever met, was General Freiherr von Falkenhausen, late German Governor-General and Commander-in-Chief in Belgium and Northern France. A member of an old family of the German nobility he had done distinguished service in the First World War, receiving the 'Pour le mérite', the highest German decoration for bravery. Until the outbreak of the Second World War he had been in China, where he was head of a military mission engaged in the reorganization of the forces of Generalissimo Chiang Kai-shek. The East, and particularly Chinese philosophy, had always exercised a great attraction on him, and as he found his work show greater and greater success he made up his mind to make his home in China. With the rise to power of Hitler, who represented everything in politics that he found most abhorrent, he even decided to relinquish his German nationality and adopt that of his new home. When, however, Nazi Germany attempted to secure the co-operation of Japan and her adhesion to the Axis power block, objection was raised to the fact that a German mission was assisting China in her fight against Japanese aggression, and orders were issued from Berlin that von Falkenhausen should liquidate his organization and return to Germany.

When this order reached him, the general reported the matter to Chiang Kai-shek, who at once said that to his great regret he could not permit him to leave China. Owing to his position, von Falkenhausen was fully informed as to every detail of China's military organization and her plans for the future and, since Germany was now flirting with her enemy and seemed even to contemplate a close military alliance, to permit him to return to Germany would be tantamount to disclosing all China's most secret information to Japan. Von Falkenhausen at once said that he had no wish to return to Germany and that he hoped that the Generalissimo would refuse to sanction his return, and would facilitate his adoption of Chinese nationality so that he could continue in his service. Chiang Kai-shek was in full agreement and von Falkenhausen wrote at length to Berlin explaining his position. The next thing that happened was that he received a telegram signed by von Ribbentrop personally, informing him that unless he left for Germany by a boat due to sail in about three weeks' time, all his property would be confiscated and all members of his family would be sent to concentration camps.

Again von Falkenhausen reported to Chiang Kai-shek who, he said, "like the fine gentleman he was", immediately told him that under such circumstances he could not of course think of preventing him from leaving the country. He was sure that China's interests were safe in his hands, and he hoped that he would find it possible to return soon and take up his duties again. He would not allow him to resign from his service but would grant him leave of indefinite duration during which he would be on full pay.

When von Falkenhausen returned to Germany attempts were made to obtain information from him regarding China's defence plans, but he absolutely refused to give any information about such matters. At that time, when he was already contemplating war, Hitler did not feel himself strong enough to take violent action against a general of such high reputation as von Falkenhausen, especially since the case of von Fritsch, who had been a victim of a Gestapo conspiracy, was still fresh in the memory of all German officers, so von Falkenhausen was permitted to return to his home. When, however, France, Holland and Belgium were overrun in 1940, von Falkenhausen was appointed Governor-General and Commander-in-Chief in Holland and Belgium. At that time it was still Nazi policy to pretend that they had entered these countries, not as aggressors, but as liberators, in the mistaken belief that large sections of the population headed by Mussart and Degrelle, the Dutch and Belgian Quislings, would be willing to co-operate with them. Von Falkenhausen was therefore appointed because he was well known for his liberal views, and it was thought that he might succeed in establishing a government which would reconcile the mass of the population to German occupation, and even bring it gradually into the Nazi camp.

Von Falkenhausen raised many objections before he would consent to accept the appointment, and when he actually did so in 1941 Holland had already been taken from him and given to Seiss-Inquart, and his command in Belgium was then extended to cover Northern France. He told me that when he heard of Seiss-Inquart's appointment in Holland he knew what that would mean for that unfortunate country, and had he not accepted the post in Belgium that country also would have suffered under the rule of some dyed-in-the-wool Nazi.

Throughout his term as Governor-General a bitter war was waged between him and the Gestapo until, when he came to Berlin one day in 1944, he was arrested on arrival and imprisoned in one of the lower dungeons in the Prinz Albrechtstrasse. He had been brought to Buchenwald a day or two before our party arrived, without ever having been interrogated or charged with any offence; he was in a very bad state, starved and verminous, and one of the first things that happened after my arrival was the delousing of his own and the two neighbouring cells.

Three or four days after reaching Buchenwald, Sippach told me one evening that they were expecting a new prisoner, an Englishman, and that very possibly he would have to share my cell as they were short of room. Of course I was delighted with this news and could hardly sleep that night; anyhow, there was a big raid on Weimar and so much disturbance that sleep would have been difficult in any case. I heard the arrival of a car and the sound of someone being brought into the cell next to mine. Next morning, when I went to wash, there was a little man with a ginger moustache in the lavatory who introduced himself as Dr. Rascher saying that he was half English and that his mother was related to the Chamberlain family. When I told him my name he was much interested saying that he knew all about my case, and that he had also met Stevens when he was medical officer at Dachau. We could not talk much at this first meeting, but I often managed to have my exercise at the same time as he and, probably because he was an SS officer, the warders raised no objection to our talking together. He was a queer fellow; possibly the queerest character which has ever come my way.

Almost at our first meeting he told me that he had belonged to Himmler's personal staff, and that it was he who had planned and supervised the construction of the gas chambers and was responsible for the use of prisoners as guinea pigs in medical research. Obviously, he saw nothing wrong in this and considered it merely a matter of expediency. As regards the gas chambers he said that Himmler, a very kind-hearted man, was most anxious that prisoners should be exterminated in a manner which caused them least anxiety and suffering, and the greatest trouble had been taken to design a death chamber so camouflaged that its purpose would not be apparent, and to regulate the flow of the lethal gas so that the patients might fall asleep without recognizing that they would never wake. Unfortunately, Rascher said, they had never quite succeeded in solving the problem caused by the varying resistance of different people to the effects of poison gases, and always there had been a few who lived longer than others and recognized where they were and what was happening. Rascher said that the main difficulty was that the numbers to be killed were so great that it was impossible to prevent the gas chambers being overfilled, which greatly impeded any attempts to ensure a regular and simultaneous death-rate.

As regards the experiments on prisoners, Rascher obviously considered that these were fully justified by the great value of the scientific results obtained. He quite obviously saw nothing wrong in exposing a couple of dozen people to intense cold, in water or air, and then attempting their resuscitation. He was in fact very proud of having discovered a technique which he said would save the lives of thousands who would otherwise have died from exposure, and said that his imprisonment was due to the fact that he had attempted to publish the results of his research into this question in a Swiss medical journal so that it might benefit British seamen who, after rescue from the sea when their ships were torpedoed, frequently died without recovering consciousness. I should say here that Rascher gave at least half a dozen different reasons for his imprisonment, and no one ever discovered what he really had done.

No, I was not at the time greatly shocked by his stories, nor, when they got to know him, were any of our fellow prisoners. We were all far too hardened to surroundings where sudden death was the order of the day. At any moment an order might come for some or all of us to be gassed, shot, or hung, and subconsciously we were all so much engaged in the struggle for survival that no one had the energy to expend in sympathy for the sufferings of unknown and anonymous people who, after all, were already dead; besides, Rascher was such a good comrade to us all. This is where the queer contradiction in his character comes in, for throughout our association with him he was distinguished by his bravery, unselfishness, and loyalty. In the difficult days that were to come he was the life and soul of our party, and although he well knew the risk, never hesitated to stand up to the brutal set of guards who had us in their power.

My meeting with Rascher was particularly interesting because he could fill in many of the gaps in my knowledge of the circumstances which had led to the capture of Stevens and myself, and the way in which it had been intended to involve me with Elser as the author of the attempt on Hitler's life in November 1939. According to what he had heard at the time, there was originally no connection at all between the two events, and the plan to capture Stevens and me had resulted from the arrest of Major Solms, through whom the Gestapo had got on the track of the conspiracy which we had been investigating. No action had been taken against the general whom we had hoped to meet as Hitler, at that time, was seeking to avoid any unnecessary friction with the General Staff; several of the minor people, however, had been arrested and in particular a colonel who should have visited us in Holland in the first instance, and who was the man who had made the first direct contact with Dr. Franz, had been intercepted and his place taken by two Gestapo officials.

When Dr. Franz went to the frontier to meet, as he thought, a friend, he was accosted by two strangers who told him that everything had been discovered and that his wife and sons were now in Dachau. If he placed any value on their lives he would have to be sensible and do what was required of him, which was to tell the British officers that they were the friends whom he had expected; he must remember that if anything occurred to arouse the suspicion of the Englishmen, appropriate action would be taken against all members of his family. Well, Dr. Franz did as he was told and my presence in Buchenwald was the result; yet, I cannot find it in my heart to blame the little man for he was certainly placed in a most terrible position. He was by no manner of means a heroic figure; just an ordinary little Bavarian whom chance had thrust into the midst of a web of plots and counter-plots.

As regards the Bürgerbraukeller bomb, Rascher said that everyone knew that this was a Gestapo fake, but he could not say exactly
what had been behind it. From all that he had heard he believed
that Goebbels had been at the back of it and that the intention
had been to arouse public enthusiasm in Munich, where there
was a sad lack of war-like spirit, by the pretence that British agents
had attempted to assassinate the Führer. When I asked whether
it had been the intention to kill a number of party members as
had actually occurred, he said no, this had been an accident as
normally they would have left the building at the same time as
Hitler. For this reason the whole matter had been rather hushed
up, for far from arousing any enthusiasm in Munich, there had
almost at once been rumours that this was just another Reichstag
fire affair, and that the people who had lost their lives had been
murdered by the Gestapo.

Rascher said that he was quite sure that at the time of our
capture Schellenberg knew nothing about the Munich affair except
what had been reported in the papers; he had, however, spent the
night with a doctor friend of his in Düsseldorf, who had suggested
that it might be a good idea to involve the two British Intelligence
Officers in the matter, and to say that they had organized the
attempt against Hitler's life, and had been caught as they were
trying to escape from Germany. When Schellenberg got back to
Berlin next day he put this plan before Himmler who did not,
however, think much of it, though he said that he would suggest
it to the Führer without whose consent nothing could be done.
As the capture of two Englishmen on neutral territory was a matter
which concerned the Foreign Office, Himmler first mentioned the
idea to Ribbentrop, who turned it down, and then to Bormann, who
was most enthusiastic and told Hitler about it at once. A week
or so later, Schellenberg was called to an audience with Hitler
and having explained his plan in detail, received the Führer's
sanction and was decorated with the First Class of the Iron Cross
for his bravery in venturing into a neutral country.

I asked Rascher what had they planned to do. "Oh, there was
to have been a big trial in Germany at which you would have
confessed to the attempt to assassinate the Führer, but Goebbels
made such a mess of things and allowed such contradictory reports
to be published that the idea had to be dropped." It seems though
that Hitler, having once sanctioned the plan, no one could go to
him and suggest that it should be called off, so Elser and I were
just put into cold storage and left to await a better day.

Rascher had been medical officer at Dachau and said that he
had attended a British officer (Colonel McGrath) who shared
quarters with Stevens. He said that Stevens himself was quite
fit and that the conditions of his life were extremely comfortable;
his quarters were roomy, he was allowed unlimited exercise in

a garden which he shared with a number of other prisoners with whom he was allowed to associate, and he was permitted to leave the camp in the company of a guard to play tennis, bathe, and even go to the theatre at Munich. I was, of course, delighted to hear that he was getting on so well, as he had really seemed to be in very bad shape at Sachsenhausen, and I had often feared that his health might have broken down.

Time passed in Buchenwald just as it always does in prison and elsewhere, but it was a cold and hungry time punctuated by air raids and my rows with the warders. The fact though that I could meet and talk to fellow prisoners made up to me for everything else, and I was really not at all unhappy. Somehow or other we managed to get hold of some news as to the progress of the war, and it became very evident that the Germans were unable to offer any effective opposition to the American advance. The warders were themselves so nervous and so anxious to understand what was happening that they allowed General von Falkenhausen to come to the guard room and listen to the daily war bulletin on the radio, so that he could mark up the position on a large staff map which he had and explain to them how near Germany was to defeat. Sippach had quite made up his mind to bolt from the camp before the Americans got there, but his timing had to be accurate as, if he bolted too soon, he might be picked up by German police and return as a prisoner. Dittman played the hero; he would never run away but would stay and fight to the last, and then, he would tell me, "I shall still have my pistol with one shot for you and one for me—you will never leave this place alive"; I was never really popular with Dittman.

By the end of March I really began to wonder whether I should live to see the end of the war, as on the 30th I had a terrific row with both Sippach and Dittman, who were waving their pistols about and telling me that they would shoot me down like a dog. They could easily have said that I had attacked them and that they had acted in self-defence. Rascher, who heard the row, warned me afterwards to be more careful as Buchenwald was very different to Sachsenhausen, and people there were often killed for far less than what I had done. My other neighbour was a Dr. Hoeppner, the brother of the General Hoeppner who had taken part in the 1944 plot and had been executed. He was the only man whom I met during my imprisonment who was an abject coward. He was a miserable worm of a man, and I really could not understand how his life could be of value to himself or to anyone else, but from the fuss he made, one would have thought that it was some priceless jewel. When he heard my quarrels with the warders he used to get into such a state of nerves that he collapsed on to the floor of the cell, and twice the doctor had to be fetched to attend to him. Of course I was sorry for him, but I also disliked him,

for fear is contagious and the last thing we wanted was anything in the nature of a general panic. I admit that things had
become very unpleasant and we had all become weak from cold
and lack of food, indeed, I wrote in my diary at the end of the
month:

> "This has been a hell of a month and has taken more out
> of me than the whole of my previous imprisonment. Doubt
> much whether shall ever get home. Probably shall be liquidated
> by a pistol bullet if our troops get too near. Only real hope is
> if troops land here from the air. The Germans say we intend
> to destroy them and see no reason to spare those of us who are
> in their power—thorough!"

On the 1st April the Americans had reached the Werra and the
sound of gunfire was faintly audible. Sippach gave orders that we
must be ready, day and night, to leave within twenty minutes, so
I packed up my gear and went to bed all standing. Next day
Dittman said that we should probably have to leave on foot and
would only be able to take with us what we could carry. I had
given quite a lot of my things away but still had a suit-case, a typewriter, and three large cartons, and I was furious at the idea that
I might have to jettison more of my belongings. On the 3rd Sippach
came in the afternoon and said that we would be leaving within
the next hour, but it was ten in the evening before we got the order
to move, and sixteen of us with piles of luggage squeezed into the
back part of a prison van in which there was just room for eight
without luggage. The front part of the van was crammed full of
billets of wood for the generator, and when we were in we were
packed so tightly that no one could move an inch.

We had just got settled when the alert sounded, and all the
military personnel bolted for the wide open spaces leaving us securely
locked in. After the 'all clear' the engine started and we moved a
hundred yards or so and then came to a standstill with the engine
still running. Fumes filled the van and Rascher called out:
"My God, this is a death van, we are being gassed". Opposite
me a glimmer of light came through a ventilator and I asked
Rascher whether they had such things in gas chambers, and he
said no, and in that case we were probably all right. After a time
we started moving and gradually some of the fumes cleared from
the van, though they remained pretty bad throughout our journey.
General von Rabenau and both our ladies fainted, and all that
we could do for them was to hold them on our united hands so
that they could lie flat until they came to.

It was a hell of a journey. The wood generator did not seem able
to propel the car at more than an average of fifteen miles per hour,
and every hour we had to stop while the flues were cleaned and

the generator refilled with firing. When this had been done they seemed to have a difficult job starting up and when the engine finally got going they had to run it for about a quarter of an hour before it developed enough power to move the van, during which time all the exhaust gases accumulated in our cell. There was no light, we had nothing to eat or drink nor, but for the generosity of Bonnhöfer, who, although a smoker, had saved up his scanty ration of tobacco and now insisted in contributing it to the common good, anything to smoke. He was a good and saintly man. Literally, we could none of us move an inch for our legs were embedded in luggage and our arms pinned to our sides; we had even small articles of baggage wedged behind us on the seats so that our sterns rested on the sharp edges of the wooden bench and soon became the seat of neuralgic pains.

We jogged and joggled along through the night, running an hour and stopping an hour, stiff, tired, hungry, thirsty, until a faint suspicion of light appeared at the ventilator. There came a time when nature, even after a sleepless night, makes certain demands, and soon there were cries from all sides, "I can't wait any longer, they must stop so that I can get out," and we started hammering against the sides of the van until it came to a sudden stop, the door was opened and a voice called: "What's all this?" Our needs were explained with the delicacy required by the presence of two ladies which the inquirer then crudely and loudly detailed to his mates outside. It was evident that we had introduced a complication which had not been foreseen in our guards' instructions, for an argument followed of which the gist was that one party said "They can't" and the other "They must", and in the end the 'musts' had it, the door was flung open and we all got out. We then saw that we were on a flat open stretch of road bare of hedges, trees, or bushes, and the question became one of how, and where. There were three guards with us. One took the two ladies across a field to a small copse in the distance, whilst we men were lined up on the bank with the other two guards covering us with their tommy guns. The ladies were prompter than we and although our backs were turned to their approach we were all of us conscious of over-exposure.

With daylight our spirits rose, whilst by the exercise of great ingenuity, in which Falconer achieved wonders, we succeeded in stowing our possessions in such a manner that the van seemed to have become twice as roomy as before. Quite a lot of the wood blocks stored in the front part of the van had been consumed during the night and there was now room there, near the window of the door too, for two people to stand, at which each of us took his turn. The guards had produced a couple of loaves of bread and a large sausage, and I seem to remember something to drink. Anyhow, we had some sort of a meal and began to take more interest in future plans. Some one recognized a village through which we passed, and after discussion the conclusion was reached that we were on our way to Flossenberg. Not so good this, for the Flossenberg concentration camp was primarily used for the extermination of unwanted prisoners.

About noon we reached Weiden, the nearest village to the Flossenberg camp, and we stopped at the police station and our guards went in there. When they came out, one of them who was more friendly than the others said, "You will have to go farther, they can't take you here. Too full." We weren't at all sorry at this news, and Rascher became quite optimistic and told us with the authority of a concentration camp expert that obviously there was no present intention to liquidate us, for Flossenberg was never so crowded that it could not accommodate a few more corpses.

We got under way again and had just cleared the village when we were overtaken by a car from which a man made signs to our driver to stop. A couple of men in police uniform got out and one opened the door of our van and called out: "Müller, Gehre, Liedig, get your things and come with us." The pile of luggage was pulled down and after a difficult search their bags were found and after a curt good-bye and 'see you later', the three men got out. Our cheerfulness vanished for we were all certain that our friends had gone to their death, and that we had seen them for the last time, but life goes on and soon we were pretending high spirits to disguise our real feelings.

After leaving Weiden there was a marked change in the attitude of the three SS guards. They had obviously left Buchenwald with orders to take us to Flossenberg, and for so long they had felt themselves constricted by the sense of an authority guiding them. When Flossenberg refused to receive us they were apparently sent off on vague instructions to continue a southward course until they found some place where they could deposit us, and so, in a measure, they felt that they shared our lot and like us were just sailing along into the blue with no certain destination. Next time that there was a stop for refuelling the door was opened and we were asked if we would like to get out and this procedure was followed each time. Once they stopped near a big farmhouse and the ladies were able to go inside for a wash whilst we men took our turns round the pump. The farmer's wife came out with a big jug of milk and a couple of loaves of bread—real good rye bread such as none of us had tasted for years. With three less in the van we were much more comfortable and everyone was able in turn to take a short nap. The window over the door was left wide open, and as it was a lovely day everything looked bright in our cage.

Just as dusk was falling we reached a large town and one of the guards told us it was Regensburg, and that if he could not

Top: View from Hotel.

Prags Wildbad Hotel near Niederdorf in the Puster Tal, South Tirol.

Below: the Hotel.

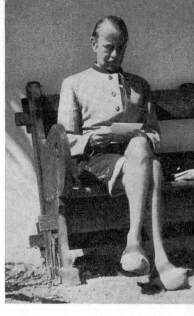

Prince Friedrich Leopold of Prussia.

Above: Dr. and Mrs. Hjalmar Schacht.

Right: Colonel Bogislav von Bonin. G.S.O.1 (Operations) with Rommel in Africa and later Operations Chief under Guderian at Hitler's General Headquarters (O.K.H.).

get us in somewhere here, he really did not know what he should do. We drove about for quite a time, stopping every now and again before some big building, and at last were told to get out, and when we did so saw that we were at the entrance of the 'Landes Gefängnis' (state prison). As we started to go up the flight of steps which led to the door two or three men in uniform, warders apparently, started to order us about very roughly until one of our own men explained that we were very important people and must be treated with consideration and courtesy. "Oh! Some more aristocrats," said one of the warders, "Well, put them with the other lot on the second floor."

We climbed up some steep iron stairs, each carrying as much luggage as he could, either his own or that of someone else if he had none. When we reached our floor a very decent elderly warder received us and said that the place was so full that we should have to sleep five men to a cell, and then let us make our own arrangements how we divided up. I shared a cell with Falconer, von Falkenhausen, Kokorin, and von Petersdorff; the two ladies were given a cell to themselves, and Heberlein went with Pünder and three others. We were given three straw mattresses to sleep on which just fitted the width of the cell, and on these we managed to pass the night. At first to our suggestion that we wanted food the warders said, "Impossible," and that "the kitchens were closed," but after a lot of argument and loud protests on the part of the members of our party, all joining in a chorus of "We want food" which soon was taken up from all cells on the floor, we were each brought a large bowl of quite passable vegetable soup, a hunk of bread, and a cup of 'coffee'.

Next morning our cell door was opened and a warder told us that we could go out and wash, and when we did so we found the whole long corridor crowded with a mass of people, men, women and children. These were the so-called 'family prisoners' (Sippenhäftlinge), the relations of people executed for complicity in the 20th July plot, such as all the surviving members of the von Stauffenberg, Goerdeler, and other families, and the relatives of German officers who, as prisoners of war in Russia, had associated themselves with the 'Free German Movement' there. Falkenhausen and Petersdorff seemed to know everybody, and soon I was being introduced right and left, and the atmosphere became more that of a big reception than a morning in a criminal prison. I met Fritz Thyssen and his wife, Goerdeler's widow and son, Mrs. Halder, and many others whose names I have forgotten. One very pretty girl whom I took to be about sixteen years of age, turned out to be the daughter of Ulrich von Hassell, who had been executed after the July plot, and the granddaughter of Admiral von Tirpitz, whose name will be familiar from the First World War. She was the wife of an Italian, Pirzio Biroli, who was an anti-Fascist, and she had

N

been arrested when visiting her mother in Germany. Her two small boys, aged four and two, had been taken from her, and she was distracted with the fear that she might never find them again.

I have described so many people that it is only fair that I should now allow someone else to describe me. Miss Isa Vermehren, in her clever and witty book, *A Journey Through the Last Act*, writing about the reunion of her own party with ours writes:

"As particularly noticeable Mr. Best must be mentioned, the Secret Service man who was 'stolen' from Holland in 1940; really, a model for the figure of the well-known international caricature of the Englishman. Very tall, very gaunt, and even stooping a little through emaciation, with hollow leathery cheeks, prominent teeth, a monocle, flannel trousers, a check jacket, and—a cigarette. Always showing his big false horse's teeth in an obliging smile and displaying that trustworthy discretion which engenders deepest confidence."

Including her comments on my teeth, I accept, and indeed am flattered by her word picture, especially since the teeth were not my own but a construction of the Sachsenhausen dentist, who possibly had used his art to make my appearance better conform to his idea of an Englishman.

It began to look as though we had come to a common decision not to return to our cells or to be locked in any more, and the warders, having been told to treat us politely, simply did not know what to do with us. I heard one old warder say to another: "You try if you can get them in; they don't seem to know that they must obey orders." Every now and again one of the warders would shout: "Everybody go to his cell," but the only result was laughter and loud cheers. Then one of them had a bright idea and food was taken into the cells and in time most of us were locked up again, but then the alert sounded and we were all marched down to a shelter in the basement where the fun started again.

From the window of the lavatory I had been able to look out over the railway marshalling yard, which was next to the prison, and really I have never seen such a mess in my life. Engines and coaches lying on their backs with their legs in the air, burnt-out coaches in long rows, and railway lines sticking up in great loops like pieces of wire.

After we got back to our floor again no further attempt was made to lock us in and, as most of us were pretty tired everything soon became comparatively quiet. At five o'clock one of our old guards from Buchenwald came to tell us that we must be moving off again, and when we got down we found our old friend 'Grüne Minna' waiting for us and in we went, this time feeling quite cheerful after this day with friends. We started off but had hardly got out of the town when our van gave a lurch and came to a stand-still; the steering had given out. Falconer, as an engineer, was called upon for an expert opinion, and since he decided that there was no way of repairing it there, our guards asked a passing cyclist to report our predicament to the Regensburg police and tell them to send a relief van.

It was a raw cold night and soon it started to rain, and as the night wore on it rained harder and harder. We had neither food, drink, nor tobacco; no relief car came and there was nothing to be done but to sit and go on sitting. Our guards were lonely, miserable, and frightened, for we were on an open stretch of road on which lay the skeletons of many burnt-out cars, and a field between where we stood and the railway was thickly pitted with bomb craters. They were quite tame now and behaved as though they were our comrades in distress; at dawn they opened the door and let us all out and we wandered about on the road trying to get back some circulation into our cramped legs. The road seemed to be quite dead and for hours no one passed us; at last a motor cyclist came along and one of our guards requisitioned his machine and rode on it back to Regensburg. When he returned he told us that another van had been sent to us the previous evening but the driver had stopped about 200 yards short of where we were and had gone back to say that he had failed to find us.

At last, at about eleven o'clock, a magnificent bus rolled up, all big plate glass windows and soft upholstered seats. We transferred our belongings, got in and soon started off again. Our nice friendly guards stayed with their broken down van and instead of them we now had with us some ten or so S.D. men armed with tommy guns which they carried at the ready. It was a delightful drive though, through lovely rolling country past quiet farmhouses and fields with every now and again a stretch of dark pines. We came to the Danube at Straubing, but the bridge had been bombed and was impassable, so we turned and continued to follow the river passing several other bridges all of which had been destroyed. Eventually we were able to cross by a pontoon bridge, and then drove along narrow winding lanes through country which became increasingly hilly and wooded. Some village girls asked for a lift, and of course when they got in and saw us they were curious to know who we were, so our guards told them that we were members of a film company on our way to make a propaganda film. The country seemed to be strong on poultry, and so many hens wanted to cross the road that our driver had quite a job dodging them, though we rather hoped that one might meet with an accident—we would all have enjoyed some nice roast fowl. I suggested to one of our guards that perhaps we might stop and see if we could beg some eggs at one of the farms, and the idea received immediate approval, but when the guard returned with a capful of eggs we got none and were left to tighten our belts and hope that we were approaching our next meal.

In the early afternoon we came to a pretty little village called Schöneberg, in the Bavarian Forest, which turned out to be our destination. We were driven to a largish white building, the village school, and were ushered into a big room on the first floor which seemed full of beds and looked rather like a hospital ward. It was a bright, cheerful room, with windows on three sides, which looked out over a delightful mountain landscape; the beds were covered with bright-coloured overlays and enormous feather beds. The door was locked and we were left to sort ourselves out; ten men and two women with a bed for each and one long table. In spite of fatigue and hunger we were all in the highest spirits, nervous, excited, and almost hysterical in our laughter. After the many hours we had spent cramped up in stuffy vans it was a godsend to be able to move about freely in a large, bright, airy room where, moreover, we felt ourselves for the first time for many months out of sight and hearing of our enemies. We each of us chose a bed and our names, with humorous comments devised by little Rascher, were written above them. The Heberlein's took one end of the room and for greater security placed the bed destined for 'Heidl' between their own. I have not yet introduced this young lady, for having little that is good to say about her I have so far tried to ignore her presence, although she was always one of our great problems.

She was a short, fair, thickset girl in her early twenties who, but for her stature, might have posed as a model for a youthful Germania. According to her own account she had worked for some Allied Intelligence Service, and had been imprisoned at Ravensbruck where she had been tortured by having two of her teeth extracted in slow motion. Later, she had become a boarder at the Sachsenhausen camp brothel, as an SS officer who was 'nice' to her had got her freed from Ravensbruck, and at Sachsenhausen the brothel was the only place where a woman could be lodged— I repeat, she only boarded there, though she seemed to have picked up much of the language and manners of her hostesses. She firmly believed that she was very beautiful and that she was desired by all men; being a good-natured girl she felt it her duty to bring joy to them, and her readiness was so great that restraint was both necessary and difficult. Her only real success, as far as I know, was with our little Russian; Wassilli became deeply enamoured, and when for a time he was separated from her sank to the lowest depths of suicidal depression. If she met with only indifferent appreciation from the other men in our party she was cordially disliked by all our women folk, and only kind-hearted Mrs. Heberlein took trouble to befriend her and shield her from trouble. Miss

Isa Vermehren, in her book from which I quoted before, describes
her as:

"An indefinable and most unpleasant young lady of whom
no one could discover what was her real name, nationality, or
language—she was put down as a spy and the only doubt was
whether she had only spied for the Gestapo or whether she had
been clever enough to ply her noble profession in the interests
of two sides at the same time."

When we had settled our sleeping arrangements and unpacked
our belongings we became increasingly aware that it was a long
time since we had eaten and that we were feeling absolutely famished.
We thumped on the door, which after a time was opened, and a
guard asked what all the noise was about. When we explained
that it was getting past our usual supper time he scratched his head,
and after some moments of deep thought, decided that the problem
was too much for him and said that he would have to ask the
officer. When this man came, a hard-bitten thug named Bader,
he told us that much as he regretted it, no arrangements had or
could be made for feeding us. This village of 700 inhabitants already
housed 1,300 refugees, and when the mayor heard that another
150 political prisoners had been wished on him he definitely refused
to allow any of his scanty reserve of food to be given to them; the
Gestapo had brought them and the Gestapo must feed them. In
this way we learned that, in addition to our party, all the people
whom we had met at Regensburg were also here; indeed, a room
next to ours was packed with men, women, and children, as I
saw when I opened the door by accident. Bader, who really did
his best to show himself from his better side, explained that he
was quite helpless as he had no more fuel for his transport, there
was no telephone, and indeed, until someone thought of our quandary
and took steps to send us food, he was afraid that we should have
to do without. So, that was that.

Mrs. Heberlein then managed to leave the room on the usual
plea, and was clever enough to find an elderly woman who seemed
to be the housekeeper and told her of our sad plight. This woman
was a real brick and at once said of course we must have food,
and she would do what she could, though unfortunately there was
very little in the village as the refugees had eaten the natives out
of house and home. Half an hour later she brought us a couple of
big basins of potatoes boiled in their jackets and some jugs of
coffee—even when we had eaten every scrap and licked our fingers
too we were still pretty hungry, but we had got used to this at
Buchenwald and did not allow it to damp our spirits. Next we
looked forward to going to bed and a real good sleep on those
beautiful soft feather beds.

The ladies retired behind a big screen which Mrs. Heberlein had induced the housekeeper to lend, whilst we men disrobed in the open as discreetly as we could. Of course 'Heidl' very clumsily knocked over the screen just as Mrs. Heberlein's clothing had reached an abbreviated stage and her own had practically ceased, whilst General von Falkenhausen evened up for our sex by modestly covering his nudity with a kimono, carefully keeping his back turned to the ladies, unconscious of the fact that his only garment was ripped open from top to bottom. In the end though we all got to bed, the light was turned out, and there were sincerely meant cries of good night all round. My bed was so soft that I seemed to float on air and very soon I was fast asleep; really, the first sound sleep for almost a week.

Suddenly we were all awakened by a noise like the firing of a machine-gun. Someone jumped out of bed and switched on the light, and we discovered Dr. Hoeppner sitting on the floor amidst the wreckage of his bed. Of course there was loud laughter, for at the best of times there was something absurd about little Hoeppner, but just then there was a repetition of the noise and this time it was my bed that collapsed. . . . It seems that when accommodation had to be found for us there was a shortage of the planks used in Germany to support the mattress on the bedframe, and someone had had the bright idea of using venetian blind slats instead. These were nice and springy but so pliable that with any sudden movement first one and then the rest would slip depositing sleeper and mattress on the floor; there were many such mishaps before we acquired the art of turning so gently that our supports were not disturbed.

Next morning, no breakfast. I still had some dried peppermint, and with some hot water which the kindly housekeeper gave us we made something warm to drink, and Rascher produced some bread which he had saved from his scanty ration at Buchenwald, which I had more than once noticed in his cell there hanging drying from a sort of clothes line. It was a poor meal but decidedly better than nothing. To wash, we were let out one by one. There was only one small basin on the landing outside our door and although there was running water there was no plug so our ablutions were very much catch as catch can. The sanitary arrangements seemed to have been constructed on the remains of a medieval *oubliette*, and both dexterity and caution were needed. My electric razor was the great success of the morning for there was a switch plug in the room and even if we could not wash properly much of the dirt could be removed with our beards. All ten men formed into a queue on which, with the excuse of showing how it was done, I secured the front place.

Mrs. Heberlein had, of course, taken over all domestic arrangements, and soon she had impressed an unwilling 'Heidl' and both got busy on make and mend, and some highly necessary laundry work. A number of the men started taking exercise by marching round and round the table while Falconer and I settled down on our beds, which were next each other, for a good talk. Falconer had been captured in Tunisia where he had been landed with a radio set from a motor-boat. By some miracle he had not been shot, possibly because he had been taken behind the Italian and not the German front. He had been taken to Sachsenhausen where he had throughout been in solitary confinement, without news from home and without himself being allowed to communicate with his family; he had spent some three years like this, and it was wonderful how he had kept up his spirits without showing the slightest sign of the privations through which he had passed. He, at all events, could tell me something about the first two years of the war before he was captured, whilst I could repeat some of the items of news which I had heard from the B.B.C. broadcasts. Rascher joined us and as he too had much of interest to tell the morning passed very quickly for us.

We could not help noticing that General von Rabenau's trousers —he was one of the marchers—seemed to show a great inclination to leave him. Before his imprisonment he had weighed, he told me, fifteen stone, and now only ten stone. A thin piece of string round the top of trousers, which had fitted his former girth, formed a most insecure suspension and, if it slipped, the worst could be expected. Besides this, his trousers did not seem to boast a single button, and through his almost mechanical movement of hitching them up under the string the adjustment of his dress became increasingly disordered so, to avoid any further unnecessary exposure I presented him with one of my spare trousers, insisting that he should put them on at once. An hour or so later he was still marching steadily round the table, and I noticed that force of habit had led him to neglect certain important buttons. As he passed us, we all made signals and when none of these was of avail, somebody stopped him, pointed, and said, "Buttons." Highly indignant, the general retorted: "I have never done up buttons for myself in my life. I always leave that to my wife."

Some of the village people to whom news of our predicament had spread, made and sent us a delicious potato salad and two large loaves of country bread. This was the only food we had that day. In the morning, von Petersdorff and I having been elected as spokesmen, we demanded the presence of Lieutenant Bader and strongly protested about the lack of arrangements for feeding us. This man Bader was a member of the chief Gestapo execution gang and passed his life in travelling from one concentration camp to another, like a pest officer engaged in the extermination of rats. We all realized that the fact that such a man had been chosen to guard us did not presage anything particularly good, but for some reason he had so far shown himself quite polite and obliging. So, too, now. He said that really he was doing everything possible to get us food; in fact, he and his men had none either; the whole difficulty arose from lack of petrol. There was food to be had at Passau but the problem was how to get it. He had now succeeded in borrowing a motor-cycle and he was going to Passau to see whether any transport was available there to bring out supplies.

He had to put up with a good deal of barracking from back-benchers who suggested that a motor-cycle might serve to take him to a good meal, but could never bring back enough to satisfy us, but Bader took everything in good part and Petersdorff handled the whole affair very well. In spite of everything, we were all lighthearted and gay; our adventures had knitted a strong bond of comradeship between all of us, and there was a complete absence of jealousy, impatience, or fear; only little Hoeppner lived in a perpetual state of panic but we had all decided to treat him as a joke, and whatever he did or said always drew roars of laughter.

The following day, Sunday 8th April, 1945, Pastor Bonnhöfer held a little service and spoke to us in a manner which reached the hearts of all, finding just the right words to express the spirit of our imprisonment and the thoughts and resolutions which it had brought. He had hardly finished his last prayer when the door opened and two evil-looking men in civilian clothes came in and said:

"Prisoner Bonnhöfer. Get ready to come with us." Those words "Come with us"—for all prisoners they had come to mean one thing only—the scaffold.

We bade him good-bye—he drew me aside—"This is the end," he said. "For me the beginning of life," and then he gave me a message to give, if I could, to the Bishop of Chichester, a friend to all evangelical pastors in Germany.

Next day, at Flossenberg, he was hanged.

That evening there was sausage, plenty of bread, and lots of potatoes for supper. We were cheerful and noisy again.

Next morning, when the shaving queue was in operation, Bader came in and called out: "Best, von Falkenhausen, Kokorin—get ready to leave at once." Everybody helped us to get our things together. Mrs. Heberlein was most apologetic because some of our laundry was not ready: "I will keep it for you and give it you when we next meet," she said, though it was clear that she, like everyone else, thought that we too had reached the station where it is all change.

We went downstairs, two of Bader's men carrying our luggage, and found waiting for us a 'Grüne Minna', and standing next to it my old friend Gogalla, very friendly and bringing me greetings from Obergruppenführer Müller. "You know, Herr Best, I told you when you were with us in Berlin that you were to be moved to somewhere where you would be comfortable. Now I am taking you to Dachau. There will be no more solitary confinement, and you will stay there until your armies reach you."

This certainly looked pretty good—we were apparently not to be executed this time, and feeling quite cheerful again I stepped up into the van.

CHAPTER IX

DR. KURT VON SCHUSCHNIGG, ex-Chancellor of Austria, in an article which appeared in the *Daily Telegraph* of 3rd March, 1946, described our entry into the 'Grüne Minna' in these words:

"Into the van came an elderly German general in full uniform, with bright red lining, the Pour le Mérite—the highest German decoration in World War I—around his neck.

After him came a slim man wearing a monocle, speaking German with an English accent. And last, half in military and half in civilian clothes, a very young Russian officer.

The first thing the three newcomers did was to roll a cigarette from the scarce supplies of the Englishman and pass it from mouth to mouth.

Then they introduced themselves as General von Falkenhausen, former Military Governor of Belgium, Mr. Best of the British Secret Service, and Wassilli, an air force lieutenant and nephew of the Foreign Commissar of the U.S.S.R., Molotov."

Having made sure that my luggage was safely stowed I followed the other two into the van. I had to climb over the legs of several people before I could reach a vacant seat at the back, but it was so dark after the bright sunlight outside that at first I was blinded and could not see who our companions were. I sat down in one corner and von Falkenhausen in the opposite one; there was no room for Wassilli who had to perch on the luggage, which was piled high in the centre. Next to me was a tall man whose face seemed familiar, although at the moment I could not place him; diagonally opposite me was Dr. von Schuschnigg whom I recognized at once. I said to my neighbour: "My name is Best," to which he replied: "Schacht"; (in Germany men always introduce themselves to each other, and it is highly incorrect to start a conversation with anyone without such prior introduction). He greeted Falkenhausen as an old friend and then introduced me to the rest of the party: Dr. von Schuschnigg, his wife, and little daughter Sissie, Colonel-

General Franz Halder, General Thomas, and Colonel Bogislav von Bonin. They had all come from the Flossenberg camp, where the Schuschniggs had been ever since their evacuation from Sachsenhausen, and, having been sitting in the 'Grüne Minna' since four o'clock in the morning, were terribly tired and stiff.

As we were leaving the room at Schöneberg, Heberlein had pushed a tiny packet of tobacco into my hand, all that he possessed and just sufficient for the very thin cigarette which I immediately rolled and which Falkenhausen, Kokorin, and I smoked with greatest delight, each taking a whiff and then passing it on to the next. When Mrs. von Schuschnigg saw this, she burst out laughing, and immediately handed round a well-filled red leather cigarette case and insisted on each of us taking one. So started our happy association with our beloved 'Camp Angel' as she was soon called by all of us. I can never express the gratitude which I feel to this beautiful, charming, and brave woman, who voluntarily shared her husband's imprisonment and put up with every hardship without a murmur. On this first day she looked terribly tired and worn and little Sissie was fractious and tearful. She kept asking: "Is it a nice prison we are going to Mummie? Why can't we go back to Sachsenhausen?" Poor little tot, she had been born in prison and had hardly ever known anything but confinement, high walls, and barbed wire. Von Bonin was the only one who could manage her, and at last she wore herself out and went to sleep, and her mother managed a short nap herself.

Schacht and I got into conversation and I reminded him of a meeting in Switzerland more than ten years earlier. He had spent many months in solitary confinement in our prison at Berlin and at Flossenberg, always with the threat of execution hanging over him, and this was the first time that he had been amongst friends to whom he could talk freely. Perhaps for this reason, on this one occasion, he behaved like a normal human being and shook off the inhibition, or the pose which normally rendered any close personal contact with him impossible.

We had a long talk about probable post-war economic problems and Schacht was at great pains to emphasize his adherence to classical economic theory, and his belief in the necessity for a return to the Gold Standard, if free international exchange of goods and services were to be achieved. Of course, at the time when this conversation took place Schacht, as indeed did all of our party, looked forward to allied victory as liberation, and still believed that the war had been waged, not against the Germans, but only against Nazi-ism.

Schacht was for me always a very tragic figure for, having the intelligence, courage, and initiative required to lead a successful revolt against Hitler, he was entirely lacking in the one essential quality of a leader, the power to attract a following. I believe that

Schacht is an extremely honest man, and one who throughout had the courage of his convictions. If at first he did not openly oppose Hitler, this was less due to shortsightedness and failure to recognize the fallacies in his programme, than to his rather conceited belief that he would always be strong enough to put Hitler in his place. Later, when he discovered his mistake and tried to find colleagues in his fight against him, his unfortunate manner or perhaps better said, affectation of superiority, set everyone against him. His manner is one of conscious rectitude, his speech incisive and didactic, and his attitude towards everybody displays the most profound contempt. He may show enthusiasm but it is purely intellectual and cold, conveying no impression that there is any real emotion behind it; Schacht thinks, but would have you believe that he does not feel. During the weeks which I spent in his company I came to the conclusion that he was in reality a shy and sensitive man, who probably felt so deeply that he had been compelled to erect a shield between himself and the outside world, and that far from being a hard and cold man he was merely a very lonely one. Whatever the truth, one thing is certain, in his attempts to find associates who would work with him towards Hitler's downfall he never succeeded in winning the confidence of those men who alone could have carried out his plans to a successful conclusion.

A dictatorship organized on modern lines has nothing to fear from any revolt by the masses; secret police, informers, concentration camps, together with control of the dissemination of information through press and radio, are sufficient to subjugate and cow the population of any country. Only a palace revolution is dangerous. With the single exception of the S.A. revolt planned by Roehm, which was so bloodily beaten down, Hitler had no difficulties with his political associates, men of straw who owed everything to him and realized that without him they would be swept away, but throughout his career he was faced by an ever-present danger from the distrust and dislike of the commanders of his armed forces. He was always perfectly well aware of this opposition and the danger which it held but, having warlike intentions, he needed his generals and could not venture to take open repressive action against them, and if they had been prepared to act instead of only giving more or less sympathetic ear to plans for action, they really held his fate in their hands. The German generals were not politically minded except that by tradition they were conservative— they were military specialists who had been trained to believe that: "Theirs not to reason why" but that their responsibility ended if they obeyed the orders of the head of the state and got on with the job of preparing for, and waging war.

In the period immediately preceding the war Schacht undoubtedly saw the dangers which his country faced, and was inspired with absolute determination to do everything within his power to destroy the Nazis, and did not shrink from the idea of removing Hitler by assassination. But all his efforts to bring his plans to fruition were, in my opinion, frustrated by the distrust and even dislike he aroused in all the men whose co-operation he tried to win, so that in the end he found all doors closed to him and the responsible military leaders refused even to see him. Since the end of the war a lot of information has been published about the numerous conspiracies which were forged against Hitler, but on this evidence any intelligent person must, I think, come to the conclusion that none of them held hope of ultimate success owing to lack of any real unity of purpose amongst the conspirators—they all lacked a commander-in-chief.

Our journey progressed with quite good speed, for the 'Grüne Minna' was powered by petrol instead of wood fumes, and at about nine o'clock we reached our destination, Dachau. Although Gogalla had already told me that we were going there, one could never quite trust anything these people said and we had learnt to require proof of the truth of their statements. We all got out and were taken into a sort of large hall at the entrance, dimly lighted and very cold, and there followed what seemed an interminable wait. There were no seats, we were hungry and tired, and for about an hour we just hung about there, our spirits getting lower every minute. At last a portly SS colonel made his appearance and with great politeness introduced himself as Obersturmbannführer Weiter, the Commandant of Dachau. With a most obliging air he made us a regular speech of welcome, even gallantly attempting, but failing, to kiss Mrs. von Schuschnigg's hand. He was very sorry that we had been kept waiting for so long, but Dachau was very crowded and it had really been most difficult to find suitable accommodation for such distinguished guests. He had done what he could but, even so, realized that the quarters to which he would now conduct us were far from being such as we expected and deserved, but really they were the best that he could provide, and he hoped that we would forgive their shortcomings.

We then walked a matter of 200 yards, some prisoners carrying our luggage, until we came to a large stone building where we were shown into what seemed to us almost luxuriously appointed cells; the luxury consisted mainly in the fact that there was a w.c. in some cells and a basin with running water in others. The Schuschniggs were given a large room and a small cell, while von Falkenhausen and I took possession of two cells which communicated with each other, with a w.c. in the one and a basin in the other; the rest of our party found satisfactory accommodation near us. We were all of us dead tired and famished into the bargain. Mrs. Schuschnigg looked as though she might faint at any moment, and my state was not much better as I was suffering from violent diarrhoea, probably an after effect of the sausage we had eaten at Schöneberg the previous day which had not tasted too fresh. After some difficulty, the kitchen being closed, a trusty found and warmed up some carrot soup which we ate; not too bad, and 'so to bed'.

Next morning we discovered that our cells were almost like normal rooms with low French windows which, although there were bars before them, we could open wide. From our room we looked out upon something almost worthy of the name of garden, with flower-beds, a plot of grass on which were standing a bench and some camp chairs; a pretty girl was talking to an SS guard. When we were up and had breakfasted on black bread and jam we were called out into the passage where we were addressed by a young Untersturmführer named Stiller, who was in charge of the building in which we were housed. He told us that we were free to go in the garden whenever we liked and could associate with any-one else we met there; we must, though, be careful, as we were expressly forbidden to speak to any people in the building who were not with our party, and if we did so the commandant would not fail to take appropriate action to prevent this taking place. He wished to allow us as much liberty as possible, but it depended on our good sense whether it could be continued. We soon dis-covered that our cells were at the eastern end of a long single story building which was called the Sonderbau (special building), and were separated from the main passage, a continuation of our own, by a steel door near which was the orderly room. This door was left open, as to get to the garden we had to pass through it. As we did so, I could see through it a long passage, at least three times as long as that on which we lived with cell doors on each side.

One of the first persons I met on our arrival in the building was the chief trusty, a man named Paul Wouwer, who in 1940 had for a time been the barber at Sachsenhausen. Of course this was a touching reunion between old friends, and we had much to tell each other about what had happened during the years which had passed. He had two pieces of news for me. One, that Ettlinger was still a prisoner at Dachau, but that after he got out of the punish-ment squad he had soon managed to wheedle himself into the good graces of the commandant and had been given a responsible job which freed him from all manual labour. The other news was, that immediately on our arrival, Georg Elser, who had been in the building for some weeks past, was taken out into the garden by Stiller and shot in the back of the neck. The man who shot him had been brought from one of the condemned cells and had been executed immediately after and both bodies had been taken at once to the crematorium. This apparently accounted for our long wait at the entrance to the camp.

Wouwer had known Elser well and had shaved him daily at Sachsenhausen; he said that when Elser first reached Dachau he was in a very low state and daily expected execution, but latterly he had become more cheerful as it was rumoured that the entire SS staff of the camp intended to bolt before it was reached by allied troops, in which case the prisoners would not be evacuated further. When Gogalla came with us to the camp he brought with him a number of orders from Gestapo H.Q. in Berlin which resulted in a renewed tightening up of discipline and, unfortunately, the execution of a number of death sentences. One of the orders which he brought with him, later came into my possession, and since it deals with our arrival and the death of poor little Elser, I am giving the translation now:

"THE CHIEF OF THE SECURITY
    POLICE AND THE SD   BERLIN SW 11.
                                       the 5. April 1945
      — IV — g. Rs   (in pencil)
Please quote date and above reference   SECRET
in your reply
(Rubber stamp)   *State affair!*

KLD Dep. VIa—F—Sb. ABw
Received: 9.4.45 | Express Letter |
Daybook No. 42/45

To the
Commandant of the KL.
Dachau
SS-Obersturmbannführer Weiter
Personal

On orders of the R(eichs) F(ührer) SS and after obtaining the decision of the highest authority the prisoners scheduled below are immediately to be admitted to the KL. Dachau.

    The former Colonel-General Halder
         „   „   General Thomas
    Hjalmar Schacht
    Schuschnigg with wife and child
    The former General v. Falkenhausen
    The Englishman Best (Wolf)
    Molotov's Nephew Kokorin
    The Colonel, General Staff. v. Bonin

As I know that you only dispose of very limited space in the Cell Building I beg you, after examination to put these prisoners together. Please, however, take steps so that the prisoner Schuschnigg, who bears the pseudonym Oyster under which name kindly have him registered, is allotted a larger living cell. The wife has shared his imprisonment of her own free will and is therefore not a 'prisoner-in-protective-custody'. I request that she may be allowed the same freedom as she has hitherto enjoyed.

The RF-SS directs that Halder, Thomas, Schacht, Schuschnigg, and v. Falkenhausen are to be well treated.

I beg you on all accounts to ensure that the prisoner Best (pseudonym Wolf) does not make contact with the Englishman Stevens who is already there.

v. Bonin was employed at the Führer's Head Quarters and is now in a kind of honourable detention. He is still a Colonel on the Active List and will presumably retain this status. I beg you therefore to treat him particularly well.

The question of our prisoner in special protective custody, 'Eller', has also again been discussed at highest level. The following directions have been issued:

On the occasion of one of the next 'Terror' Attacks on Munich, or, as the case may be, the neighbourhood of Dachau, it shall be pretended that 'Eller' suffered fatal injuries.

I request you therefore, when such an occasion arises to liquidate 'Eller' as discreetly as possible. Please take steps that only very few people, who must be specially pledged to silence, hear about this. The notification to me regarding the execution of this order should be worded something like this:

On . . . on the occasion of a Terror Attack on . . . the prisoner in protective custody 'Eller' was fatally wounded.

After noting the contents and carrying out the orders contained in it kindly destroy this letter.

Signature: illegible."

'Eller' was, of course, the pseudonym of Elser just as mine was Wolf and Stevens's 'Fuchs' (fox).

It is perhaps worth noting that the above letter, although written to the camp commandant, was contained in an envelope addressed to Untersturmführer Stiller with a note that, in the event of the latter's death, it should be destroyed unopened. Stiller appears to have been a direct representative of the SD at Dachau and thus, although a subordinate, possessed of more real authority than the commandant. This was directly in line with Nazi policy which, as is the case in Soviet Russia, always took care that every man holding a position of any importance was kept under observation. There was another man, a Hauptscharführer, who appeared to spy on Stiller in turn.

Although for the better part of the first week after our arrival I was really very ill with dysentery, getting so weak that I could hardly stand, I have the most pleasant memories of the days we spent, a band of absolutely united friends, in that garden at Dachau.

Our two charming ladies, Vera von Schuschnigg and Gisela Rhode, looked after me with the utmost devotion and each in turn brought me little gifts, such as eggs, which they had been able to obtain, for both were voluntary prisoners and could visit Munich when they liked. I managed to get hold of the camp doctor, but when I asked him to prescribe something for me his answer was: "We need all the medicines we have for our own wounded. Why should I give anything to an Englishman?" Anyhow, Wouwer managed to get me some medicinal charcoal which I swallowed in vast quantities and Rhode brought me an electric warming cushion which I later learnt he had borrowed from Pastor Niemöller, and gradually I got better. By this time though I had got so thin (I weighed under eight stone against my normal weight of twelve) that when I went under the shower the joke was made of calling me Gandhi.

For the first week of our stay at Dachau our little group from the 'Grüne Minna' remained the only inhabitants of our part of the building, and we came in contact with no one else except the Rhodes who, as it were, lived on the other side of the Iron Curtain. They were young people, he about thirty-five and she in her early twenties; she very sweet and pretty, and he a long, lanky, and rather untidy 'intellectual'. He was head of a big radio firm at Munich and a few months before we reached Dachau had been denounced by an employee for listening to foreign broadcasts. He had been arrested by the Gestapo who, suspecting that he might have used the facilities of his business for the purpose of espionage, had resorted to physical violence in the hope of forcing him to confess. He had been flogged in all due form whilst his wife had been knocked about during interrogation and had received an injury above her eye which affected her sight. The Gestapo succeeded in establishing the fact that, even if he were not a spy, he was certainly an opponent of the Nazi regime, and at one time it seemed quite probable that they might have him shot out of hand.

Rhode owed his escape to the fact that he claimed to be on the point of discovering a means of putting the ignition system of enemy planes out of action by a special radio beam and, as at that time Hitler was immediately interested in any idea, however fantastic, which might add to the list of secret weapons upon which his last hopes of victory were based, Rhode's life was spared. He was brought to Dachau and given a large room which he filled with all manner of complicated radio equipment and ostensibly continued his search for the magic ray which would end hostile air attacks on Germany, though really all that he did besides some research work in the normal course of his profession, was to listen to B.B.C. broadcasts and to the conversations between the leaders of British and American planes as they passed over the camp. As he spent most of the day with headphones over his ears he could listen to whatever stations he liked without danger of being spotted.

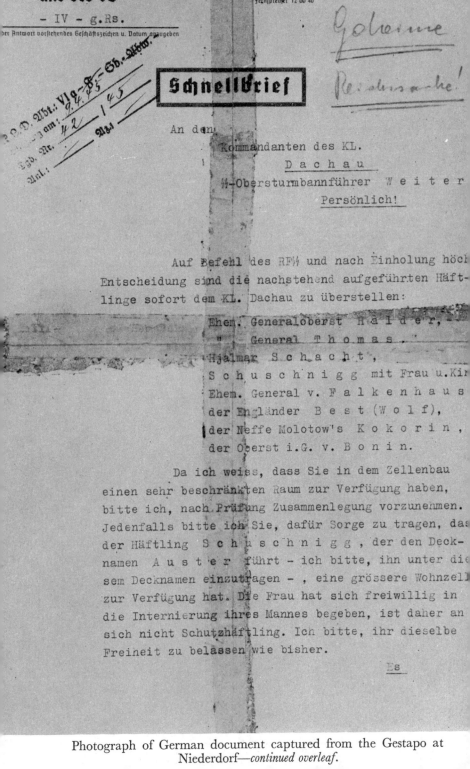

Chef der Sicherheitspolizei
und des SD

– IV – g.Rs.

Bei Antwort vorstehendes Geschäftszeichen u. Datum anzugeben

Berlin SW 11, den 5.April 19

Prinz-Albrecht-Str. 8

Fernsprecher: 12 00 40

Geheime

Reichssache!

Schnellbrief

An den

Kommandanten des KL.

D a c h a u

SS-Obersturmbannführer W e i t e r

Persönlich!

Auf Befehl des RFSS und nach Einholung höch[st]
Entscheidung sind die nachstehend aufgeführten Häft-
linge sofort dem KL. Dachau zu überstellen:

Ehem. Generaloberst H a l d e r ,
" General T h o m a s ,
Hjalmar S c h a c h t ,
S c h u s c h n i g g mit Frau u.Kin[d]
Ehem. General v. F a l k e n h a u s[en],
der Engländer B e s t (W o l f),
der Neffe Molotow's K o k o r i n ,
der Oberst i.G. v. B o n i n .

Da ich weiss, dass Sie in dem Zellenbau
einen sehr beschränkten Raum zur Verfügung haben,
bitte ich, nach Prüfung Zusammenlegung vorzunehmen.
Jedenfalls bitte ich Sie, dafür Sorge zu tragen, das[s]
der Häftling S c h u s c h n i g g , der den Decknamen A u s t e r führt - ich bitte, ihn unter diesem Decknamen einzutragen - , eine grössere Wohnzell[e]
zur Verfügung hat. Die Frau hat sich freiwillig in
die Internierung ihres Mannes begeben, ist daher an
sich nicht Schutzhäftling. Ich bitte, ihr dieselbe
Freineit zu belassen wie bisher.

Es

Photograph of German document captured from the Gestapo at
Niederdorf—*continued overleaf.*

Es ist eine Weisung des RFSS, dass
H a l d e r , T h o m a s , S c h a c h t ,
S c h u s c h n i g g und v. F a l k e n -
h a u s e n gut zu behandeln sind.

Ich bitte, auf jeden Fall besorgt zu
sein, dass der Häftling B e s t (Deckname
W o l f) keine Verbindung aufnehmen kann mit
dem dort bereits befindlichen Engländer S t e -
v e n s .

v. B o n i n war im Führerhauptquar-
tier tätig und befindet sich in einer Art Ehren-
haft. Er ist noch aktiv Oberst und wird es vor-
aussichtlich auch bleiben. Ich bitte, ihn daher
besonders gut zu behandeln.

Auch wegen unseres besonderen Schutz-
häftlings "Eller" wurde erneut an höchster Stelle
Vortrag gehalten. Folgende Weisung ist ergangen:

Bei einem der nächsten Terrorangriffe
auf München bezw. auf die Umgebung von Dachau is
angeblich "Eller" tötlich verunglückt.

Ich bitte, zu diesem Zweck "Eller" in
absolut unauffälliger Weise nach Eintritt einer
solchen Situation zu liquidieren. Ich bitte besorgt zu sein, dass darüber nur ganz wenige Per-
sonen, die ganz besonders zu verpflichten sind,
Kenntnis erhalten. Die Vollzugsanzeige hierüber
würde dann etwa an mich lauten:

"Am .... anlässlich des Terroran-
griffs auf ..... wurde u.a. der
Schutzhäftling "Eller" tötlich ve
letzt."

Nach Kenntnisnahme dieses Schreibens
und nach Vollzug bitte ich es zu vernichten.

One of the first things that was done after our arrival was the construction of an air-raid shelter in our garden, which was nothing more than a shallow hole dug in the ground roofed over with timber and a thin covering of sods—hardly strong enough to withstand a large shell splinter. Nevertheless, whenever Allied planes passed overhead, which generally occurred two or three times daily, we were all driven in to take shelter and, what was far more annoying, the same at night. It was rather funny the way my life seemed to fluctuate in value. At Sachsenhausen I was supposed to take cover but didn't, at Berlin and Dachau, I was given no choice, while at Buchenwald it was the guards and not I who went to ground.

Our garden had originally been an execution yard, and that part of the building in which we were housed had contained the death cells. These had been redecorated and partly rebuilt to accommodate a party of distinguished Roumanians, and since they had objected to the presence of a gallows in their place of exercise and to executions being carried out there during their meal times, steps had been taken to convert it into a garden. When we arrived this work had not been quite completed and a prisoner, who acted as gardener, was busy making a new bed near one of the walls. He pointed out to me thousands of pit marks on the wall and described to me how prisoners had been brought in through a narrow doorway, ordered to turn with their faces to the wall, and had then been shot through the back of the neck. He said that digging up the beds he had removed a hundredweight and a half of pistol bullets. This gardener was a most amusing little fellow. He had originally been a circus clown and had travelled pretty well all over the world—he always acted and looked like a clown too. During the war the Germans had an economy campaign in the use of fuel, and in their press advertising used drawings of a scrubby, grubby little man whom they called 'Kohlenklau' (Coal pincher) and, as our little friend looked very like him, he was always known by this name. He was very knowledgeable, and as he was apparently free to go wherever he liked in the camp he had much interesting information to give. For some reason he seemed to have a liking for me and I found him most useful.

The Schuschniggs had been able to bring their radio set with them from Sachsenhausen, and every afternoon we went to their room to hear the German war bulletin at three o'clock, after which our three generals and von Bonin would carefully mark up positions on a map, analyse every statement made, and finally deliver considered judgment on the military situation, reconstructing truth out of propaganda. These debates were most interesting, and I am sure that very few prisoners of war have ever been privileged to listen to discussions between an ex-C.G.S., two full generals, and the late G.S.O.(1) Operations, of the enemy's staff. My presence certainly made no difference of any kind in the freedom of such discussions, for none looked upon me as an enemy; I was just one of the family, a family firmly cemented by the bond of common danger. I had many most interesting conversations with these officers, and even if it would not perhaps be indiscreet to repeat what was told me, in any case it would be out of place in this book. Anyone though who is interested to know more cannot do better than to read Liddell Hart's book, *The Other Side of the Hill*, in which he gives details of his conversations with German generals who told him almost exactly the same things that I heard from them in Dachau. They were all men who hated Hitler bitterly; hated him most of all because he had involved their country in a war which from the first they had declared could not be won—whether they would have felt the same hatred for him had he been willing to accept advice and to postpone war until a propitious moment, I dare not venture to say. Who should blame them? Certainly none were men given to rattling the sword in its scabbard, or had any wish for war, but first and last they were Germans for whom their country came first, and when she was in danger could be counted on to perform the duties for which they had been trained with the utmost devotion.

Generals in mufti tend to look very much like anyone else, but our two generals, Halder and Thomas, had absolutely nothing of the popular conception of a German officer about them; indeed, nothing distinctively German at all. Travelling in a suburban train from London, Halder would probably have been taken for the secretary of some important and highly respectable company, and Thomas for a lawyer. The attitude of both men towards the war was purely professional, and both seemed to derive a certain satisfaction from German defeat since it tended to prove that war waged in defiance of established General Staff theory could never be successful. In numerous conversations with them I never had the impression that either felt any personal responsibility for the events which were rapidly leading to the destruction of their country—these were matters of politics and as such, entirely out of their range of interest. They were soldiers who, copying Moltke, regarded war dispassionately as though it were a game of chess; as long as they were players they devoted their best skill to the game, planning their moves and moving their pieces without thought of any purpose beyond that of playing strictly to rule. Hitler was for them an intrusive amateur who, ignorant of the rules, did not play the game.

During our hours in the garden, our ladies, Vera von Schuschnigg and Gisela Rhode, held court, sitting on deck-chairs with all men their slaves. We did not talk about our own circumstances, indeed, for most of the time we did not even feel that we were prisoners—the sun shone, it was peaceful, and we were free to talk without fear of being overheard. The ladies, and that applies to all the women prisoners I met, showed the most perfect courage; that of simply ignoring the fact that danger existed—I cannot attempt to express what we men owed to them for this cheerful heroism and for the way in which, through their own behaviour, they re-educated us in the manners of civilized life, which for us were so far distant as to have become almost forgotten. Then there was little Sissie, aged four, who had never known such freedom or experienced life in such wide open spaces before. She had immediately the freedom of the house and for her there were no taboos, and no enmities. People for her were divided not into prisoners and jailers, but into nice people who gave her cake and sweets and uninteresting people who had nothing. She went everywhere and knew everyone. Every day she came back laden with the treasures which she had accumulated, chocolates, cake, sweets, and even some things which might pass as toys—everywhere she passed she left sweetness and new hope behind her. I, alas, had neither cakes nor sweets and so was unworthy of her attention; nevertheless, I was sufficiently happy watching her and envying her unconscious adaptation to the strange conditions of our life.

At meals little Wassilli came to the cells of von Falkenhausen and myself, and, indeed, was always with us as much as possible. He was a very lovable sort of boy, quite unspoilt and unaffected, though strangely like his uncle Molotov in appearance. He could understand German quite well, but spoke it in a schoolboyish fashion which often added savour to the things which he said:

"Stalin very beautiful man." "He love my mother very much." "She go to him every day after supper." "Stalin very lazy man and hate work; he like good eating, good drink, and beautiful girls." "Stalin marry a girl from my class at school and love her very much, but he soon get tired." "Stalin always let Politbureau do what it like but my mother read all the letters which come to him and if she see too many people don't like what done she tell him and he say Politbureau must do other things." "Stalin beautiful character and never cross about anything but like much to laugh."

Wassilli said that his father was one of the heroes of the October revolution who had lost his life fighting the Whites; he had been a great friend of Stalin's and his mother was the person he liked and trusted most. They lived in a house on the Red Square in Moscow, as Wassilli proudly said, with eight rooms and two servants; if they wanted a car this was provided from the Kremlin. He seemed, from what he told me, to have closer relations with Stalin than with his uncle who was inclined to look upon him as a lazy young devil who would never do much in life: "Molotov always busy. He do all things that Stalin doesn't like and so people don't like him like Stalin." I asked him once why on earth he and Stalin's son had been sent on such a dangerous mission as being parachuted amongst Russian partizans behind the lines. His answer was: "This great honour. Stalin can't trust other people to go away from army as perhaps never come back and join Germans. Lots Russian officers and soldiers desert and fight for Germans so Stalin send me and other family of party leaders, but now Stalin very cross that I am prisoner. I must fight till dead, but my feet frozen and I could only lie down so Germans made me prisoner. Other prisoners shot or sent to labour camp after war and perhaps I too be badly punished."

Another time, talking about Russian prisoners who died or were executed at Sachsenhausen, I spoke about the Nazi terror His answer was: "German terror, ten, fifteen men, Russian terror ten—fifteen thousand men. What will you?" "Prisoners no good in war and no good after war. No man fight if easy be prisoner. In Russia, if man won't fight, is shot; if becomes prisoner, is also shot—so better fight."

The general impression I got from my conversations with him was that he and everyone else in Russia lived in conditions of complete insecurity, and that these were accepted as quite natural and normal. He belonged to a privileged class, had had a good education, and, as long as Stalin held the reins, could look forward to promotion and favouritism; yet, he also had obvious fear of returning home after the end of the war, and the words: "I think Stalin he very angry with me," constantly recurred in our talks. For the future, his ambition was to be sent on some diplomatic mission abroad, and then he said: "I stay away and don't go back to Russia any more." His ideal was to go to live in America.

The Rhodes knew Stevens well and told me a lot about his life at Dachau. Although I had caught a glimpse of him once or twice as I looked down his corridor when I went to the garden, I had made no attempt to enter into contact with him as obviously this was one of the things which were forbidden and I felt, that in any case, it would not be long before we could meet freely. The 14th April was my birthday and Stiller having provided some bottles of wine, we had a little celebration in the evening in an unoccupied cell which we used as a general sitting-room. We enjoyed this so much that next day, having managed to get hold of a cask of beer (Dachau and all contents of the canteen were being sold up, it seemed) we had a beer evening at which one of the warders, quite a pleasant young fellow, came and entertained us with songs to a lute. He and another warder named Lechner were professional musicians and had originally been in the army; both had been wounded and after recovery, instead of returning to their units had been drafted into the SS—to their great disgust. They were nice, well-behaved fellows, who treated all of us with the utmost courtesy, and obviously felt that they stood closer to us than to the professional jailers, some of whom looked to me pretty evil.

After our beer evening had ended and we were all ready for bed, one of them whispered to me, "stay behind for a bit." Shortly afterwards Lechner came in, bringing with him Stevens. He looked to me very fit and almost unchanged since I had last seen him. As soon as he came in he flung his arms round me and kept saying how glad he was to see me again. After this we sat down and talked about our experiences over a bottle of wine which Lechner brought in, telling us at the same time, that Stevens must not stay too long.

That same morning I had had a long letter from Colonel McGrath hidden in a basketful of Red Cross delicacies which, having heard of my birthday, he had most kindly sent. Of course I thought that he had only sent me some of his surplus, but when later I got to know him personally I found out that his parcels had been stolen just as mine had been, and that he had practically cleared himself out in order to make me this present; he was a most kind and generous Irishman. In his letter he told me about his stay in cell No. 38 at Sachsenhausen, and of having once caught sight of me there though he had been unable to make his presence known to me. He had been wounded and captured during the Dunkirk period, and had for a time been commandant of a prisoner-of-war camp reserved for Irishmen, whom the Germans always deluded themselves into believing might be induced to transfer their allegiance from Great Britain to her enemies. McGrath took advantage of the more favourable conditions accorded to Irish prisoners to organize escapes and, when the Germans tumbled to it, was transferred to the Bunker at Sachsenhausen where he was kept in strict solitary confinement, being allowed neither to send, or receive letters. When I met him in 1945 he had been without news from home for three years, and suffered greatly from anxiety about his aged mother who, in fact, had died in the meantime.

Although Gogalla had assured me that we should be allowed to remain at Dachau until it was reached by our troops, we had not been there long before it became obvious that the Gestapo intended to keep hold of us as long as possible, and it was again rumoured that we were to be transferred to the Berchtesgaden area to become hostages, whose lives could be bartered for those of Nazi leaders if a last stand were made in the so-called Southern Redoubt. On the morning of 17th April we were told to pack up and be ready to move at two hours' notice. Of course there was much speculation as to our destination and as we waited about in the garden, hour after hour, Rhode brought us news that we were going to Switzerland to be handed over to the International Red Cross, that we were to be moved to a château on the Lake of Constance, and finally, that we were to be taken across the Brenner to Italy.

In the afternoon there was an influx of new guests, amongst whom were M. and Mme. Leon Blum, Herr and Frau Fritz Thyssen, and several other people whom we had already met at Regensburg;

from them we learnt that all the other 'Sippen Häftlingen' had also been brought to Dachau and I was able to find out from Kohlenklau that they had been quartered in the camp hospital. The Blums had the cells which von Falkenhausen and I had occupied, and several other members of our party had been rendered homeless, but until long after dark we were kept hanging about in the garden with the possibility that at any moment orders might come for us to get under way. At last Stiller came and told us that we were to stay at Dachau yet a little longer as it had been found impossible to find other accommodation for us; he was going away himself to see what arrangements he could make.

By this time I had managed to get on pretty good terms with Stiller, who was a weak, uncertain sort of fellow, and before he left us I suggested that the best thing he could do was to fail in his mission so that we could stay quietly where we were. The Americans had reached the Danube, it could not be long before they broke through the very weak German line and overran the Munich area. Stiller was inclined to listen to advice of this kind, for like most other officials at the camp he was pretty well scared out of his wits— afraid of what might happen to him if he fell into the hands of the victorious Allies and yet still, perhaps, more afraid of what might be his fate if he disobeyed orders; he was one of those men who always agree with the last adviser and are consequently quite undependable. From one of the trusties we learnt that, in addition to the newly arrived prisoners, another convoy had also reached Dachau, which consisted of a number of British and Greek officer prisoners. As no accommodation could be found for them they had remained in their prison van and it was said that they were being taken farther south that night; from what we could find out, it seemed probable that they were men whom the Schuschniggs had met at Flossenberg. Stiller went off that evening, and it was said that he had gone to make arrangements for the reception of these men at another camp.

It was getting on for ten o'clock in the evening before any definite arrangements were made to house our party, and then von Falkenhausen and Wassilli were moved right to the end of the long passage past the iron door, whilst I was given the cell No. 72 which we had so far used as a sitting-room. I did not like this separation from my two friends and next day asked whether I could not join them, and as a result was given a cell next to von Falkenhausen, with Niemöller as a neighbour on the other side. I cannot remember whether I had met Niemöller before, but rather think that he had visited us in our garden. He enjoyed far more freedom than most and spent a great part of the day walking swiftly with a purposeful air along the passages; he was very kind to me when I entered into possession of my new cell, offered me wine and made me some good coffee. He was obviously pretty well at the end of his nervous strength, no wonder either after an imprisonment of nearly ten years, and did not seem able to settle down to anything, even to connected conversation.

At the end of the passage where we were there was a door which could be used to shut off some six cells from the main corridor, and at first an armed guard stood there, apparently to prevent any of us from passing; at all events he made difficulties about my going to von Falkenhausen's cell which was just outside the barrier. Niemöller went out to inquire the meaning of this restriction and succeeded in arranging that we could rejoin the rest of our party in our old garden. To get there meant, of course, passing along the main corridor, and inevitably several prisoners came out of their cells and spoke to us as we passed, amongst them Stevens, who took me into McGrath's cell, which was next to his own, so that I could thank him for his most welcome birthday present. Later in the day when I again passed along the passage to my new cell I was hailed, and to my great delight found Müller and Liedig who had just arrived from Flossenberg. Both of them looked in very bad shape, through starvation and the beatings which they had received; Müller's face in particular was bruised and puffy from blows received with a rubber truncheon—but at all events they were alive.

Neither could understand why they had not been executed, for on the 9th April there had been a regular holocaust among the more important political prisoners at Flossenberg; our old companions Captain Gehre, General von Rabenau, and Pastor Bonnhöfer had all three been killed, and Admiral Canaris and General Oster, the two chiefs of the Army Intelligence Service, had been put to death by strangling in the cruellest possible way; besides these, hundreds of others had been liquidated. Müller and Liedig had been practically without food since they were taken out of our 'Grüne Minna' at Weiden on the 4th April, and after the privations endured at Buchenwald were just about on the point of collapse. The day before Mrs. Rhode, who was always much concerned about my emaciation, had given me a bottle holding about a quart of cod-liver oil. I had already drunk quite a lot of it for, starved of fat as I was, it tasted like nectar. I fetched the bottle from my cell and gave it to my two friends who, drinking in turn, finished every drop in about five minutes both declaring at the end that it was the best drink they had ever had.

During the afternoon the rest of our party from Schöneberg turned up, the Heberleins, Rascher and Heidl, Falconer, Pünder, and Höeppner, and all were permitted to come to our garden which was becoming rather overcrowded, but that evening Rascher and Heidl were both taken to cells in the main corridor and locked in. When little Wassilli saw his beloved Heidl he almost went off his head with joy, but she took not the slightest notice of him, having apparently taken up with little Rascher, so that it was quite appropriate that these two should be removed together from our circle. That evening, when we went to our cells to go to bed, I found Wassilli in the depths of suicidal depression, and I was really afraid that he might do himself some harm for at Sachsenhausen he had already made a couple of attempts to kill himself. His cell was opposite to mine and I went to have a look at him during the night—he was in deep sleep and next day was as cheerful as ever. There were six cells in our little block occupied on the one side by myself, Niemöller, and Kallay, ex-President of Hungary, and on the other, by Wassilli, a son of Field Marshal Badoglio, and the younger son of Admiral Horthy—distributed in other cells on the main corridor were all the ministers belonging to the last Hungarian Government under Horthy.

Almost every time that I passed along the main corridor, going to or coming from the garden, Stevens would pop out of his cell for a brief chat. I did not much like this for I had heard that strict orders had been given that we were not to meet, and I felt no inclination to ask for trouble just for the pleasure of exchanging a few inanities with him, even though he said that it was quite safe and no one would give us away. Be it as it may, on the 21st April Stiller came into the garden and called to me: "Herr Best, please get your luggage ready, you are moving to other quarters." A hurried farewell to my friends who all looked as though they never expected to see me again, and indeed I myself had my doubts, and off I went to my cell to pack. When I got there Niemöller came in and said, "It's quite all right, Best—I have found out all about it—you are only being moved to the brothel where the other foreigners are—I will come and see you there tomorrow."

Just as I was ready with my packing the alert sounded and I had to go to the shelter while there was quite a heavy raid on Munich—the evening before Munich had had its worst raid, when it was said that British planes dropped 140 ten-ton bombs and practically wiped out the whole centre of the city—although we were some ten miles away, the shelter in which I was, rocked about like a ship at sea, and when I went near the entrance I was almost blown off my feet. After the all clear sounded I set off in the company of an SS guard with a prisoner carrying my baggage. It was not a long walk, a couple of hundred yards or so past a number of huts, and I noticed that several were surrounded by barbed wire and guarded by sentries armed with tommy guns—I asked the guard what they were and his answer was typhus. There were a few emaciated figures lying within the enclosures but I could not see whether they were dead or alive.

We reached a hut, exactly like the others which housed the camp prisoners except that it, too, was surrounded by barbed wire and a sentry was standing at the entrance. I went in and was met by a trusty who said that the place was very full and that the only bed free was with the bishop as his room-mate had been executed the previous evening. I thought to myself, 'a billet with a bishop in a brothel', sounds quite original and so I accepted the proposal with thanks and was taken to a large cell, no, it could better be called a room, where I found a pleasant faced elderly Frenchman who was the Roman Catholic Bishop of Clermont Ferrand.

He was very kind and agreed at once to allow me to share his room telling me that his previous room-mate had been a French general named, as far as I can remember, something like Destrelle, who had been shot the evening before as a reprisal for the execution of some SS men in France. Like the bishop himself, he had been taken from France during the German retreat as a hostage.

In addition to the bishop, three other Roman Catholic dignitaries were also imprisoned in the brothel, and it seems that the choice of this particular billet had been intended as an insult to their cloth. The SS had, however, reckoned without their host for with a bishop, a canon, and two priests, the purification of any place of every vestige of sin was mere child's play. Holy water had been made and every nook and cranny thoroughly scrubbed and purified until, with an easy conscience, it had been found possible to sanctify one of the rooms as a chapel where Mass was celebrated daily at the appropriate hours.

The population of the brothel was one of mixed nationalities, and although at the time I was very angry at having been removed from the society of my friends the Schuschniggs and the others, it turned out in the end to be a good thing, for it gave me an opportunity to make the acquaintance of other prisoners with whom I was to be associated in the future. There were five Russians, two generals, a colonel, a lieutenant, and an orderly; eight Scandinavians, most of whom had served with the R.A.F.; four Italians, a Swiss, a Lett, and a Czechoslovakian major, and during the following days I was able to get on friendly terms with all. The Russians were particularly kind and immediately after my arrival gave me tobacco and invited me to their rooms for drinks. The Scandinavians were rather inclined to keep themselves to themselves and had established their mess in one of two big rooms of which there were four, two at each end of the barrack. Although I often visited them for a chat I had my meals and spent most of my day in the room on the left of the entrance, opposite to which was the place where food was distributed and if necessary warmed up.

With me were the priests, four Italians, General Garibaldi, Colonel Ferrero, and two rather mysterious men, one of whom was said to have been a commissioner of police at an important town. Garibaldi was a grandson of the famous Italian revolutionary and had been a leader of the French Maquis; I believe that the same was true of Colonel Ferrero. There were also several others who used this room, amongst whom were a Czechoslovak, Major Jan Stanek and a Swiss, M. Mottet, who had been condemned to death but somehow or other had escaped execution. General Garibaldi, who wore prison clothes, had been sent in from the camp to act as servant, but beyond occasionally plying a broom to create the impression that he was performing his duties, he did no work and was treated as one of us. When I first arrived, there was a trusty, a German, who really did all the work and did it very well, but a day or two later he was taken away for execution and in his stead came another Czechoslovak general staff officer. After this, all prisoners took their turn in cleaning up and generally looking after the establishment.

When I first met the Russian officers I naturally told them about Wassilli and that he was at Dachau at that moment. This threw them into a state of tremendous excitement and crowding round me they almost mobbed me in their eagerness for news, for they had heard nothing of him since he was removed from their camp. Then they all started talking about his companion, Lieutenant Joseph Stalin—did he know that he was dead? According to what they told me, Lieutenant Stalin had suffered greatly from depression after the failure of the attempt which he had made to escape with Wassilli, and one day he had suddenly rushed to the barricade round the camp and seized hold of the electrified wire. The shock did not kill him but apparently he could not release his hold, and as he writhed in agony he kept shouting to the guard to shoot him which eventually one of the men did, killing him instantly. As far as I can remember it was stated that this took place on the 25th August, 1944.

Niemöller did come to visit me on the day after my arrival and told me that there was a faint prospect that we might be permitted to stay at Dachau until it was relieved. Stiller had so far been unable to find any place where there was room for us, and although he had been sent off again to try to find accommodation across the Brenner in the Italian Tirol, Niemöller had advised him, just as I had before, to take the opportunity to vanish. The trouble with him was, and this applied to most Germans, that he could never shake himself free from the habit of obedience to orders even though he was himself convinced that he was foolish to pay any more attention to them. It is all very well to criticize them for this slavish subservience but the idea that orders were sacred and must be obeyed without question had been so drummed into them from earliest childhood that it had become almost the most marked German characteristic. When men of the upbringing and intellectual calibre of German generals seriously considered themselves bound by an oath which had unconstitutionally been extracted from them by Hitler, and were prepared to watch the destruction of their country rather than break it, one need not be surprised if the idea of disobedience never even entered the minds of the rank and file.

I had plenty of evidence that although separated from my friends I was not forgotten, and almost daily little presents were brought me which they had saved for me out of their own scanty stores; Mrs. Blum was particularly kind as she sent me quite a large packet of her husband's tobacco, which was far better than anything which I had smoked for a long time. Indeed, both the Blums were kind and very brave people whose behaviour throughout was an example to all. Never for a moment did they show the slightest sign of fear or even that they were conscious of being prisoners—they were with us, they were the friends of all their fellow prisoners, and our jailers simply did not seem to exist for them. M. Blum, always perfectly turned out, was so absolutely what one expected him to be that he was almost a caricature of himself, with his inordinately long legs and rather stork-like gait, raising himself on his toe with each step.

During the time when I was in the first building I had often discussed with Rhode the possibility of entering into communication with the American forces on the Danube, as he said that he knew of people prepared to make an attempt to get through the lines. He wanted me to write a letter which his men could take with them, but this seemed to me rather too risky, particularly since I had no other proof of Rhode's bona fides beyond what he had told me himself, and all that I was prepared to do was to permit the use of my name, to which I added a code number by which I could be identified. Not long after my removal to the brothel Rhode sent me word that one of his men had almost certainly succeeded in getting through and that he was now planning to follow him himself; the SS guard, who generally accompanied him on his trips outside the camp, had agreed to go with him, so that with luck he should be able to reach the battle area without great difficulty. Frankly, we were all rather annoyed that no effort was made to relieve us, for we were convinced that if paratroops had landed either near us or at Munich they would have met with practically no resistance; indeed, from all that we could learn, apart from a few small detachments of SS men such as concentration camp officials and men employed on staff jobs, the whole area was pretty well devoid of troops. A few days after Rhode's man was supposed to have got through to the American lines there was greatly increased air activity over the camp, with planes apparently engaged on reconnaissance, and we all got highly excited hoping for speedy delivery.

Life in my new quarters was not too bad, though I greatly missed the apparent freedom of the old garden. Here the building was closely encircled by wire entanglement, and there was only just room for two to walk abreast round the sides and back; a guard at the front prevented us from passing. Gradually I got to know all my fellow prisoners as I made a point of talking to each in turn. At the beginning there was a strong tendency for prisoners to clump together, according to their respective nationalities, and as this, of course, was a possible source of weakness should the necessity for any joint action arise, I did everything I could to break down these national barriers and in the end I think that I can claim to have met with considerable success. I got on extremely well with the Russians and spent a lot of time with them in their rooms, but otherwise they were not good mixers, and throughout there was a Slav block which could not be completely assimilated. All the officers were strongly anti-Stalinists and laughed at the idea that after the war there could ever be any real co-operation between the U.S.S.R. and the West—they all claimed to be Communists and to belong to the school of Lenin; Stalin, they said, was nothing but a dictator and his policy had nothing to do with communism. I think it is probable that all of them had deserted to the Germans who had hoped to make use of them in their war against Russia; as they would not agree to take up arms against their country they had been handed over to the Gestapo, and so came to be treated as civilian rather than military prisoners of war.

On the 24th April we had a visit from Stiller, who after all had not been able to make up his mind to desert, and were warned that we should be leaving at five o'clock that evening. At three-thirty, just as we had finished packing, we saw about half a dozen fighter planes dancing over the camp and obviously firing on some ground target; Garibaldi, who knew the layout of the camp said that they were firing at the transport park, and a little later we got word that five buses which were ready to take us on our journey had been shot up and that we should not move that day. We were to be ready at five o'clock on the next day. Our hopes rose to fever point and I really began to believe that Rhode's man had been able to get my message through and that steps were now being taken to prevent our removal.

When the afternoon came, we all clustered round the window from which the transport park could be seen, waiting for our friends the fighter planes. Time went on, three, four, and five o'clock. We were told to put our luggage on trucks which some prisoners had brought when, at last, there was a renewed sound of low-flying planes and of firing. Back into the building and to our window. Six or ten planes diving at the transport park and apparently firing with their guns as well as machine-guns; a burst of fire and some puffs of smoke. Three of five buses set on fire and thirteen casualties was what we heard. No move apparently that day either, and we all did a sort of dance, jigging from one foot to the other. After about an hour a renewed order to move and this time we really did so. Three buses had been destroyed, but three lorries had been brought in from Munich to replace them—instead of travelling comfortably in buses our journey was to be made on hard benches in lorries.

On the previous day some new guests had come to us from the camp, all men dressed in the ordinary camp prisoners' clothes; they were Prince Frederick Leopold of Prussia, Prince Xavier de Bourbon, Dr. Richard Schmitz, the Mayor of Vienna before Austria's annexation by Hitler, and Baron Cerrini, Prince Frederick Leopold's secretary; somehow or other too, the trusties Wouwer and Kohlenklau had also managed to join us with the intention of accompanying us wherever we might be going. All these men had been through the mill of ordinary camp life, but being of the stuff of which good prisoners are made, had suffered hardship and indignities without breaking down. Prince Xavier and Dr. Schmitz looked thin and worn, but Prince Frederick Leopold was in fine fettle, having had a job in the canteen for some time. He had had a very bad time having been forced to do the hardest manual labour. He had nearly died from diphtheria and was given no medical attention of any kind. After his recovery the camp commandant had a happy thought, and made him errand boy and batman to the prostitutes at the brothel, but nothing broke his spirit and he always came up smiling. He was descended from a collateral branch of the Hohenzollerns and had always lived in Austria. Even before he joined us I had heard quite a lot about him as he had made himself generally loved in the camp, where he was called 'Pat' by everybody, and on our way out, all the prisoners lined up to see us go, and he could hardly make his way past them; so many hands were stretched out for him to shake.

When we reached the camp entrance we found a comfortable looking bus and a canvas covered lorry. With Prince Frederick Leopold next to whom I was walking I directed my steps towards the bus, but as I was about to get in I was stopped by Stiller and told that I was to travel in the lorry; as I later learnt, this was because Stevens was already in the bus and Stiller was still trying to obey the injunction to keep us apart. I had quite an argument with Stiller before I would consent to move over to the lorry, for I was really feeling very weak and I dreaded the idea of another uncomfortable cold night journey, but he was adamant and in the end I had to give way. There were four rows of seats in the lorry and I was lucky enough to get a place close to the entrance, from which, at least, I could see something of the country through which we were passing. Müller and Liedig sat next to me and I found that most of the people from the brothel, with the exception of the bishop and his colleagues, were also travelling with us. At the last moment little Wassilli was pushed in so I introduced him to the Russians; from that moment he went Slav and disappeared so completely behind the curtain that I scarcely saw anything more of him.

We passed through Munich lurching like a ship at sea as we bumped our way over rubble and hastily filled bomb craters—the ruins were still smouldering and the air was thick with smoke— I had lived and studied in Munich and knew every inch of the city, but all that I could see on our passage through the centre were the ruins of gutted buildings behind a wall of rubble that filled the roadway from side to side. After leaving the city we were all eager to see which direction we would take; whether the new motor road to Berchtesgaden or the road through Landsberg to the Lake of Constance, both of which places had been indicated by camp prophets as probable destinations, but from time to time we got glimpses of a river on our left which could only be the Isar, and when we entered the foothills of the Bavarian Alps it became certain that we must be going towards Innsbruck, the Tirol, and perhaps places farther south.

We came to a place called Mittenwald just as the alert sounded and this seemed to rattle our driver so much that he took a wrong turning and landed us in a blind alley. The other buses had followed us and now it was quite a business to extricate the heavily laden vehicles and in the end we all had to get out. It was pitch dark and I was seriously tempted to disappear into the woods near the road, but decided that the escape of any one of us would certainly make things worse for the others and that it was therefore my duty to stay put. We seemed to have a couple of the world's worst drivers, for it took them endless time to get out on to the proper road again and our guards were slanging them and telling them that the planes would be overhead at any minute and we should all get killed. At that time all roads leading to passes through the Alps were being regularly and badly shot up by our planes in order to prevent any large-scale movement of troops and munition to the Southern Redoubt. It all went off well though, the vehicles were straightened out on the road and we all got in, thirty-nine people in the lorry and twenty-two in each of the buses—I noticed that there were at least two more lorries behind us which seemed to be filled with luggage and SS guards—we started off again and had hardly got clear of the place before we heard the sound of bombs bursting behind us.

We jogged along all night, our driver showing a great inclination to leave the road at several steep and nasty bends which he had to negotiate, once bumping a low wall at the side so hard that we nearly tipped over. Just as dawn was breaking we reached Innsbruck but making no stop passed steadily through its sleeping streets. Where on earth were we going now? Unless it was the intention to take us to the Swiss frontier our destination must be Italy and our road be over the Brenner, but soon after leaving Innsbruck we turned down a side track off the main road and came to a stop before a gateway guarded by SS sentries, with beside it a large single story building, obviously just another concentration camp which, as we later discovered, bore the name of Police Education Camp Reichenau, which meant, of course, that it was the police which did the educating.

We all got out and were taken into the building where we found a room that was a cross between a railway waiting-room and a restaurant; it was, I believe, the canteen of the troops employed at the camp. We were given some bread and sausage and mugs of *ersatz* coffee and after that we just sat and sat, too tired to bother about what was to happen next. I can't remember how long we stayed there, but eventually we were told to clear out, and when we got outside we found that it was a lovely hot day, more like mid-summer than spring, and that the camp was in a beautiful valley surrounded by high mountains with the town of Innsbruck seemingly just above us. The building where we had breakfasted was on the left side of the entrance, and on the right was an enclosure which advertised itself to our nostrils as what it was. I saw a man with straw-coloured hair, dressed in khaki shirt and shorts, obviously an Englishman, enter there, so I followed him in and introduced myself.

He was Lieutenant-Colonel Jack Churchill, and he told me that there were a number of other British officers in the camp who had come there from Flossenberg; no doubt the convoy which we had heard of at Dachau. I remembered Colonel Churchill's capture very well, as the German papers had carried long stories about how a close relative of Winston Churchill had been taken prisoner on an island off the Dalmatian coast, and from the fuss which was made one would have thought that this event was a great step towards victory. One of the guards saw me talking to Churchill and I was called back to rejoin our flock, which was then moved farther into the camp and left to stand about in the middle of a broad path, until one of the Dachau guards who had accompanied us was induced to provide some benches on which we could sit.

One of the Dachau warders was an Austrian of about sixty-five; in peace-time he was a railway guard, and he always treated us as first-class passengers from whom substantial tips might be expected. He was fond of telling how, at the beginning of the war, he had been enrolled in the SS and sent to Dachau where, he was told, he would only have to stay for five months, after which he would be free to return to his railway work—but he had been there ever since. He was in charge of the supply of luxuries to us prisoners, and for weeks we had been on his tail for tobacco which he had promised but which had never materialized; on this day, though, he suddenly appeared with a large basket and said that at last he had been able to get hold of some tobacco, and that he had half a packet (one ounce) for each of us. He said that we must pair up so that each man could fetch the ration for himself and another.

This was started quite fairly, but very soon each of us was fetching a packet for himself, and before long the old man's basket was empty, although half of our party declared that they had had nothing. He said that we must all have had our share as he had certainly had half a packet for each of us, but with a clamouring mob around him, shouting at him, and jostling him, he gave way and promised to fetch more, which he did—all along we had suspected that he had intended to collar half of the tobacco supplied for us, as it seemed unlikely that half packets would have been issued as a ration.

When he had at last satisfied our demand for tobacco we raised the question of food, and after some noisy argument he went off, and after a time returned with some prisoners carrying big baskets containing sandwiches of bread and sausage and a couple of buckets of normal coffee hog-wash.

We were all very tired after our all-night journey and anxious to get to some place where we could lie down. It was terrifically hot in the sun, and nowhere was a spot of shade to be found. The night journey had been cold, and warned by past experiences, we had all of us dressed as warmly as possible and were in no state to enjoy the Tirolese sunlight. There were several of the warders from Dachau with us and to each in turn we appealed for billets, but were told that the camp was full and that a barrack was being cleared for us; it was not until evening that we were told to move and were taken to a long wooden hut which was to be our new home. There were several parallel lanes in the camp with these huts on either side, and when we came to ours I saw that the huts opposite were occupied by British officers and men in other military uniforms. Our hut was divided into a number of small rooms containing double-tiered wooden bunks, with filthy looking straw mattresses and blankets. There were thirteen of us in our room and when we had all got in with our luggage there was hardly room to move.

As soon as I had parked my gear I went across to the opposite huts where I made the acquaintance of the British officers. There was Colonel Churchill, whom I had already met, and also Captain Peter Churchill; then there were a number of the survivors of the massacre after the mass escape from Stalag Luft III of 23rd March, 1944; men who had taken part in the breakout and whose lives for some mysterious reason had been spared. There were Wing Commander ('Wings') Day and Flight Lieutenants Sydney Dowse and B. A. 'Jimmy' James; all three heroes of numberless escapes. Also in these huts were four Irish soldiers, a rather mysterious Belgian or Frenchman who said that he had served in the R.A.F., and Mr. Greenewich who had been British Passport Control Officer at Sofia; then there were five Greek generals headed by the Commander-in-Chief of the Greek armies, General Papagos, and a couple of Polish air force officers.

It was a wonderful experience meeting these people, as it was the first time in nearly five and a half years that I had been able to talk freely to men of my own race, men too, who by virtue of their indomitable courage and refusal to accept defeat were the heroes of all their fellow prisoners. They were all extraordinarily nice and kind to me but in my heart I felt very much ashamed that, whilst they had broken out of prison time and again, I had done nothing but sit in my cell leading the well-fed life of a prize poodle. Instead of telling of their own adventures they pretended interest in my tales of the Sachsenhausen Bunker, where they had all been guests for a time.

Some prisoners wheeling garden water-carts appeared and these turned out to contain our supper; a watery vegetable soup. After we had eaten, to bed, and as we were so few, each of us got an upper bunk. I was very tired and went to sleep at once, but in the morning there were loud complaints from all the others, whose night had been passed in a vain fight with bugs. I am one of those lucky people whose blood is disdained by all insects that bite, and so I had noticed nothing of this disturbance, but von Falkenhausen and Thomas, who had slept on either side of me, complained bitterly that all the bugs from my bunk had moved over to them in columns of four and had almost eaten them alive, and their skin certainly did look rather mottled.

I remember little about the next day except that the washing facilities of the camp were deplorable and the lavatories open cess-pools. The weather was gloriously fine and sunny, but we were all feeling unsettled and nervy wondering what had been happening at the front, and what the immediate future held for us. We saw some of the camp inmates, most of whom seemed to be Frenchmen who had belonged to the Maquis—all looked half-starved and were dressed in rags; amongst them was a party of French girls who were in rather better state and had energy enough to cheek their guards and shout comments on our appearance. Part of the camp was fenced off as a sort of kitchen garden, and I was told that about six men who were working there were American airmen who had been shot down. I think that it was Greenewich who managed to speak to them and who told me that these men had had a terrible time and had been absolutely starved—they certainly looked more like skeletons than living men, and it was pitiful to see their slow and laboured movements as though they had to call up all their reserves of strength to move a limb. This was really the first view at close quarters that I had had of the sufferings of the inmates of concentration camps.

We, for our part, had quite a good midday meal, for Canon Neuhäusler, one of the clerics I had met at Dachau, had managed to get a guard to fetch a large parcel of provisions from Innsbruck which he shared with us. Although no SS man was supposed to

P

take any part in Christian observance of religion, it was most noticeable how anxious were those who had been Roman Catholics to keep on the right side of our priests. Neuhäusler was Canon of Munich Cathedral and had been the chief assistant of Cardinal Faulhauber in the fight against the Nazis; a most unassuming man he was a loyal friend to all his fellow prisoners, and did much to ease their lot.

In the early afternoon five or six large buses arrived, and after waiting for some time at the entrance the Schuschniggs, Blums, Thyssens, and others of our Dachau party, together with all the other men, women, and children, whom we had previously seen at the prison at Regensburg, were brought into the camp. They also had been travelling all night and were tired, hungry, and dirty; as had been the case with us, too, there was nowhere for them to rest. The best that we could do for them was to offer them our quarters which, even after being warned about the bugs, they accepted with every sign of delight. Stiller had also arrived with the party and button-holing him I managed to get from him an admission that we were moving again that night to the Italian Tirol; he said that he was taking us to an hotel there where we would await the arrival of our troops, and that his orders were to see that our liberation should be effected in an orderly manner. He was, as always, very friendly and polite, but his assurances did not ring true to me and I had a shrewd suspicion that he was holding a good deal back—there was one thing I did not like at all, and that was, that I had seen Lieutenant Bader and a considerable number of his S.D. men in the camp—if it was the intention to permit our liberation, why had Bader and his men, whose function was the liquidation of unwanted prisoners been sent with us?

Our situation did not look any too good to me, and as the day passed several people told me of snatches of conversation between the guards which they had overheard, which indicated that they did not consider our expectation of life any too good either. I did everything that I could to allay people's fears and assured everyone that I was quite certain we should come through safely, for several seemed to be thinking of attempting escape and I was pretty sure that any action of this nature would arouse the murderous inclinations of Bader's men. If only we could get safely into Italy and our guards away from their home ground we might have a better chance of organizing opposition to their plans. I talked this over with Colonel Churchill who had the most definite escape plans and, as I thought, convinced him that our best plan would be to see the thing through together.

My Dachau friends brought with them the news that little Rascher had been shot the previous evening. When he went to the window in the door of his cell to take in his supper he was met by a pistol bullet instead of the expected bowl of soup.

Undoubtedly he deserved his fate, which probably spared him the ordeal of trial and hanging at Allied hands, yet I could not help feeling sorry, for we had been through much together and always he had behaved with gallantry and been our loyal comrade.

Just before sunset that evening the whole party, now numbering over 130 people, embarked in buses assembled at the entrance; I believe that there were five in all as well as the lorry in which we had travelled from Innsbruck. I managed to get into a comfortable bus with my Dachau friends after a little difficulty with Stiller who had intended to put Stevens in with McGrath, who was already in the bus. I said that I had already done my share of uncomfortable travelling and as Stevens was ten years younger than I, it could do him no harm to do a spell as well; McGrath backed me up, so I was able to do this last bit of my long journey under conditions which approached luxury. As a matter of fact I was so thin and my stern so sore that I was afraid if I did any more sitting on hard seats my bones would come through my skin.

There were, of course, the usual delays before everything was ready for departure, and it was about nine o'clock by the time we got started. There followed the usual night journey in pitch darkness but from the first there was no doubt about the direction: we were on our way across the Brenner and to Italy. We jogged along at the usual fifteen miles an hour until we got to the top of the Brenner, where the convoy came to a halt and remained motionless for over an hour. There must have been some moon for I can remember that everything around seemed to be in ruins—near where we were stationed there was a concrete bunker and most of our guards went to earth there. Later we heard that we had stopped in this desolate spot in the hope that there might be an air raid, for these were of nightly occurrence, in which case we should all have been shot down and our death attributed to bombing. Luckily, the weather was very cloudy and there was no air raid.

Dawn was just breaking when we completed our traverse of the Brenner and continued along the lovely road which leads to Bozen. We had, however, heard rumours that our destination was a village in the Puster Thal and sure enough, when we reached Franzensfeste, we turned left on the road leading to Lienz and Klagenfurt in Austria. Dr. Schuschnigg, a Tirolese by birth, was familiar with every inch of this part of the country and knew the name of each village. At about nine o'clock our convoy came to a halt, and then turned to the right along a narrow road and over a level crossing; then there was another stop and much discussion between Stiller, Bader, and the rest of our guard. Our bus, and two or more others, were then backed out of the side turning on to the main road again, lined up, stopped apparently for good, and we were told that we might get out.

It was an open stretch of road with fields sloping to a copse on one side and a railway line on the other. Sentries armed with tommy guns took up positions along the road at intervals of about ten yards, and we were permitted to exercise ourselves between them and the buses. I managed to get hold of Stiller and asked him what was the plan. He said that he had intended to take us to a nearby hotel but had learnt that this was occupied by an air force staff and he really did not know what to do next; could not indeed do anything until he had found some petrol, as the tanks of his transport were almost empty. The general impression was that Stiller not only could not do anything but did not much want to, and it looked rather as though he were adopting only passive resistance to Bader's wish to liquidate the whole lot of us, and thus be free to move to a better spot with whatever loot could be obtained from our luggage. The great idea, though, still seemed to be to hope for an air raid as an excuse for shooting us down.

I was by this time on pretty good terms with quite a number of our guards, including some of Bader's men who had been with us at Schöneberg, and although they would have shot us if ordered to, they did not seem at all keen to begin—one or two to whom I talked seemed to think that it would not be a bad idea to make a start by shooting Stiller and Bader, but although I was encouraging, the idea was not put into practice. Stiller was quite obviously scared and inclined to favour our survival in the hope that we might put in a good word for him if he were captured by our troops. He was senior in rank to Bader and had thirty of his own men to Bader's twenty, none of whom had the slightest wish to be involved in mass murder; most were quite decent fellows, many of them old Wehrmacht soldiers who had been drafted into the SS after their recovery from wounds. Could Stiller be induced to act?

The problem seemed to me one which could best be settled amongst the Germans, for I had already gone about as far as I dared in my attempts to influence Stiller and his men, so I got Schacht and Thyssen together, as the plutocrats of our party, and suggested that the time had come for a little bribery and corruption; would they put up the money for a substantial reward if Stiller agreed to take us all to the Swiss frontier so that we could cross to safety? They were quite ready to act as bankers and agreed on an offer of 100,000 Swiss francs, but neither they nor anyone else was prepared to approach Stiller and make him an offer; they were not even willing to come with me while I put it up to Stiller.

While this conversation was going on, Dr. von Schuschnigg was recognized by some cyclists who passed him and these reported his presence to a certain Dr. Ducia, a leader of the underground resistance movement who happened to be in the nearby village of Niederdorf. Not long afterwards, Ducia himself came along and, after a talk with Dr. von Schuschnigg, spoke to Stiller and told him that he could arrange for the feeding and billeting of his party in the village. Ducia went backwards and forwards several times between our car park and the village before Stiller would agree to any move being made, but in the end, as he and his men also felt the pangs of hunger, agreed to a mass movement towards the village and food. Ducia had already told us that we would be quite safe from air attack as he had succeeded in communicating with the American Army by clandestine radio; he also said that once we were in the village he hoped to find some means of assuring our safety—perhaps the Allies might be induced to make a landing by air to relieve us.

The distance to the village was about a mile and I walked between General Thomas and Fabian von Schlabrendorf, one of the only surviving participants in the 20th July plot. Just as we were entering the village there was a call of "Thomas! Thomas!" and a lieutenant-general standing by a building on our left rushed in a state of great excitement to General Thomas and threw his arms round him in affectionate embrace, and ·then both left the ranks and went away together. In the village Ducia led a number of us into an hotel where he said we should be given food, and then took the rest on somewhere else. Can you imagine our joy and excitement at being in a real hotel, welcomed by a friendly pro-prietress and brightly clad Tirolese waitresses? First we took it in turn to have a real good wash and then we all sat down at a long table and steaming bowls of food, a sort of stew of liver and mushrooms were brought in—would we like some wine? Would we! We were a charabanc load of beanfeasters—all shouting and laughing—and eating and drinking.

Halfway through our meal Thomas came in with the news that the town major, the lieutenant-general who had welcomed him, was one of his oldest and best friends and was most eager to help us. There followed a long discussion as to what action could be taken and how Thomas's friend could help. I put forward the argument that as we were now in army operation area the general commanding should be warned that if anything happened to us he would certainly be held responsible by the Allies. Thomas said that he did not know General Vietinghof, the general commanding the German southern armies, personally, but at this von Bonin said that he knew him extremely well. In the end it was agreed that Thomas should take von Bonin to his friend and try to get permission for him to telephone to Vietinghof and both went off on this mission.

After dinner we all walked back to our buses which, since they carried all our worldly possessions, we could not afford to neglect, then came a hitch. My bus, which was the last in the queue; started, ran a hundred yards or so, and then stopped—no petrol.

There was only the driver and one guard with us, and they could not leave us to go to the village for help, so there was nothing for it but to wait in the hope that someone would pass and take a message; but no one did and as time went on it began to look as though we were stranded for the night. At last the guard agreed that one of our party should go to the village and ask for help, and I think that it was von Schlabrendorf who went; anyhow, the result was that one of the other buses came back and took us in tow. I had been very worried at the delay for naturally I was eager to hear the result of Thomas's and von Bonin's attempt to get the army to intervene in our predicament.

When we got to the village we were met by Ducia, who had arranged billets for all; quite a number of the men would have to put up with beds of straw at the town hall, but von Falkenhausen had arranged a room for himself, Thomas and me at Hotel Bachmann, and when I got there Andy Walsh, one of the Irish soldiers with McGrath, was waiting to look after me and my luggage, having apparently decided to act as my batman. There was no news of Thomas and von Bonin and no one had seen or heard anything of them since they left us after dinner, so as there were rumours that wine was to be had at the hotel if one talked prettily to the proprietress, McGrath and I decided to try our luck and found our way to the kitchen. A couple of our guards, Fritz, the quartermaster-sergeant, and one of Bader's men, were already there with a bottle of wine before them so, hoping that there was some truth in the saying 'in vino veritas', and that it might be possible to extract some information from them, I asked whether we could join them, to which they gave cordial assent. It was obvious that the bottle on which they were engaged was far from their first and their mood was distinctly mellow.

Fritz was by turns lachrymose and truculent, talking about his wife and innocent children, or about how he would never be taken prisoner alive, and Bader's man was in the glassy-eyed stage which presages an imminent 'pass-out'. The kitchen was warm and brightly lighted and our hostess, although it was near midnight, was still busy with pots and pans at her kitchen stove, apparently preparing a meal for herself and family. I told Fritz what a good fellow he was and how well he had always behaved towards us, and he told me that he looked upon me as a dear friend and proposed that we should drink Brüderschaft. I said that I would certainly put in a good word for him when he fell into the hands of our troops, which started him off blustering again and boasting how many tommies he would take with him. When he calmed down again he said: "Yes, I know you are my friend and would help me if you were alive." Then he pulled a paper out of his pocket and spelling through it he said: "Here is the order for your execution; you won't be alive after tomorrow."

"What nonsense is that," I said. "Surely no one is going to be such a fool as to shoot any of us at this stage of the war. Why, the whole lot of you will be prisoners yourselves in a day or two." This started him off again saying that no one would ever take him prisoner, and that all SS men would fight to the last, and his glassy-eyed friend revived sufficiently to start muttering "Shoot them all down—bum, bum, bum—bump them all off is best," and he began fumbling at his pistol holster.

"No, it is quite certain. See, here it is in black and white—an order from the Reichssicherheitsdienst in Berlin," and Fritz pushed a paper under my nose. He waved it about a good deal and I could not read it all, but it was an order that the following prisoners must not be allowed to fall into the hands of the enemy and were to be liquidated should there be danger of this occurring. Then followed a long list of names which, as it reached to the bottom of the page, was probably continued on the back which I did not see. I saw the names of Schuschnigg, Blum, Niemöller, Schacht, Müller, Falkenhausen, Thomas and Halder, as well as Stevens and myself.

"You surely don't mean to tell me that Stiller will be such a fool as to carry out this order—why, I have been talking to him today and he assured me that we could rely upon him to hand us over safely to the Americans when they reach here."

"Stiller! Don't you make any mistake about it. It is Bader who runs this show, and he says he is going to liquidate all the prisoners —he has had his orders to do so for the past three months, and Bader always carries out his orders."

"Now, Fritz," I said, "we have just drunk Brüderschaft, surely you don't intend to take part in killing me."

"Ja, Herr Best—but what can I do? You are all going up to a hotel in the mountains tomorrow which, after you have all been shot will be set on fire. I don't like it at all. I know what shooting people with these tommy guns is like, half of them are not properly dead—the bullets are too small and you can't aim properly—so a lot of people won't be dead when the place is set on fire." He thought deeply for a time and then continued, "Herr Best, you are my friend. I will tell you what we will do. I will give you a sign before they start shooting and you come and stand near me so that I can give you a shot in the back of the head (Nackenschuss)—that is the best way to die—you won't know anything about it—I am a dead shot—never miss." Then he went on to explain the special technique of killing people pleasantly by this means. "You mustn't touch them with your pistol for then they may flinch and your shot go astray. No, you have to aim very carefully as the bullet must take a certain line to kill a man instantly and—you must do it quickly. I can do it without looking, almost."

He pulled out his pistol and said: "Just turn round and I will show you."

"Don't be silly! How can I see what you do behind my back—why you might have an accident and shoot me now." He turned to his pal and said: "You turn your head so that I can show Herr Best how to give the 'Nackenschuss'." But he only stared, muttering again about "bump them all off" and, with a sweep of his arm knocked bottle and glasses from the table.

Our further conversation was inconclusive. The other man passed right out and lay with his head and shoulders on the table and Fritz became more and more melancholy as he told me how his wife and innocent children had no idea that he had killed hundreds, no thousands of people, and that war was a terrible thing, but that it was all the fault of the Jews and plutocrats in England and America—the Führer was a good man and only wanted peace, and so did the common people everywhere, but the Jews were a pest which destroyed everything in its path.

McGrath, who did not understand German had left us some time ago, and as I was feeling pretty well dead tired I took the first opportunity I could of going too. When I got up to our room I found only von Falkenhausen who said that he had heard nothing of Thomas and von Bonin. I did not tell him of my talk with Fritz as there was nothing that we could do, and the more people that knew, the greater likelihood of panic. Of course it would have been a simple matter simply to pull out and escape for we were in a friendly country and I would have had no difficulty in finding a hiding place. As a matter of fact, one member of our party did escape that night. It was, I think, a cowardly action, such as even the bravest man is sometimes guilty of—luckily his escape was never discovered by our guards for if it had been, it would certainly have led to their taking precipitate action against the rest of us. My consolation is that he did not get far but spent an uncomfortable, and very cold week, wandering about in the mountains until he was found by the American troops who relieved the rest of our party.

It was not until about 3 a.m. that Thomas turned up. He and Bonin had spent all the time waiting for a reply from General Vietinghof who was not at his headquarters when they first rang up. They had spoken to his Chief of Staff who had promised to speak to the general, but it was after two before he rang them up again with his answer. Vietinghof admitted at once that the war was at an end, and that although his orders were to retire fighting to the Dolomites, he was trying to arrange for an end to hostilities. Certainly no harm must come to any prisoners in his army area, and he promised that he would send an officer with a company of infantry at once with orders to ensure our safety. He promised also to notify the Americans where we were and to ask them to regard the Niederdorf area as neutral ground—if forced to retire he would not establish any fighting line there.

This news was most heartening and for the rest of that night we put in some intensive sleep—I did, though von Falkenhausen complained that I had kept him awake by grunting like a wart hog in between loud snores. Early next morning von Bonin and Liedig came along and we held a council of war. Bonin told us that the officer whom Vietinghof had promised to send had arrived, but that he had only fifteen men with him and moreover had no authority to take any military action against the SS and SD detachments if they refused to allow him to take charge of the prisoners. Later, I spoke to him myself. He was a very charming, correctly behaved young officer, but so afraid of exceeding his authority that he was of little use to us in our present position. We all felt that if he were to start parleying with a man like Bader his weakness of character would be so apparent that it would only make the position worse, so we decided that the best thing would be for von Bonin to try and get him to stay put and refrain from any action for the time being. For our part, we would get hold of Stiller and see whether we couldn't put the wind up him.

As I left the hotel I ran into Stiller, so seizing the opportunity I said that we should like to have a talk with him and asked him to come up to my room. None of his men were about at the moment and, as we all looked pretty determined, Stiller obviously thought it safer to do as we asked and came upstairs with us like a lamb. Von Bonin had a pistol and we had decided that if Stiller proved difficult he would not leave the room alive. The four of us sat down at a table and I started up: "Herr Obersturmführer, you told me that your orders were to ensure our safety until you were able to hand us over to our advancing troops. Now we have heard a lot of rumours which seem to indicate that you are either unwilling or unable to carry out this intention and that plans are afoot to liquidate the whole lot of us."

"No, Herr Best, really, I want to do the best for you—you have nothing to fear from me—Colonel Stevens knows me well and can tell you that I have always treated prisoners well—it is all the fault of Bader—I had a big row with him last night when I told him that I would not allow any of you to be harmed and he threatened to bump me off 'mich niederzuknallen'. You can count on me to do anything that I can to help, but I can't do anything with Bader."

"Well, you say that you want to help but can't, so that's not much good to us, as we most certainly are not going to allow you or anyone else to murder us. We have therefore decided that I shall take over command from you. Do you agree? Can I count on you for loyal co-operation?"

Stiller received the suggestion with enthusiasm and agreed at once. He said, though, that he could do nothing about Bader and his men and that I would have to fix this up myself. "Bader is a most dangerous man. He belongs to Major Stavisky's special detachment which does nothing but extermination; he knows that his number is up if he ever falls into the hands of the enemy and thinks that he may as well be hung for a sheep as a lamb." I then told Stiller that von Bonin had established contact with General Vietinghof and that we now had the support of a company of Wehrmacht Infantry—if Bader made any difficulty, we would soon settle his hash. I then asked him to do two things. First to tell Bader about our military support and, secondly, to convene a meeting of all the prisoners in our party for twelve o'clock at Hotel Bachmann, so that he could formally hand over to me, to both of which he agreed.

As von Bonin, Liedig, and I were leaving the hotel we ran into McGrath and 'Wings' Day, to whom I told the arrangements which had just been made.

"Oh, you are hopelessly out of date, Best. It's all fixed up. Garibaldi is going to stage a rising tonight with his Italian partisans, occupy the village and take all of us up into the mountains."

I was absolutely horrified at this suggestion. I had seen something of Garibaldi's so-called partisans—just a lot of village youths who had tied red scarves round their necks for the occasion, just as a little while back they had probably cried Viva Mussolini! or Heil Hitler! How on earth could they hope to overpower the German troops and occupy the village whilst some 140 men, women and children were roused from their beds and taken to the mountains? I did not at all like to feel that my own plan was in opposition to the wishes of my fellow countrymen, but most certainly I must endeavour to scotch this idea of an armed rising. The hitch came at a most inconvenient moment too, for Bader had still to be dealt with, and until his teeth had been drawn no great reliance could be placed on Stiller's promise of co-operation. It was then about ten o'clock and the assembly of the whole party of prisoners was to be called for noon, so there was only two hours left in which to get the whole tangle sorted out. To deal with McGrath and Day's opposition, which received support from Stevens, I decided to invoke the forces of democracy and said that of course I did not want to force my opinions on anyone and suggested that a committee should be formed to decide our course of action.

We went round to the town hall, where Garibaldi had established himself on the top floor, and got him to agree to the idea of a committee in spite of strong objections voiced by Colonel Ferrero, and it was decided that we should call a meeting in Garibaldi's quarters at eleven. I then set to work to appoint the committee and in addition to Day, McGrath, Garibaldi, and Ferrero, asked Bonin,

Liedig, Canon Neuhäusler, Major Stanek, General Papagos, and General Priwalow, one of the Russians, to serve as members.

Next, I went with von Bonin and Liedig for a conference with the officer sent by von Vietinghof, but found him very nervous and disinclined to take any definite action. After some argument in which von Bonin said that, as his superior officer, he would accept full responsibility, he agreed to allow his men to make a display of force by setting up a couple of machine-guns on the square trained on the SD lorry. Stiller had obviously told Bader about his conversation with us as he and his men were assembled near their lorry and were holding a conclave of their own. Von Bonin and I went up to them and said: "Throw down your arms or else those guns will go off." To our surprise they obeyed without a murmur and, as fast as they threw their sub-machine-guns out of the lorry, these were whipped up by Italians with red scarves who only lacked a weapon of some sort to turn them into full-blown partisans. After this was over Bader became quite humble and pleaded with us to use our influence to get him some petrol so that he and his men could move off.

Then, up we went to the third floor of the town hall and found the rest of the committee assembled. For me everything depended on Garibaldi and on getting him to call off his partisans; I had seen a lot of him while we were both staying at the brothel at Dachau, and I felt pretty sure that he was far too intelligent a man to wish to resort to force if a peaceful solution could be found, and so I concentrated on winning him over to my side. My knowledge of languages gave me a considerable advantage for although Garibaldi, whose mother was English, could speak that language, the Germans and General Priwalow spoke only German, and General Papagos only French, so that I could always tide over awkward moments by engaging in a bit of interpreting. The main trouble came from Colonel Ferrero who absolutely refused even to listen to any suggestion that his uprising should be cancelled, and ultimately, when he saw that I was gaining the support of Garibaldi, flounced out of the room shouting that whatever we might arrange he at all events was going on with the original plan.

The line I took with Garibaldi was that at the present juncture he must consider matters not as a prisoner desiring release but as an Italian. We were in the Tirol, in a part with a predominantly German population which nevertheless, after the First World War, had been handed over to Italy, and which he, as an Italian, certainly did not wish to see returned to Austria. Supposing he carried on with his plan for an armed rising and anything went wrong, and men such as Blum or Schuschnigg were wounded or killed. Might such an event not possibly weigh the scales against his country when the question of the future of the Tirol came to be decided? I explained what had been arranged with the Wehrmacht and told of the abdication of our jailers. Why resort to violent action when, in my opinion, everything could be arranged without friction? To my great joy Garibaldi agreed with me at once, saying that he was a man of peace and certainly preferred a solution which could be attained without recourse to force. Of course with Garibaldi prepared to call off his show the matter was really settled, but I put the whole question up to the committee and met with no more opposition. Both McGrath and Day said that they had no faith in promises made by Germans, but that possibly I knew best, whilst of the other members only General Papagos said anything. His view was that steps should be taken to get into contact with the International Red Cross at Geneva, and asked whether I would endeavour to have a telegram or wireless message sent to it, and to this, of course, I agreed.

At noon I found all my fellow prisoners assembled in the café of Hotel Bachmann, and Stiller called out that he was no longer responsible for their safety and that Herr Best would tell them more. Von Bonin and I then climbed on to a table, and he in German and I in English and French told of the arrangements which had been made, and that everyone could now consider himself a free man. Until we were actually relieved by allied troops though, everyone must be very careful and not move far from their billets. I then told them of arrangements which were being made for our whole party to move up to an hotel in the mountains where we could feel ourselves perfectly safe under the guard and protection of the Wehrmacht. There was a little applause and then a voice from the floor: "I notice from the names given of the members of the committee that France was not represented, and therefore propose that His Highness Prince Xavier de Bourbon should be appointed to the committee to safeguard the interests of France and the French members of our party." I thought to myself: 'Good old League of Nations, come to life again,' but explained politely that when forming my committee I had not thought in terms of nationalities, but had only asked those gentlemen to help who were in a position, owing to their special knowledge or influence, best to serve the interests of all members of our group.

We had some sort of a midday meal, and then most of the afternoon was filled with discussions with Bonin, Liedig and Ducia. The latter, I found, had known all about the Italian plot, and told me that if it had not been called off he would have mobilized the Standschutzen (Tirolese underground) and would have prevented any attempt by Garibaldi to move us from Niederdorf; he could have called up several hundred men while Garibaldi had less than eighty—we had therefore escaped the danger of outbreak of civil war in the night. Although I had told my fellow prisoners that we were moving up to a hotel, the plan was still very much in the air, and Ducia had to do a lot of running about before it was really fixed up, as the hotel was empty and locked up, and he had to get hold of the proprietress to open it up. Eventually everything was satisfactorily arranged, and it was decided that we should move there next day, and Ducia then set about arranging for transport to take us and our baggage—no easy matter at this stage of the war.

By the time these matters were settled I was all in, and without bothering about food or anything else went off to bed. The day had not been perfect, but at all events it had at last come to an end.

CHAPTER X

THE 30th April, 1945, found us no longer prisoners, but yet not free; we were more in the position of some passengers in an old-time sailing ship crossing the ocean—we had mutinied and removed officers and crew, but did not yet know how our further course was to be set nor who would navigate. None of us had had news from home for many months, nor did those who filled our hearts and our thoughts have any idea where we were or whether we were living or dead. Of what was happening in the world we had only the most sketchy knowledge. We had learnt that the war in Italy was almost at an end, but knew practically nothing about events to our north, or that Berlin was invested, and Hitler near his end. There were 136 persons, men, women, and children, whose ages ranged from four to seventy-three, and who belonged to seventeen different nationalities. We had no money, no food, and no one was now responsible for seeing that we were housed and fed.

Very few of our group of prisoners ever realized the difficulties of our position, or how grateful they should be to Tony Ducia, his assistant, Dr. Thalhammer, and the people of Niederdorf, who made themselves responsible for our well-being, and without hesitation opened up their secret stocks of hoarded foodstuffs and contributed their last reserves. Remember, these were the last days of the war; all communications were disrupted and this isolated little village in the mountains could hardly hope that fresh supplies would reach it—I know that the inhabitants fully realized the position—and yet, food, wine, and tobacco poured in, and we became the richest and best-fed people for miles around. It was a triumph of organization on the part of Dr. Ducia, and a miracle of generosity on that of the population of Niederdorf.

For our Tirolese friends, for von Bonin, Liedig, and me, it was a very busy day, as a host of things had to be arranged before our move would be possible. First of all the proprietress of the hotel where it was intended that we should be housed had to be fetched from Brixen. The hotel itself was in the mountains 5,000 feet up and about five miles distant from Niederdorf; it was normally closed during the winter, but had now been shut since the beginning of the war, so that it was certainly unprepared for the reception of guests, and there was some doubt whether our stay there would be feasible. As soon as Frau Emma Heiss, the proprietress, arrived, Ducia and Liedig went up to inspect and brought the news that, although we would have to rough it a bit at first and everyone would have to take a hand in running it, we should be able to make ourselves fairly comfortable whilst, since it could be reached only by a single narrow road, it would be simple to put the place in a state of defence. Ducia's next problem was to arrange for transport to take us, our luggage, and necessary provisions up —a most difficult task, but one which, with the help of the German town major, he succeeded in solving.

Meanwhile, von Bonin was busy with the Wehrmacht, arranging for our security as far as could be done with the very slender force at his disposal. Von Bonin telephoned several times to Southern Army Headquarters and received the promise that a front-line infantry company would be sent for our protection and placed under his orders, but at the moment the only concrete evidence we had that we were under army protection was the arrival of two cases containing sixty bottles of Italian brandy and another of Asti; a present from General von Vietinghof. For my part, my task was to try to keep the members of our group from scattering too much, and to encourage those who were inclined to pessimism regarding the future. The first task was most difficult, for the idea of freedom had gone to the heads of the younger members of our party, and they had scattered wide over the whole district and, a far as I could make out, were engaged in scrounging for such delicacies as eggs and anything else to be found in farm larders. The whole neighbourhood was vastly excited by our arrival in their midst, and everyone was delighted to be able to do something for us.

The morale of all the prisoners was good, except that some of the ladies who had been separated from their young children, and had no idea of their whereabouts, were much aggrieved because I could offer them no hope of being able to communicate with their relatives in Germany. Most of them had been imprisoned long before the disruption of communications even approached its present state, and they could not understand that there were now no postal facilities of any kind available. I did what I could to comfort them, but I was feeling so ill myself that I fear on occasion I gave way to impatience, and to my present regret gave answers which must have seemed rather unfeeling.

Liedig went up to the hotel early in the afternoon, as we thought it better that when our people went up there they should find rooms reserved for them, just as they would have in peace time.

Not only this, but we thought that it would probably be preferable if national groups were as far as possible kept together; there was also another problem—the hotel had been closed for so long that it was doubtful whether it could be adequately heated, especially since it was really only a summer resort. Although there was central heating no one knew whether there was any fuel—when we got there we found that the heating plant had been frozen and consisted of a mass of burst pipes—and, as we had a number of elderly people, some attempt must be made to provide warm rooms for them at least. Two of our ladies, Miss Elisabeth Kaiser and Mrs. Kate Gudzent, went with him, and for the whole of our stay there gave devoted service as our secretarial staff. In the early afternoon a start was made with the transport of our party up to our new sanctuary, women and children first, while von Bonin, Ducia, and I stayed until the last, sorting out all the luggage and other belongings which had been forgotten. We had told Stiller that we had no objection to him and a few of his men coming up with us if they were unarmed, and that we would speak in their favour when our troops reached us. Stiller badly wanted to come, but in the end was too afraid that even now the long arm of the Gestapo might reach him, and decided not to; eleven of his men, however, did come, one of them bringing with him his wife and daughter who had mysteriously made their appearance in Niederdorf.

When at last I got up to the hotel I found that everyone had been found satisfactory quarters, and that a start had already been made to prepare something in the way of an evening meal. Mr. and Mrs. Mohr, who seemed to have technical knowledge of the business, had taken charge of the kitchen with the two Dachau trusties, Wouwer and Kohlenklau, as their staff. The younger women and girls were also making themselves useful in the arrangement of rooms, sorting out bedding, etc. Liedig had reserved rooms for us Britishers at one end of the second floor; nice big rooms, but like most, unheated. The first thing, indeed, that struck me when we entered the hotel was the intense cold which was really like that of a refrigerator. We were 5,000 feet up, and the end of April is really too early for such a height; in Niederdorf it had been quite warm, but by the time we got up to the hotel it had begun to snow and from the look of it, we might be in for a heavy fall. On that evening the only rooms which could be warmed were the kitchen and a big room next to it which had apparently been the hotel café, and which became our communal living- and dining-room.

The name of our new home was, as I only discovered after my arrival, Hotel Prags Wildbad—or, as it is called in Italian, Lago di Braies. It was a big place with over 200 bedrooms, and under normal circumstances, must have been most comfortable; the situation is absolutely perfect, and when I first went into my bedroom and looked out of the window the beauty of the view quite took my breath away. I saw below me a lake of purest emerald, entirely surrounded by pine trees growing at the base of jagged mountain peaks that seemed to shut us in away from the rest of the world; not a ripple moved the face of the water and the indescribable mountain silence, a silence that you seem to hear, filled the pure cold air. I went out on to the balcony, and in spite of the cold, could not for long drag myself away from the loveliness before me—for five and a half years I had been starved of the beauties of the world, and to me scenery is the one thing of which I never grow tired and which, however familiar, always retains its unabated charm.

When I went downstairs again I found that a really magnificent meal had been prepared and everyone seemed gay and happy— our party ate with such good appetite, indeed, that thirty more rations were drawn than our total number. There was so much to eat that I am sure that everyone had enough with his own allowance, but the prison spirit still endured and those extra rations must have been smuggled up to bedrooms just to be held in reserve in case bad times should come again. It made things very difficult though, for a lot of people were left without food until more could be produced by our cooks. After dinner the proprietress, Mrs. Emma Heiss, announced that she had a small amount of wine left and invited those who cared, to come down to the Weinstube in the basement, where we formed an extremely gay and carefree party. Again though, there was another lamentable proof that the honesty of ex-prisoners could not be trusted, for while we were having our own little party more than fifteen gallons of wine were abstracted from the cellars which Frau Heiss had left unlocked, and as a result of this, and other similar events, no little time and ingenuity had to be devoted in the future to ensuring that each member of our party got his allotted share only of the good things provided for us by the generosity of our hosts.

This was the first time in my life that I had ever had anything to do with the running of an hotel, but it had to be done, and I believe that it was well done; I am, in fact, rather proud that very soon the majority of our guests looked upon Liedig and me, and on all those who took an active part in management and service, as foreordained to minister to their comfort. Liedig became staff manager, and I a cross between host and hotel porter, with questions on every subject in the world being shot at me without intermission wherever I went.

Hugh Falconer, as our wireless expert, got hold of a radio set almost as soon as he arrived and spent most of his time listening for news and issuing bulletins at frequent intervals. On the first evening when he was listening to a B.B.C. broadcast, one of the SS men who had come up with us and who obviously did not

Dr. Kurt von Schuschnigg, late Austrian Chancellor, with his wife and Sissie on the boat on their way to find a new home in the United States.

Group-Captain H. M. A. "Wings" Day, R.A.F., D.S.O., O.B.E., A.M.

quite appreciate his changed status, started to make a fuss, saying that it was forbidden to listen to foreign broadcasts; for a moment there seemed to be every prospect of an ugly scene but luckily von Bonin came along and soon put the man in his place. McGrath was also extremely active though I never quite understood what his functions were. He had turned out in an extremely smart uniform, with which he wore a red-topped artillery forage cap, and certainly lent an air of military tone to the proceedings; he was a charming and generous fellow, but at times I found his attempts to introduce a martial element in our pleasant casual life slightly trying.

To return to the subject of the acquisitiveness of prisoners, two rather amusing incidents occur to me. In our sumptuous bedrooms we had each of us large soft pillows and an eiderdown, and on the day after our arrival one person after another who had a room on the third floor came to complain that pillows and eiderdown had been taken from their rooms, and to ask why this had been done. As we knew nothing about this Liedig went at once to look into the matter, with the result that he found all the missing bedding piled up high in the bedroom of one of our party. Everything was returned to the rightful owners and nothing was said about the matter to the culprit who, I am sure, had acted automatically and sub-consciously. Later on I had proof of this in my own case, for although I had been in a measure the director of the hotel and responsible for the equitable distribution of all comforts, when I came to pack my things before leaving for freedom and home I found tins of milk, spam, and butter, tobacco and all manner of other things hidden in my room, which I must have brought there quite unconsciously—certainly, no one was more surprised than I when I found them.

Before coming up to the hotel I had been to see General Gari-baldi again, and had succeeded in making my peace with Colonel Ferrero. They, however, decided to stay where they were in Niederdorf and organize their force of partisans; both had suc-ceeded in finding magnificent uniforms befitting their rank and had turned the town hall into General Staff offices and quarters. Their spirit was so warlike that I was rather afraid that enthusiasm might run away with discretion, and that they might attempt to place the village under Italian rule and so precipitate something like a civil war in which they would be in a hopeless minority; I therefore arranged with von Bonin that he should go down next day and see whether he could not calm them down. He had dinner with Garibaldi whom he found most reasonable and afterwards, in a meeting which he arranged with Ducia, agreement was reached for co-operation between the Italians and the German Tirolese on the basis of majority rule in the villages in the Pustertal.

Dr. Thalhammer, who deputized for Ducia, came up in the

evening with news that the Tirolese Gauleiter Huber with a considerable force of SS had left Innsbruck and were on their way to Bozen; that is, far too close to us to be pleasant. What made this news worse was the fact that our original Wehrmacht guard had been recalled and the company of infantry which was to replace them would only arrive late next day; conditions were most unsettled as deserters were drifting back from the Italian front, and many of them would not have hesitated at murder if he saw a chance of getting hold of civilian clothes. The young people of our party were still exploring the district, going down to the village or visiting neighbouring farms, and it was most difficult to get them to realize how dangerous it was to wander far afield.

On the next day, the 2nd May, a notice was posted asking all members of our party to assemble in the lounge and we then told them what we knew of the position, and made a special plea that no one should go far from the hotel. From then on we held such meetings daily, when Liedig would first give an address in German, which I then interpreted in French and English. It was a curious thing that, whilst I could manage all right in French I found English most difficult. Not only had I deliberately put English as much as possible out of my mind during my imprisonment, but I had not yet learnt to manage my false teeth in this language, although with German they gave me no trouble of any kind.

On this same day Mr. Ducia came up with the news that the town of Bozen was not to be defended, but would be evacuated when the American forces reached it, which they were expected to do next afternoon. Ducia said that he thought that it might be possible to reach Bozen, and in any case he intended trying, and asked me whether I, or someone else, would care to come with him. I should dearly have liked to have gone myself, but decided against it for two reasons; my health, and the fact that I was needed in my present post. In any case, it seemed to me that the first chance of such an escape rightly belonged to 'Wings' Day as a culmination of the five or six attempts which he had already made, so I asked him whether he would care to go and received his immediate assent. As I knew more about the local situation than he, he asked me to write a letter to army headquarters, which I did, and then we set about dressing him up for his trip, for obviously, as he would have to pass through the German lines, he could not very well travel in Air Force uniform. I had a rather dressy black overcoat which fitted him, but my hats were far too small, so one was borrowed from Prince Philip of Hesse, Hitler's one-time representative with Mussolini. Poor Prince Philip had been arrested shortly after the fall of Mussolini, but had no idea that his wife, the Princess Mafalda, had also been arrested, and when the news of her death at Buchenwald was given to him broke down completely.

Ducia had brought a large supply of cigarettes and tobacco with him, which Miss Kaiser and I had the pleasure of distributing, going from room to room and being welcomed as though we were bringing manna from heaven. We had some difficulty with ladies with young children who claimed an allowance for each, but in the end Miss Kaiser ruled that no one under the age of eighteen was entitled to tobacco, and was adamant towards the pleas of mothers for extra rations. We had also instituted a system whereby everyone had a ration card, which was date stamped when food rations were fetched at meal times; everyone could have a second helping if desired, but we insisted that all food must be eaten in the dining-room and that none might be taken to the bedrooms except in the case of people who were ill and confined to bed, as was the case with M. and Mme. Leon Blum.

On the morning of the 3rd May a plane flew over dropping leaflets of which we were able to collect a few. These carried an announcement from Field Marshal Alexander to the effect that General von Vietinghof with all troops under his command had surrendered, and instructing all German military units in the district to refrain from further hostile action and to await further orders at their stations. There was great rejoicing by us all.

Later the same day four men wearing the red neck-scarfs which identified them as partisans, arrived at our hotel by car, and demanded to see Mr. Leon Blum and Molotov's nephew. The leader of the party claimed to be a French officer and said that he had orders to remove both Blum and Wassilli to a place of safety in the mountains. I told him that whilst there was no objection to his seeing any member of our party I certainly could not permit him to remove anyone from the hotel; I pointed out that we were in a sector which fell into the Anglo-American operation area, and that I had already taken steps to enter into communication with our H.Q., and could not accept a decision from another quarter regarding the disposal of any of the people under my charge. These men were at first inclined to be difficult, but when I told them that we had a guard of some hundred Wehrmacht soldiers, and that I should not hesitate to have them arrested and detained until the arrival of a competent authority, they calmed down; I sent someone to show them to the rooms of the Blums, and of Wassilli, and not long afterwards they came down and went away.

Of course, had M. Blum expressed a wish to go with them I could not very well have done anything to prevent it, but I was certainly not going to be bullied by these fellows who came in waving their tommy guns about in most truculent fashion. From what they said, they did not belong to Garibaldi's contingent, but were members of some communist gang from Cortina. I do not know what they said to the Blums or to Wassilli, but just as we

Q*

were starting our usual noontide meeting someone came to me and whispered that the latter was leaving the hotel carrying a suit case. I went out of the front door and caught him up before he had gone very far, but he refused to come back with me, saying: "I don't want to be slaughtered." I understood this to mean that he was afraid of what might happen to him when we were relieved by British or American troops, and told him that he would be quite safe and that I would look after him until he could be sent safely home, but he was in such a panic that nothing that I said had the slightest effect. He was so determined to leave that only by physical violence could I have prevented him, and so I was reluctantly obliged to let him have his own way; a sentry posted on the road leading to the hotel later reported that he had been picked up in a car by our visitors of the morning. From what I learnt subsequently from his friends it appears that it was not our troops of whom he was afraid, but that he believed that if he were returned to Russia he might be executed or murdered by the troops in whose hands he was placed; he believed, it seems, that the Kremlin had ordered the immediate execution of all prisoners of war returned from Germany.

Late in the evening Mr. Ducia turned up again and reported that Day and he had fulfilled their mission. The American troops had not entered Bozen as soon as had been expected, but they had found them a little farther south of the town. Day and he had been immediately flown to Army H.Q. at Florence, where Day had remained whilst Ducia had been sent back to tell us that immediate steps would be taken to relieve us. The two men had a pretty tough journey to Bozen as Ducia's car broke down, and they had had quite a long march through the mountains which proved rather a strain to Day who was, of course, quite out of training. What pleased me most about the whole thing was the fact that 'Wings' Day had at last succeeded in escaping for he had actually passed through the German lines the day before their surrender. He was an absolutely splendid fellow who won the affection and trust of everyone who knew him—modest, unassuming, he was yet the born leader, and there was nothing that I regretted more than the fact that we did not see eye to eye at Niederdorf when he favoured a revolt by Garibaldi's partisans to my more pacific solution.

He has, however, since told me that he thought I had acted for the best, and that he had favoured Garibaldi's plan mainly because he considered it his duty as a British officer to carry on the war against the enemy wherever and whenever he could. He was shot down in October 1939; that is, a month before my own capture, and in spite of his long imprisonment and an unparalleled series of attempted escapes, two of which were nearly successful, he allowed nothing of the strain through which he had passed to show.

When, after his return to England, he was awarded the D.S.O. and O.B.E. for gallantry shown as a prisoner of war, I think that every ex-prisoner felt that these honours had been conferred on their finest representative in recognition of their own sufferings.

I was worried about little Wassilli, and talking the matter over with McGrath we came to the conclusion that the best thing would be to enlist the aid of General Garibaldi, who perhaps, through his gang of toughs, might be able to find out what had happened to him. I therefore asked Major Treiber, a quiet middle-aged Wehrmacht officer, who had been sent to us by Army H.Q., if he could perhaps arrange for transport so that we could go down to the village that evening, and he at once offered to take us down in his own car. When we got there, we found that Garibaldi had completely taken possession of the town hall, and before we could get to his apartments on the third floor we had to run the gauntlet of some fifty or so of his men who, at the sight of the German officer with us, waved their tommy guns about in most alarming fashion; luckily, someone had the sense to ring up the general, who gave orders that we were to be taken up to him. He was much interested about the case of Wassilli whom he knew quite well, and promised to do what he could to help, though when it came down to bedrock, it was pretty evident that his authority ran in Niederdorf only, and that the men who had abstracted Wassilli from our midst belonged to a rival organization with which he was not even in touch.

Long afterwards I heard that poor little Wassilli had been taken up to some mountain refuge by his communist friends, and in the cold there had again suffered frost-bite in what remained of his feet and, lacking proper medical attention, died of gangrene. He was a thoroughly nice, ingenuous lad, and during our long association I had become very fond of him, so that the news of his death gave me a great shock and still causes me sorrow—it was all so entirely unnecessary as he was perfectly safe with us, and would, of course, have received every care after his liberation.

As we passed through the village I saw the Gestapo lorry standing derelict on the square. On the advice of von Bonin the town major had refused to provide any petrol, and eventually Stiller and Bader had set out with the intention of marching to Bozen, and it was later rumoured that they had been attacked on their way by Italian partisans, and several of them, Stiller included, captured and hanged from telegraph poles along the road. Whether this story was true or not was never established, but they certainly deserved anything they got. Earlier in the day a search was made of their lorry, and in it were found nearly 200 Belgian Red Cross parcels addressed to prisoners at Dachau, which they had stolen, and which were then brought up to us.

Next morning, the 4th May, Andy Walsh came into my room just as I had finished dressing and said: "The whole place is full of those Ities, and they are opening the doors of all the rooms and threatening the ladies with their guns." I rushed downstairs, and when I reached the hall found General Garibaldi talking to an American officer; half a dozen American soldiers were also standing by. I went up to the officer, who introduced himself as Lieutenant Ashe, and said that he had come up with an advance detachment which would shortly be followed by the rest of the company; they had made a forced march throughout the night in order to rescue us. I explained that whilst we were getting on quite all right I would be much obliged if he would get rid of the Italian partisans who were upsetting all our arrangements, and disturbing the women and children of our party. He saw the sense of this at once, and in a very few minutes had shooed the whole lot of them off the premises.

I had a few words with Garibaldi, who said that he had only come up to the hotel to show the Americans the way and to render assistance should our German guards offer any resistance. I then explained the position to Lieutenant Ashe and asked that consideration should be shown to the German officers and troops who had protected us from the Gestapo. While we were talking, Captain John Attwell arrived with the bulk of the company, S Company of the 2nd Battalion of the 339th U.S. Infantry Regiment, and immediately took steps to disarm all the German troops. I introduced Major Treiber and the two von Alvenslebens to him; they were cousins and the second of them had come with the German infantry regiment which had guarded us at the hotel. All three were very sad at the idea that they were now prisoners of war, and I made a strong plea to Captain Attwell to make a favourable report about them to H.Q.

Next on my programme was breakfast. Our American friends had travelled light throughout the night and were both tired and hungry; they seemed to have expected to find us in extremis, and were certainly surprised when, within an hour of their arrival, they found themselves sitting down to a magnificent breakfast, and being waited upon by a number of pretty and very charming girls. To cope with this sudden addition to our ration strength I had the Red Cross parcels, which we had retrieved the day before, opened, and so had ample supplies for everybody. It was a source of pride to me at the time that during this first day, when they themselves were without supplies, we were able to provide our rescuers with three square meals, and even with cigarettes.

Although we had not been in any danger since we arrived at the hotel, it was nevertheless a very great relief to have the Americans with us, and for me particularly, it meant the ending of a responsibility which, in my poor state of health, was almost more than I could cope with. I am a very temperate man; often months pass without my touching alcohol, but since our arrival at Prags I had almost been living on General von Vietinghof's brandy, drinking the best part of a bottle a day. It was the only way in which I could keep going, and apart from giving me the energy I required, the unaccustomed drink seemed to have no effect on me at all. Now that I have had experience of the *métier* I look with new respect on hotel and restaurant staff, for I know how difficult it must be to meet all the exigent demands of customers with never failing urbanity. Although I liked most members of our party, and sympathized with all, I often found it most difficult to avoid giving very sharp replies to some of the absurd inquiries and requests which they showered on me.

The American Army did us proud. It is simply astounding what trouble they took to promote our comfort and security, and what nice fellows they were too. There was a spontaneous, almost childlike kindliness shown to us by all of them; something which showed their interest in us, and in the events which had led to their arrival, of which no sophisticated European would have been capable—they thought everything wonderful, said so, and obviously enjoyed being with us. They seemed to be entirely devoid of national hatred, and their behaviour towards the Germans in our party was just as friendly as to all others; perhaps even more friendly, for our pretty girls were all German. There seemed to be amongst them men of all nationalities, men who spoke German, French, and even Russian, and yet, all bore the stamp of being citizens of the U.S.A. and showed that they were proud of it. Almost as soon as they arrived a net was put up and games of hand-ball were in progress in which everyone was free to take part. Others discovered rowing boats and made up parties on the lake. In association with the prisoners there was no distinction between officers and men.

Of course with the arrival of the Americans the excitement amongst the prisoners mounted to fever heat, and I could not move a step without being buttonholed by some agitated person who wanted to know whether letters and telegrams could be sent or, if Germans, whether they could go home—for all, it was liberation, and I do not think that it entered the head of anyone that for many it was to be the threshold to a new and arduous long imprisonment.

Checking up on the prisoners we found that in addition to Wassilli, several others were missing: a Russian general, Heidl, and her latest friend, Captain van Wymeersch. The last named was soon found, as he had gone for a joy ride in a derelict German car, had turned it over, broken his leg, and been taken to hospital. When Captain Attwell heard of this, he put a guard on the road to the village and gave orders that no one might leave the grounds of the hotel. There was a good deal of murmuring about this, as it made everybody feel that something of new-won freedom had been lost, but personally, I wished that I had had power to exercise similar authority long before, and thus could have prevented Wassilli from running away.

On the next day a convoy arrived bringing supplies of all kinds—the finest that the American Army had in the way of rations and comforts. With it came two American colonels named Peebles and English, also Captain Warren Chester Cobb from Battalion H.Q. I discussed the question of supplies with these officers, and asked them whether it would be possible to provide clothing for some of the prisoners who had not even a change of linen. Of the course of that day, the entry in my diary reads: "A lot of trouble with many people." My memory is of having people who wanted to know something which I could not tell them, tagging about after me wherever I went. Apart from this, these days were very pleasant. I had my meals with the American officers, and spent much time with them, though in the evenings I was generally with my old friends the Schuschniggs, Falkenhausen, and others from Dachau. In the evening we were suddenly inundated by a mob of press and news-reel photographers; I have never before experienced such an excitement and such a rush. For a while every corner of the hotel was illuminated by flashlight bulbs; every instant I would be blinded by someone popping one off in my face and then, in a moment, all were gone, having satisfied their ambition to photograph Niemöller, Blum and Schuschnigg.

On the 6th May Brigadier-General Gerow and his adjutant, Lieutenant Buckridge, arrived, and after some discussion with them an announcement was made regarding our evacuation. General Gerow said, that although he did not want to hurry anyone or cause them any inconvenience which could be avoided, he would have to move us out as soon as practicable and moreover, everyone would have to be taken south as all communications with the north were broken. He would not be able to move us all in one party, but hoped to be able to do so in two, and he asked that we should try to arrange amongst ourselves who should go with the first and who with the second party. He spoke very nicely and showed great consideration for all. His speech was then translated by Russian and Greek-speaking soldiers, whilst I followed in German and French. I had already promised my fellow prisoners that I would stay with them to the last, and when I told General Gerow this he was very pleased. I had suggested to him that it would probably be best to evacuate first all prisoners of allied nationality, and also one or two others such as Niemöller and the Hungarians, and this was agreed upon, the date of departure being fixed for the 8th.

Next morning a doctor and a dentist arrived and I had a busy morning arranging appointments for various people who wanted attention and acting as interpreter, and in the evening some dozen press correspondents came and interviewed our celebrities, when again I had to do the translating. One way or another I never seemed to have a moment free, and during our entire stay the only time when I left the hotel was on the evening when I went down to the village in search of Wassilli. We were all up bright and early on the 8th as General Gerow wanted to get the convoy started at nine o'clock, and there were in all eighty-five people to move. McGrath had volunteered to make the arrangements for getting the passengers assembled, but having failed to get a list of the available transport so that he could allocate people to certain cars, the whole thing was a bit of a muddle and the convoy was nearly two hours in starting. When it did, it was quite an impressive sight with armoured cars in the van and the rear and a flight of fighter planes overhead.

General Gerow was anxious to get everybody evacuated as soon as possible, and we therefore arranged that the second batch should leave on the 10th. Several people seemed sorry to be leaving, but in the end all agreed to the plan. I arranged that all cars should bear numbers, and let the individual members of our party arrange their own groups of three or four for the journey, allotting a car to each. I was up at six seeing to the luggage, and on the stroke of nine I was able to report to the general that everyone was aboard and that he could give the sign for our departure.

The journey was a long and tiring one; twelve hours in a staff car reminded me of past journeys by prison van. The roads over which we had to pass were in an appalling condition, and for long stretches practically non-existent. Almost all bridges were a tangled mass of girders, and often the only possible route lay along the river bed of the Piave, but our convoy kept going, and exactly at 9 p.m. we arrived at Verona where we found everything ready for us at a very nice hotel. There was a good dinner followed by a wonderful sleep. Next morning we were taken by car to a flying field and loaded into three planes with Naples as our destination. It was a lovely clear day, and as we flew fairly low we had an excellent view of the country, one of the crew pointing out different landmarks. We passed over Rome and then over Monte Cassino, where the pilot came down so low that the scarred battleground could be clearly seen. We reached Naples at about eleven, where I was immediately taken charge of by a Major McDonagh and Colonel Hicks, who took the greatest trouble to find my gear, searching for it themselves as the planes were unloaded. All the rest of my friends were taken into a sort of customs house, where I was allowed to visit them to say good-bye; they were sitting in rows on benches, looking rather desolate at the news that I must leave them; indeed, I was sorry to go for we had been through much together and a warm spirit of friendship had grown up between us.

McDonagh took me to lunch at the officers' club and then by

car to Caserta, where we were met by Colonel Hicks, who conducted me to a magnificent caravan, all polished walnut and chromium fittings, and complete with every luxury from radio to cocktail bar, which he told me was to be my quarters. Then to dinner with him at the officers' club in the palace.

Next morning a batman brought me breakfast in my caravan, and I went to meet Colonel Hicks at the palace, who conducted me to a number of different staff departments where I reported on the prisoners of our party. Everybody was extremely kind to me and much interest was taken in my opinions. Lunch again at the officers' mess, where I was introduced to a very charming young lady, Senior Commander Olive Grant, A.T.S., who from that moment took charge of me and looked after me as though I were a baby. As a matter of fact, all these lady officers who seemed to run G.H.Q. were something quite new in my experience, and they really scared me to death for fear that unwittingly I might commit some unpardonable solecism when speaking to them. They were all so terribly efficient and businesslike, and yet they were just a lot of pretty and charming girls. I was told by one lady that I was to be sent home by air, and that I had only to say when I wished to leave and she would see that a place was reserved for me on the plane. Then, when I said that I should like to see my prisoner friends once more, so as to be sure that they were comfortable, Olive said at once, of course you can; they are at Capri and we can go there tomorrow, and it was therefore arranged that we would do this, and my return to England was fixed for Tuesday, 15th May.

On Sunday morning Olive called for me with a car and took me to Naples where she gave me lunch at the officers' club; rather funny to be taken out like this by a girl, but, of course, I had not a penny and was entirely dependent on charity. After lunch we went down to the port where Olive pulled strings and twisted some senior naval officers round her fingers with the result that we were soon on a launch which took us to Capri. The day was dull and misty, and the view of the Bay of Naples was no more inspiring than that of any other place in the fog; we could not even see Vesuvius—indeed, all that I had seen of Naples was dirty, shabby and war worn. When we reached Capri the sun was shining and the place looked most inviting. There was, however, a hitch in Olive's arrangements for there was no car for us, and no one seemed to know anything about us or even to want to.

We hung about on the quay side for nearly two hours when another launch arrived and on it I saw the Schuschnigg family, who told us that they had until then been living on the mainland, but were now going to a villa lent to them by friends on Capri. An American officer in a jeep came to meet them and took them up the hill promising to come back and fetch us in a few minutes. Just then two or three more jeeps came down to the quay and out of them stepped my three generals, von Falkenhausen, Thomas, and Halder; Dr. Schacht, Prince Philip of Hesse, von Petersdorff, and one or two others, and were taken by American military police to the launch which had brought the Schuschniggs. An officer who was in charge allowed me to jump on to the launch and say good-bye; all the men were greatly upset by this sudden separation from the rest of their party, particularly General Halder who was thus once again taken away from his wife after their reunion at Prags.

Our car, a jeep, arrived, and we drove up a steep and winding road until we stopped before a very pretty white-painted hotel in the village of Anacapri, and going in I found a number of old friends wandering in rather melancholy fashion round a small and overgrown garden. As soon as they saw me they started telling me of their woes. They were not allowed to leave the grounds of the hotel, greatly as they desired to enjoy the beauties of the island, nor had they any money with which to buy wine, and the water was so highly chlorinated as to be well-nigh undrinkable. Otherwise they were highly satisfied with the quarters and the food provided for them. After conversation with several old friends separately I got all the people at the hotel, the entire German contingent from Prags, but for those whom I had seen leaving on the launch, to assemble in the hall of the hotel, and then made an attempt to explain the position to them. For the moment they could not be moved to their homes for all communication with Germany was disrupted; for the same reason it was for the time being impossible for them to write or telegraph to their relatives; I was in the same boat for although I had tried to communicate with my wife, I had so far heard nothing from her, and in fact, had no idea where she was. For everybody the watchword was 'patience', and we should now be satisfied with the thought that the war was over and that we had come through alive.

When I had finished speaking, Mrs. Heberlein started off and said that they should all be thoroughly ashamed of themselves, complaining instead of being grateful—they had only been in Capri for two days, and it was unreasonable to expect that everything would be perfect at once—they should remember how the Gestapo, Germans like themselves, had treated them. Really, after this talk the spirits of all seemed to have risen very considerably, and when I promised that I would speak to the authorities when I got back to the mainland and hoped that they would be given more freedom soon, they all got quite jolly. Only poor Mrs. Halder was very sad; she and her husband were a most devoted couple, and it hit her very hard again to be separated from him so soon after they had been reunited. I did what I could to comfort her, but it seemed that when the men were taken away something was said about their being war criminals, and this made her fear the worst.

There was an American major in charge of the hotel, or better said, of the internees, and he invited Olive and me to have dinner with him. He then told us that there was another party of ex-prisoners on the island in a hotel a few hundred yards away, so we decided to go there after dinner and see who was there. As we went out of the hotel we met Dr. and Mrs. von Schuschnigg in argument with the military policeman before the door, and very much upset because he would not permit them to enter. I went back to the major who, when I explained that the von Schuschniggs had originally belonged to the party which numbered many friends of theirs, immediately gave permission for them to come to the hotel whenever they liked.

When we reached the second hotel we found only very few people there; merely a sort of residue consisting of men who could be classified neither as ex-enemies nor allies. The Hungarians were there, also Major Stanek and other Czechoslovaks, and the Swede Edquist; all the other Scandinavians had been treated as British officers and had remained on the mainland. Lacking ladies, this hotel seemed much duller than the other, and the spirits of all the men there were very low. I promised to do what I could for them, but said that probably their stay at Capri would only be short as I was sure that arrangements would be made for them to return to their own countries.

After a short stroll about Anacapri which was a very lovely place which I should dearly love to revisit, we went back to the hotel and turned in early as we had been told that our launch left at eight o'clock next day, and if we wanted a car down we must be ready at seven. At breakfast I introduced Fey Pirzio-Biroli to the commandant, as she was absolutely distracted about her two little sons, aged two and four. At the time of her arrest they had been taken from her by the Gestapo who told her that they would be sent to a home under assumed names, and she was terribly afraid that being so young they might forget their real names and she would be unable to trace them. Of course the major could not really do anything to help, but it comforted her to talk about her troubles to someone who seemed to be in authority, and as she was an extremely pretty woman she was given a most sympathetic hearing.

When we got back to Naples, Olive had first to wangle a car from somewhere to take us back to Caserta, and this she did with her customary efficiency. Whilst we were waiting for it she again took me for lunch at the officers' club, and we discussed what could be done to help the people at Capri. She took a lively interest in the problem, and after some thought said that she would take me to department G, something which she thought could help. When we got to Caserta we went to the rabbit warren of a palace, and under her sure guidance climbed stairs and traversed long passages until we reached a room guarded by an American woman officer, and after a conversation between the two ladies who both seemed to be named Darling, I was ushered into a Brigadier-General Spofford, or Spofforth, who was certainly one of the brightest and most understanding people I had yet met. He appreciated the position at once and promised to do what he could to help; he thought though, that it would be better for me to have a talk also with the British Minister, Mr. Macmillan, and immediately rang him up, making an appointment for me at five o'clock. Macmillan was a man of similar calibre to Spofford, and without hesitation promised to arrange that the women and children should be given freedom to go where they liked on the island, and that the priests should be allowed to leave the hotel to attend Mass.

When we left after this interview and were on the way to the mess, I more or less collapsed, and before I knew where I was Olive had hauled me up to some medical department where an American doctor stuck a thermometer in my mouth, and after looking at it said: "You are going to hospital at once." I protested that this was impossible as I was flying to England next day, but he would not listen to reason, said that I had a temperature of over 102 and that I would be taken to hospital at once; when you get there you will be in British hands, and they must decide for themselves what to do with you. Olive had a further talk with him, and when we got down to the courtyard there was an ambulance waiting into which we got, and Olive was not satisfied until she had handed me over at No. 2 General Hospital and arranged for me to be kept there; then, off she went again to fetch my luggage from the caravan.

When the M.O. came along and examined me he pulled a long face and said that I ought never to have been walking about in such a state, but should have been put in hospital immediately I arrived. It was no use my explaining that I was in far better health than I had been for months; he simply would not understand that after I had stood five and a half years' imprisonment it would take a lot to kill me, and that in any case it would do me far more good to get home to May than to be shut up in a beastly hospital. Well, there I was, and there it seemed I must stay. On subsequent days the M.O. said that it would be at least a month before I should be fit to travel, and I really began to feel quite desperate—if I had still been in Germany I should have been put into a prison van or a draughty lorry and sent on long journeys, and it seemed absolutely ridiculous to suggest that I was not fit for a comfortable translation by air to England and to my wife. They were all most kind to me at the hospital, and apart from people sticking pins into me to get blood tests and X-ray photographs of my inside I was left pretty well free to do as I liked so long as I did not leave the hospital grounds.

After the first day I did not stay in bed but spent that part of the day which was not occupied by meals (I seemed to be fed every two hours at least) in visiting other patients who, unlike me, were confined to bed. There was a very nice crowd of men there, and from them I could learn something of the war which in Germany had, of course, escaped me. Every day Olive came to see me, bringing me oranges, cigarettes and other delicacies, though the best thing that she brought was her charming presence; then, once a day there was the visit of the matron. She was most impressive. She bore the crown and two stars of a full colonel and numerous ribbons, and had something of the manner and presence of Queen Victoria with all her autocratic majesty. Her attitude towards me was one of benevolent toleration which seemed to tell me to be a good little boy and do what the nice doctor told me; although I was probably the elder she invariably reduced me to the status of a boy of six.

As the days passed I got more and more anxious and despondent; all tests had proved negative, and I had been cleared of T.B.C., malaria, dysentery, mumps, yellow fever, and measles, I was classified as a case of mild pyrexia of unknown origin, which simply meant that I was slightly feverish as I had been for months past, and yet they would not let me go. Meanwhile, it seems that my chiefs in London had entirely lost trace of me, and all that they could do was to telegraph to May to say that I was safe and somewhere in Italy. Towards the end of the week I was visited by the Chief Intelligence Officer from Naples, who had at last run me to earth, but even he could do nothing to get me released as long as the M.O. would not agree that I was fit to travel. Then I had a piece of luck, the R.A.M.C. major who had been looking after me went on leave for the week-end and Lieutenant-Colonel Easton came to examine me. He was a splendid fellow and at once understood that my principal complaint was worry at not being allowed to go home. He said that if I would promise to stay in bed for two days and be very careful not to do anything for myself on the journey, such as carrying my own luggage, he would let me leave on Monday.

No seat could be got on the plane then, but Olive fixed everything up, for the following day and on Tuesday the 22nd May she called for me with a car and drove me to Naples where we were met by the Intelligence Officer and taken to the plane. I was the only civilian but people were most kind, and someone immediately gave up his seat so that I could sit in front. There was only a short wait before the plane started off and soon we were airborne and I was at last returning from that journey on which I set out on the 9th November, 1939. What should I find? It was lovely weather when we started, bright sun and summer hot, but as we crossed the sea towards France little wisps of cloud appeared

which, as we passed through them, made a noise like the beating
of hail. Over France there was brilliant white cloud beneath us
which dropped in a sheer precipice as we came to the Channel;
then, before us I saw a dense threatening black wall, cloud over
England, which seemed to express my own fear that I was returning
home to an England I did not know, myself probably changed
beyond recognition and, as so often before, I wondered whether
one has ever the right to go back. Then in the cloud I seemed to
see May's face before me, and I knew that one person in the world
at least wanted me and would have patience whilst I fought the
battle which faces every prisoner who returns.

FINIS

Chagford,
   6th April, 1949.

APPENDIX

Nominal roll of the prisoners of war, political prisoners, and hostages who reached Niederdorf in the South Tirol, on 28th April, 1945.

BRITISH

H. M. A. DAY; Wing Commander, R.A.F.
JOHN McGRATH; Lieutenant-Colonel, R.A.
'JACK' CHURCHILL; Lieutenant-Colonel.
R. H. STEVENS; Lieutenant-Colonel.
HUGH FALCONER; Squadron-Leader, R.A.F.
SYDNEY H. DOWSE; Flight Lieutenant, R.A.F.
BERTRAM JAMES; Lieutenant.
PETER CHURCHILL; Captain.
WADIM GREENEWICH; Civil Servant.
S. PAYNE BEST.
THOMAS CUSHING; Soldier.
ANDREW WALSH; Aircraft fitter.
PATRICK O'BRIEN; Soldier.
JOHN SPENCE; Soldier.

RUSSIAN

PETER PRIWALOW; Major-General.
IWAN G. BESSENOW; General.
W. BRODNIKOW; Lieutenant-Colonel.
NIKOLAUS RUTSCHENKO; Lieutenant.
WASSILLI KOKORIN-MOLOTOWSK; Lieutenant.
FEDOR CEREDILIN; Soldier.

FRENCH

LÉON BLUM; Prime Minister.
MADAME LÉON BLUM.
GABRIÉL PIGUET; Bishop of Clermont-Ferrand.
PRINCE XAVIER DE BOURBON-PARMA.
JOSEPH JOOS; Journalist.
R. N. VAN WYMEERSCH; Lieutenant, R.A.F.

Dutch

Dr. J. C. van Dijk; Minister of Defence.

Danish

Hans Lunding; Captain.
Jörgen L. F. Mogensen; Vice-Consul.
Max J. Mikkelsen; Captain Merchant Service.
Knud E. Pedersen; Captain Merchant Service.
Hans F. Hansen; Marine Engineer.
Adolf T. Larsen.

Norwegian

A. Daehle; Naval Captain.

Swedish

Carl Edquist; Company Director.

Polish

Alexander Zamoyski; Major.
Stanislaw Jensen; Pilot-Officer, R.A.F.
Jan Izycki; Pilot-Officer, R.A.F.

Czechoslovak

Dr. Imrich Karvas; University Professor.
Jan Stanek; Major, General Staff.
Josef Rozsevac-Rys; Journalist.
Josef Burda; Merchant.

Greek

Alexander Papagos; Commander-in-Chief, Greek Forces.
Joan Pitsikas; Lieutenant-General.
Constantin Bakopoulos; Lieutenant-General.
Pamajotis Dedes; Lieutenant-General.
George Kosmas; Lieutenant-General.
Nikolaos Grivas; Corporal.
Vassilis Dimitrion; Soldier.

Yugoslav

Hinko Dragic.
Dimitrije Tomalevski; Journalist.
Novac Popovic; Postmaster-General.

Swiss

Armand Mottet; Engineer.

Austrian

Dr. Kurt von Schuschnigg; late Austrian Chancellor.
Mrs. Vera von Schuschnigg.
Maria-Dolores von Schuschnigg (Sissie).
Dr. Richard Schmitz; Mayor of Vienna.
Dr. Konrad Praxmarer; Journalist.

Italian

Sante Garibaldi; General.
Ferrero; Lieutenant-Colonel.
Amechi; Civil Servant.
Burtoli; Civil Servant.

Hungarian

Nikolaus von Kallay; Prime Minister.
Peter Baron Schell; Minister of the Interior.
Geza von Igmandy-Hegyessy; Member of the Upper Chamber.
Nikolaus von Horthy, Jr.; Member of the Upper Chamber and
    Ambassador.
Andreas von Hlatky; Secretary of State.
Julius Kiraly; Police Chief.
Aleksander von Ginzery; Artillery Colonel.
Josef Hatz; Major.
Samuel Hatz; Schoolmaster, retired.
Desiderius von Onedy; Civil Servant.

Lettish

Gustav Celmins; Professor.

GERMAN

DR. HJALMAR SCHACHT; President German Reichsbank.
DR. HERMANN PÜNDER; Secretary of State.
PRINCE PHILIPP VON HESSEN; Ambassador.
DR. ERICH HEBERLEIN; Ambassador.
MRS. MARGOT HEBERLEIN.
FRANZ HALDER; Colonel-General, late C.G.S.
ALEXANDER BARON VON FALKENHAUSEN; General, late C.I.C.
    Belgium and North France.
GEORG THOMAS; General.
BOGISLAV VON BONIN; Colonel, General Staff.
FRANZ LIEDIG; Naval Commander.
MARTIN NIEMÖLLER; Clergyman.
JOHANN NEUHÄUSLER; Canon of Munich.
DR. ANTON HAMM; Chaplain.
KARL KUNKEL; Chaplain.
WILHELM VON FLUGGE; Director.
FRIEDRICH LEOPOLD PRINCE OF PRUSSIA; Landed Proprietor.
BARON FRITZ CERRINI; Private Secretary.
DR. JOSEF MÜLLER; Lawyer.
BARON FABIAN VON SCHLABRENDORFF.
DR. HORST HOEPNER; Businessman.
HORST VON PETERSDORFF; Colonel.
FRITZ THYSSEN; Industrialist.
MRS. ANNELIE THYSSEN.
MISS HEIDL NOWAKOWSKI.
WILHELM VISINTAINER; Circus Clown.
PAUL WAUER; Hairdresser.

So-called "SIPPENHÄFTLINGE" or Family Hostages—
all German

MRS. GERTRUD HALDER; wife of General Halder.
MISS ANNELIESE GISEVIUS; School Teacher.
DR. GUSTAV GOERDELER; Physician.
MRS. ANNELIESE GOERDELER.
ULRICH GOERDELER; Lawyer.
MRS. IRMA GOERDELER.
DR. MARIANNE GOERDELER.
MISS BENIGNA GOERDELER.
MISS JUTTA GOERDELER.
MRS. KÄTE GUDZENT.
BARONESS VON HAMMERSTEIN-ECQUORD.
ARTUR VON HAMMERSTEIN-ECQUORD.
ILSE-LOTTE VON HOFACKER.

MISS ANNA-LUISE VON HOFACKER.
MASTER EBERHARD VON HOFACKER.
MRS. THERESE KAISER.
MISS ELISABETH KAISER.
ARTHUR KUHN; Patent Agent.
MRS. LINI LINDEMANN.
MRS. FEY PIRZIO-BIROLI.
WALTHER COUNT VON PLETTENBERG; Cotton Importer.
GISELA COUNTESS VON PLETTENBERG.
MISS ISA VERMEHREN; Singer.
MRS. INGEBORG SCHRÖDER.
MASTER HARRING SCHRÖDER.
MASTER HANS-DIETRICH SCHRÖDER.
MISS SYBILLE-MARIA SCHRÖDER.
ELISABETH COUNTESS SCHENK VON STAUFFENBERG.
MARKWART COUNT SCHENK VON STAUFFENBERG.
MARIA COUNTESS SCHENK VON STAUFFENBERG.
ALEXANDER COUNT SCHENK VON STAUFFENBERG; University Professor.
MARIA GABRIELE COUNTESS SCHENK VON STAUFFENBERG.
INEZ COUNTESS SCHENK VON STAUFFENBERG.
ALEXANDRA COUNTESS SCHENK VON STAUFFENBERG.
OTTO-PHILIPP COUNT SCHENK VON STAUFFENBERG.
CLEMENS COUNT SCHENK VON STAUFFENBERG.
JOSEF MOHR.
MRS. KÄTHE MOHR.